IRISH ARCHITECTURAL AND DECORATIVE STUDIES
Volume VI, 2003

IRISH ARCHITECTURAL AND DECORATIVE STUDIES

THE JOURNAL OF THE IRISH GEORGIAN SOCIETY – VOLUME VI, 2003

IRISH ARCHITECTURAL AND
DECORATIVE STUDIES
The Journal of the Irish Georgian Society
Volume VI, 2003

Published by the Irish Georgian Society
© Irish Georgian Society and the authors, 2003.
All rights reserved.

ISBN 0946846 979

This annual journal continues the publishing
tradition of the Irish Georgian Society's *Bulletin*
(38 volumes, 1958-1997).

Edited by Dr Nicola Figgis

Design   John O'Regan (© Gandon, 2003)
Production   Nicola Dearey
                                  Gunther Berkus
Printing   Nicholson & Bass, Belfast
Distribution   Gandon, Kinsale

Produced for the Irish Georgian Society by Gandon
Editions, which is grant-aided by The Arts Council.

Gandon Editions, Oysterhaven, Kinsale, Co Cork
tel +353 (0)21-4770830 / *fax* 021-4770755
gandon@eircom.net / www.gandon-editions.com

The Irish Georgian Society gratefully
acknowledges the grant-aiding of this book by
THE PAUL MELLON ESTATE

front cover and flap
Irish wallpapers of the eighteenth century:
– 'Smith' wallpaper from Belvedere, county
  Westmeath *(cover)* (courtesy NLI)
– Wallpaper from Lady Kildare's Room at
  Castletown House, county Kildare *(top)*
  (courtesy Castletown Foundation)
– Wallpaper from Bellamont Forest, county Cavan
  (bottom) (courtesy John Coote)

back cover and flap
An unpublished watercolour by James Malton:
– John Soane's *Elevation and Plan of a Dog-house
  designed for a nobleman Romae 1779 (cover)*
– Mussenden Temple, Downhill, county
  Londonderry *(top)* (courtesy National Trust
  Photographic Library; photo Mike Williams)
– Mausoleum at Downhill, county Londonderry
  (bottom) (courtesy National Trust Photographic
  Library; photo Steven Wooster)

The Irish Georgian Society aims to encourage an
interest in and the preservation of distinguished
examples of architecture and the allied arts in
Ireland.

Further information – and membership application
details – may be obtained from:
THE IRISH GEORGIAN SOCIETY
74 Merrion Square, Dublin 2
tel +353 (0)1-6767053 / *fax* 01-6620290
e-mail info@igs.ie

IRISH ARCHITECTURAL AND DECORATIVE STUDIES

THE JOURNAL OF THE IRISH GEORGIAN SOCIETY – VOLUME VI, 2003
EDITOR: NICOLA FIGGIS

———

Foreword

THE KNIGHT OF GLIN

IT IS VERY SAD TO REPORT THE DEATH OF SIR PAUL GETTY, WHOSE CHARITABLE TRUST supported our *Journal* from volumes II to IV. His philanthropy in England to the National Gallery and many other institutions is well known, and it is agreeable to note his support for an Irish institution, considering his family's Irish antecedents.

Naturally we wish to record how enormously grateful we are to the estate of the late Paul Mellon, which continues to underwrite the cost of this publication. As a result of this support we are now able to spend more funds on colour plates. We are very excited by the quality and variety of our contributions, and it is gratifying that we are attracting considerably more scholarly material.

Beginning in this volume, and continuing next year, we will be publishing some stimulating articles covering the history of Irish patronage and painters. We have Sarah Drumm recording the Irish patrons of the great pastellist, Rosalba Carriera, and Toby Barnard concentrates on collecting in Ireland in the eighteenth century. We greatly look forward to his new book *The Grand Figure: material worlds of Ireland, 1641-1770*, which will be published by Yale University Press next year. His exhumation of the bones of Irish material culture in the eighteenth century is going to be of enormous value to all of us working in this field.

Other articles in this *Journal* cover subjects as diverse as wallpaper, Waterford glass, and an archbishop's patronage of books. Additional eighteenth-century topics include the subject of how Lord and Lady Kildare organised their great house at Carton, and, earlier in the eighteenth century, Dean Swift's minimal observations on architecture.

As to the nineteenth century, we have a new insight into the designing of University Church, and leading on to the twentieth century, Hugh Lane's decorative schematic visions for his stillborn gallery of modern art in Dublin. Returning to architecture, our studies range from railway stations to dog kennels! It is welcome to record that our former president and co-founder still whets our appetite for architectural peccadillos.

Authors' biographies

TOBY BARNARD is a fellow and tutor at Hertford College, Oxford. He has written extensively on seventeenth and eighteenth-century Ireland. *A new anatomy of Ireland: the Irish Protestants, 1649-1770* was published by Yale University Press in 2003; a companion volume, *The Grand Figure: material worlds of Ireland, 1641-1770*, will be published in 2004. He is an honorary member of the Royal Irish Academy

RONALD COX is Research Fellow and Director of the Centre for Civil Engineering Heritage at Trinity College Dublin, which he founded in 1995. He has published widely in the fields of civil engineering heritage and engineering biography. He is co-author with Michael Gould of *Civil Engineering Heritage: Ireland* (London 1998).

SARAH RHIANNON DRUMM carried out research on Rosalba Carriera's Irish patrons for her MA (NUI, 2001). She is currently an M Litt. student at the Department of the History of Art, University College Dublin, investigating artists who visited Ireland during the eighteenth century.

MICHAEL GOULD is Honorary Senior Research Fellow, School of Civil Engineering, The Queen's University of Belfast, and has published widely in the fields of general and historical civil engineering and local government administration. He is co-author with Ronald Cox of *Civil Engineering Heritage: Ireland* (London 1998).

THE HON DESMOND GUINNESS is a leading authority on Irish houses and castles, and a pioneering force behind the Irish Georgian Society, of which he was president from 1958 to 1991.

MICHAEL MCCARTHY is Professor of the History of Art at University College Dublin and is the author of *The Origins of the Gothic Revival* (Yale 1987), and editor of and contributor to *Lord Charlemont and his Circle* (Dublin 2000).

PATRICIA MCCARTHY is a research student in the department of the History of Art and Architecture at Trinity College, Dublin. Her book on the architecture of the King's Inns will be published in 2004.

JOSEPH MCDONNELL has just completed a research fellowship in the history of art at University College Dublin. He is the author of several works, including *500 Years of the Art of the Book in Ireland* (Dublin and London 1997).

PHILIP MCEVANSONEYA is Head of the Department of the History of Art at Trinity College Dublin, with research interests in British and Irish art.

JOSEPH MCMINN is Professor of Anglo-Irish Studies at the University of Ulster at Jordanstown. He is author of several works on Swift, including *Swift's Irish Pamphlets: An Introductory Selection* (1991), *Swift: A Literary Life* (1991), and *Jonathan's Travels: Swift and Ireland* (1994). He is currently writing a study of Swift's relationship with the non-literary arts.

ANNA MORAN is a graduate of the MA course in the History of Design and Material Culture, run jointly by the Victoria & Albert Museum and the Royal College of Art, London. She lectures in design history at the Institute of Art, Design & Technology, Dun Laoghaire, and the National College of Art & Design, Dublin.

DAVID SKINNER is a specialist in the conservation, reproduction and history of historic wallpapers.

———

1 – Wallpaper from Lady Kildare's Room at Castletown House
(courtesy Castletown Foundation)

Flocks, flowers and follies: some recently discovered Irish wallpapers of the eighteenth century

DAVID SKINNER

ESPITE THE SURVIVAL OF A NUMBER OF WALLPAPERS FROM AROUND 1780 onwards in Irish houses, until now very few examples of early to mid-eighteenth-century papers have been found, while physical evidence of early furnishing textile usage in Ireland is still more scant. With one notable exception – the opulent gilt leather hangings of around 1730, still in the saloon of Loreto Abbey, Rathfarnham, Dublin – our knowledge of Irish interior decoration in the early eighteenth century has been restricted to stucco work, surviving panelled interiors, or contemporary written references to less permanent materials.[1] Expensive, movable tapestry hangings have survived from the period, but not the less permanent weaves used for hangings and curtains, such as the crimson mohair curtains ordered by Mrs Delany for Delville, her Dublin home, in 1744, or the crimson damask used in her bedchamber.[2] Elaborate papered schemes like the print room at Castletown or the Chinese room at Carton both in county Kildare have survived from the 1750s and 1760s, but not the simpler patterned wallpapers which begin to be described in Dublin newspaper advertisements in the late 1730s.[3] Recent conservation work in four Irish houses of the early eighteenth century (Castletown, county Kildare, Belvedere, county Westmeath, Bellamont Forest, county Cavan, and No. 10 Henrietta Street, Dublin) has resulted in the discovery of a number of wallpapers and one textile wallcovering from the period when the use of wallpaper was starting to be widely adopted in Irish houses. Seen in context, these discoveries throw new light onto how wallpapers and textiles were incorporated into interior schemes.

Three floral wallpapers found in Castletown, Bellamont Forest and 10 Henrietta Street show stylistic and technical similarities which suggest that they may have originated in the same Dublin workshop in the second quarter of the century. Unusually, all three papers are printed onto ungrounded paper – that is to say, paper which has not been given any base colour – a feature which does not appear to have any equivalent in contemporary English or European practice and may be indicative of a local industry at an early and technically unadvanced stage. In each case the outline of the pattern is block-printed in black, and the colours added somewhat crudely by stencil.

The paper found in Lady Kildare's Room at Castletown (Plate 1) is identical to that found in the ante-room at Henrietta Street, and both papers were clearly printed from the same block. The pattern of small flowers and leaves on trailing stems is set against an all-over, imbricated background pattern of pin-dots, probably intended to represent quilting in black-stitch. Wallpapers made 'in imitation of Tapestry or Needlework, fit for hanging of Rooms' were advertised by Dublin paper-stainers Bernard and James Messink of Blind Quay in 1746,[4] while similar examples found in England date from the first decade of the century.[5] The Henrietta Street example was used with an unusual fretted border, printed in black, blue and yellow, very similar in style to that used with the paper found at Bellamont Forest (Plate 2). Technically similar to the first two papers, the Bellamont paper has a pattern of trailing stems of flowers and foliage combined with gardening implements and baskets, but without the pin-dot ground.

In all three cases, the papers were the earliest in a sequence of wallpapers found at that location, with no traces of earlier decoration beneath them. The Castletown example was applied to a stretched hessian lining in a cupboard in Lady Kildare's room, beneath three layers of later papers. In Henrietta Street the paper was found in the ante-room, a first-floor room created out of the original 1730s stairwell of the house some time between 1761 and 1772, when a new stairway was constructed at the back of the house. The fragments of wallpaper were attached to pieces of oak recycled from an apartment – possibly a bedroom or boudoir – destroyed when the new staircase was built, and used to line the walls of the ante-room. In Bellamont Forest the paper was found beneath a later Georgian paper, both of which predate the fire which damaged part of the house in the 1770s. It seems by no means unlikely that these papers and borders are the work of a Dublin paper-stainer of the 1740s, possibly James or Bernard Messink, or else John Russell, whose name first appears in 1737.[6]

From the above it is clear that wallpapers were used in private rooms in Ireland early on in the eighteenth century. In No. 10 Henrietta Street, significant evidence relating to the use of wallpapers and textile hangings in formal, public rooms has come to light, broadening our knowledge of the variety and hierarchy of materials used in the early to middle part of the century. The survival of extensive evidence of the earliest decoration of the first-floor rooms in 10 Henrietta Street is due to changes in taste which occurred around 1770 towards a plainer, less ornamented style of decor. Built around 1730 for the first Luke Gardiner, possibly designed by Sir Edward Lovett Pearce, the house underwent some remodelling by his son Charles Gardiner from around 1755, and was further altered and extensively redecorated when Luke Gardiner the Younger inherited it in 1769. Some time after Luke the Younger moved into the house in 1772, the outmoded wainscoting in the four principal first-floor rooms was lined from the dado to the cornice with stretched hessian and paper to provide a flat finish, preserving earlier decorative material intact beneath the hessian. Most of this hessian was taken down in the 1960s and replaced with sheets of hardboard, and it was when this hardboard was removed in the course of recent conservation that the original oak panelling and early wallpaper and textile fragments, hidden since the 1770s, were revealed. In the Yellow and Blue drawing rooms (the names come from a 1772 inventory),[7] the walls above the chair rail were finished partly in fielded panels of polished oak, partly in rough oak planks laid horizontally to form a flat surface.[8] The areas of rough timber had originally been covered with paper or textile hangings, some of which have remained in place. In the Blue Drawing Room, extensive amounts of blue flock wallpaper with a small geometric pattern were found (Plate 3), while in the Yellow Drawing Room, fragments of yellow woollen material were discovered, together with remains of a battening system used to attach fabric. The walls of the ballroom – an addition of the 1750s or 1760s – were treated the same way, but using pine painted pale grey, instead of polished oak. No conclusive evidence of the original hangings in the ballroom survives, although traces of a plain crimson flock paper may indicate the earliest scheme. This division of wall space into areas of panelling and hangings is not unique to Henrietta Street. In Castletown House, Louisa Connolly's bedroom on the first floor, although altered in some ways since the 1720s, also combines areas of fielded pine panelling painted pale grey, with a large area of rough pine sheeting intended for hangings. A tiny fragment of green flock paper and larger fragments of block-printed and hand-coloured 'tree of life' pattern wallpaper found in Louisa Connolly's bedroom both date from the eighteenth century, and indicate the type of hangings used in conjunction with the painted panelling (Plate 4).

In No. 10 Henrietta Street, the fashionable remodelling of the rooms to provide plain surfaces undertaken in the 1770s is reflected in contemporary advertisements such as that of Michael Boylan of Grafton Street in 1777, advertising 'Plain Papers now so much used in London and Dublin', and listing some of the more popular colours in use, including 'Pea Green, verditer, Blue, Peach ... Queen's Brown, Hair Stone, lemon'.[9] Between the early 1770s and 1829 the walls of all four first floor rooms at 10 Henrietta Street were decorated in a succession of schemes using plain blue or green verditer distemper. Initially, the plain-coloured walls were

2 – Wallpaper from Bellamont Forest, county Cavan
(courtesy John Coote)

3 – Blue flock paper at No. 10 Henrietta Street, Dublin
(photo Andrew Smith)

4 – Fragments of 'Tree of Life' wallpaper from Louisa Connolly's bedroom at Castletown House
(courtesy Castletown Foundation)

relieved with narrow block-printed paper borders, while the later schemes were fin-ished with elaborate, multicoloured flock borders, fragments of which survive, and which probably date from the time of Charles John Gardiner, 2nd Viscount Mountjoy, who lived in the house from 1798 to 1829. The geometric flock paper in the Blue Drawing Room clearly precedes these schemes, and therefore dates from the time of the first Luke Gardiner, or possibly that of his son Charles Gardiner who lived there from 1755 to 1769. Precisely how old the paper is impossible to determine. Pigment analysis of the ground colour indicates that Prussian blue was used, a pigment which was first advertised in 1710 and in widespread use by the mid-1730s. Historically, the very early use of flock paper in Dublin is indicated by the existence of the exam-ple in the Royal Hospital, Kilmainham,[10] and by Dublin newspaper advertisements of the 1740s advertising flocked papers.[11] The coarse quality of the paper in the Blue Drawing Room, and a certain lack of sophistication in the way it is applied to the wall, also support an early date, as does the absence of any evidence of an earlier scheme.

The fragment of yellow cloth found in the Yellow Drawing Room of No. 10 Henrietta Street is of some interest, given how rare it is to find early furnishing tex-tiles *in situ*. As in the Blue Drawing Room, the walls were divided into areas of fielded panelling and areas of rough oak planks, although it appears that the Yellow Drawing Room was the more important of the two apartments, being larger in area and having more elaborate doorcases. The piece found was around two inches wide and approximately five feet long, and was formed from three widths sewn together.[12] It looks like a piece cut from the top or bottom of a large panel, intended for use as a curtain or a wall hanging. The strip of cloth had been nailed across a gap in the rough oak sheeting lining the wall, presumably as a preparatory measure in order to prevent the passage of air and dust through the gap from soiling the wall hangings. Evidence of the battening system used to attach the hangings was also found, but as only a few yellow threads were attached, it is impossible to be absolutely certain that the strip of cloth nailed to the wall was the same as that used for the hangings themselves. The woollen cloth is of a type known as 'harateen' or 'moreen', com-monly used for furnishing in the eighteenth and early nineteenth centuries, and men-tioned frequently in inventories. It was made with a worsted warp and a thicker worsted weft to form horizontal ribs, then finished by watering and stamping with a vermicular pattern. Authorities differ as to its former social standing. While in later years their use seems to have moved down market, in the late seventeenth and early eighteenth centuries worsted materials similar to harateen were evidently used as wall hangings in the smartest rooms, along with silks.[13] In Temple Newsam in the 1730s, on the other hand, chairs covered in more expensive material had their backs covered in harateen,[14] while moreens are frequently mentioned as curtains and bed curtains in colonial American homes or in housekeepers' rooms in English houses. Its presence in the Yellow Drawing Room is thus slightly enigmatic: were the walls actually hung with yellow harateen, or was this merely a draught-proofing strip recycled from a humbler part of the house as a preparation for a more expensive textile?[15] Whatever its true role, it seems that the harateen was probably manufactured in Ireland, as an advertisement placed in the *Dublin Daily Advertiser* of 1736 by Edward Wale 'of the Black Swan in High Street' makes clear. Wale states plainly that he 'makes and sells all kinds of Kidderminster, Parragons, Herrattens, and Cheney for Houshold Furniture'.[16]

The wallpaper found at Belvedere, county Westmeath, is perhaps the most interesting on a number of counts (Plate 5). A large and well-preserved section of this paper was found during recent conservation work when a partition was removed from one of the two bedrooms of the house, which was designed by Richard Castle for George Rochfort, Lord Belfield and later Earl of Belvedere, in 1740. The paper's manufacturer, a Mr Smith, incorporated his name into the design (Plate 6), thus giving us the first known link between a recorded Irish paper-stainer and a surviving example of work.[17] A 'Samuel Smith, paper-stamper' of Upper Ormond Quay is listed in the *Dublin Directory* of 1778, while his descendants appear to have carried on the business at that address, and later in Nassau Street and Capel Street, until the 1830s (Plate 7).[18] This exuberant pattern presents a profusion of birds, trees, fruit, flowers, architectural elements and follies, arranged with cheerful disregard to proportion, and which seems to echo so closely the spirit of Rococo fantasy of the house and its folly-strewn demesne that it is hard to believe that the paper was not chosen or commissioned by the 1st Earl himself. Nevertheless, as is so often the case without corroborative documentary or architectural evidence, it is frustratingly difficult to date the paper with any accuracy. Rochfort died in 1774, four years before Samuel Smith's first listing, so Smith would have had to have been in business some years prior to his first recorded mention if the paper were to have been made by him during the Earl's lifetime. It may be that the paper was printed by an earlier 'Smith' of whom no record survives. Like the early floral papers described above, the Belvedere paper is printed on ungrounded paper, the outlines block-printed in black with the colours added by stencil or additional blocks. While this technique might suggest a date in the 1740s or 1750s, aspects of the draughtsmanship point to a later date. The arrangement and treatment of the flowers is quite similar to English printed linen and cotton designs of the 1770s,[19] while the general style, and the handling of the trees in particular, recall plate-printed Irish toile designs of the 1770s to 1780s. A date after the 1st Earl's death cannot be ruled out.

In the manner of printing, the 'Smith' paper may provide evidence of a unique aspect of the Dublin printing industry in the eighteenth century, noted by

The WHOLESALE AND RETAIL
PAPER HANGING MANUFACTORY,
No. 11, UPPER ORMOND-QUAY.

SAMUEL SMITH, Junr.

RETURNS his sincere Thanks to his FRIENDS and the PUBLIC, for the very
great Encouragement they have been pleased to favour him with, since his Com-
mencement in Business; begs Leave to inform them he makes all Sorts of the most
elegant and fashionable white and coloured FLOCK and MOCK FLOCK PAPER,
figured PAPER, of all Sorts and newest Patterns; ORNAMENT FESTOON, and
other Borders, equal to any made in ENGLAND.——He colours PLAIN ROOMS,
HALLS, STAIR-CASES, &c. in the neatest and best Manner.

☞ WHOLESALE DEALERS and COUNTRY PURCHASERS will find it much to
their Advantage to examine his PAPER, which he will sell on the lowest Terms.

✦ ✦ ✦ PRINTED BY W. PORTER, No. 11, SKINNER-ROW. ✦ ✦ ✦

Ada Longfield. Whereas in England and France textile and paper printing were carried on quite separately, in some Dublin factories they were carried on side by side, as, for example, that of Thomas Ashworth of Donnybrook, who described himself in a petition for parliamentary aid of 1755 as a 'Linen, Cotton, Callicoe and Paper Printer'.[20] The 'Smith' paper from Belvedere unites aspects of both technologies in that the colours are applied in transparent glazes from light to dark, rather than in opaque layers from dark to light, as was the general practice in wallpaper printing. Some of the glazes are combined to produce secondary shades. This technique, the unusual width of the paper, and the scale of the design all suggest contemporary fabric printing practice as applied to block-printed cottons and linens.[21]

Before leaving the subject of the Belvedere paper, it might be relevant to touch on the question of design and authorship in the Dublin wallpaper industry. A survey of the advertisements recorded by Mrs Leask shows clearly that the principal source of designs for Dublin paper-stainers was London. There was of course no copyright protection at the time, and at the start of each season the wallpaper makers of Dublin would travel to London, returning with examples of the latest patterns, which would quickly be copied and advertised for sale. Extravagant claims for the quality, fashionability, and cheapness of the product recur constantly in the advertisements, but the notion of originality of design simply does not feature.[22] The Belvedere paper is one of only three eighteenth-century Irish fabric or wallpaper designs whose authorship is known, the other two being the 'Volunteer furniture' printed by Edward Clarke at Palmerstown in 1783, and the linen union toile printed by Robinson of Ballsbridge during the 1770s or 1780s.[23] These three designs stand out from the generality of anonymous and more conventional designs by virtue of certain shared characteristics. These may perhaps be described as cheerful whimsicality, a two-dimensional, flattened perspective, and an almost cartoon-like manner of drawing. Based on English or French models, they have a distinct local flavour, and it is these few appealingly unrefined compositions (pending further discoveries) that constitute what might be called an Irish school of pattern design.[24]

———

opposite

5 – 'Smith' wallpaper, Belvedere, county Westmeath

6 – Close-up of 'Smith' paper showing urn and 'Smith' inscription

7 – Samuel Smith, billhead (courtesy NLI)

ENDNOTES

[1] For a description of the leather hangings at Loreto Abbey, see J. Cornforth, 'Aglow with Golden Leather', *Country Life*, 26 November 1987, 62. It is John Cornforth's view that this is the only set of early eighteenth-century leather hangings still in their original location in the British Isles.

[2] A. Day (ed.), *Letters from Georgian Ireland* (Belfast 1991).

[3] Documentary references to the activities of Dublin paper-stainers in the eighteenth century were extensively researched and published by the late Ada Longfield (Mrs H. Leask). Virtually all the references to newspaper advertisements quoted in this article are from her 'History of the Dublin Wallpaper Industry in the 18th Century', *JRSAI*, lxxvii, 1947.

[4] Advertisement in *Pue's Occurrences*, 17 June 1746, cited in Longfield, 'History of the Dublin Wallpaper Industry in the 18th Century', 107.

[5] A. Wells-Cole, 'Flocks, Florals and Fancies' in L. Hoskins (ed.), *The Papered Wall* (London 1994) 35. A paper found in the 'Ancient House' in Stafford with a similar pin-dot ground pattern is dated 1700-1710.

[6] An intriguing link between the three papers is that each of the three houses in which they were found is associated with Sir Edward Lovett Pearce. The coincidence may probably be ascribed more to the small number of paper-stainers active in Dublin at the time, however, than to the patronage of a particular manufacturer by the leading architect of the day.

[7] National Library of Ireland, Gardiner Papers, Henrietta Street Inventory; PC11(6). The inventory was taken in 1772 when Luke Gardiner the Younger returned from the Grand Tour and took possession of the property. The names given to the rooms are of interest in that they suggest the use of each room at the time, and even the colour scheme. The inventory also lists the pictures hanging in each room. See also J. Coleman, 'Luke Gardiner, an Irish Dilletante', *Irish Arts Review Yearbook*, 15 (Dublin 1999) 160-9.

[8] Paint scrapes indicated that all the visible interior woodwork, doors, dado panelling, shutters, etc. were of polished oak.

[9] Advertisement in *Faulkner's Dublin Journal*, 5 April 1777, quoted in Longfield, 'History of the Dublin Wallpaper Industry in the 18th Century'.

[10] D. Skinner, 'Irish Period Wallpapers', *Irish Arts Review Yearbook*, 13 (Dublin 1997) 52-61.

[11] John Russell 'at the Indian Woman in Bride Street, Paper-Stainer' is recorded as early as 1737, advertising papers both 'flocked and plain' in the 1740s, while James and Bernard Messink of the Blind Quay made wallpapers 'in imitation of Coffoy' – a term used to describe figured woollen velvet.

[12] Each width was woven to a width of 24 and a half inches.

[13] P. Thornton, *Authentic Decor; London* (1993) 56-8.

[14] *ibid.*

[15] In a letter to the author, Mr John Cornforth states that woollen cloths come far down the hierarchy of materials, and that he would be surprised to find moreen or harateen used in a drawing room of the period. However, he also suggests that Dublin or Irish interiors may have been less 'stratified' than those in London. He also points out that in the recently refitted English Rooms at the Victoria & Albert Museum, the walls of the drawing room from (London's) Henrietta Street have been hung with glazed, plain blue mohair. The effect of this would have been very similar to that of the harateen in No. 10 Henrietta Street, Dublin, which, with its impressed pat-

tern, would have been, if anything, more decorative.

[16] *Dublin Daily Advertiser*, 19 October 1736. Advertisements placed by other woollen manufacturers in the same year indicate the wide range of fashionable furnishing and dress woollens available, all – as one advertiser put it – 'of Irish Matter and Make'.

[17] In a similar fashion, the manufacturer of the plate-printed Irish toile of the 1770s or 1780s in the National Museum of Ireland incorporated his name ('Robinson Balls Bridge') into the design.

[18] National Library of Ireland MS 8,037(1). A billhead of Samuel Smith Junior lists wallpapers and borders supplied to Lord Killeen, possibly in 1797, although the date is indistinct.

[19] See in particular the block-printed linen in the Victoria & Albert Museum, T.227-1931, illustrated in W. Hefford, *The Victoria and Albert Museum's textile Collection: Design for Printed Textiles in England from 1750 to 1850* (London 1992) 63.

[20] *Journals of the Irish House of Commons*, v, 1 Nov 1755, cited in Longfield, 'History of the Dublin Wallpaper Industry'.

[21] The pattern is printed onto sheets measuring 26 inches across by 21 inches up and down. The vertical repeat of the pattern is 42 inches, thus half of each repeat could be printed onto one sheet of paper. This is entirely counter to normal practice at the time. Wallpapers in England and Ireland were almost universally printed onto 21-inch-wide paper, the sheets being joined together into rolls before printing.

[22] This reliance on London fashions as models of taste has been borne out by the discovery of several wallpapers printed in Dublin which are identical, with very minor variations, to examples located in English houses. The flock paper of around 1700 in the Royal Hospital Kilmainham, the 1820s Gothic paper from the library at Malahide Castle, and a floral paper of the 1760s from Eustace Street, Dublin, all have equivalents in England. I am indebted to Mr Robert Weston of Hamilton Weston Wallpapers for drawing my attention to the English examples of the last two.

[23] The most talented Irish designer of the time, William Kilburn, left Dublin soon after completing his apprenticeship for England, where he rapidly achieved success and rose to the top of his profession.

[24] Similarities between the treatment of the trees in the Volunteer furniture and the work of the French topographical artist Gabriel Beranger have led to suggestions that he may have been involved in the design, although there is no documentary evidence to support this view.

———

1 – Interior of University Church, Dublin
(*photo Jacqueline O'Brien; courtesy J.A. Gaughan, NEWMAN'S UNIVERSITY CHURCH (Dublin 1997)*)

University Church:
towards a stylistic context

MICHAEL McCARTHY

T HE ARCHITECT OF UNIVERSITY CHURCH, JOHN HUNGERFORD POLLEN, WAS THE first writer on its architecture.[1] He doubled as Professor of Fine Arts for the new University, and his fifth lecture in that capacity, devoted to the material origins of its decoration and the sources of the iconography of its ornament, has been reprinted recently in the booklet of Fr Gaughan, as it had informed the earlier booklets of Dr Curran and Dr Kane.[2] It is hardly useful for me to offer further remarks in detail on the fabric and furnishings of this exquisite building – an oasis of seclusion and privacy chanced upon with surprise and delight in the public space of St Stephen's Green, between façades of rivalling grandeur of the surrounding houses.

The entrance to the church is a later addition, the gift of Fr Anderdon (Plate 3).[3] In keeping with the High Victorian brick polychromy of the firm of Sir Thomas Deane,[4] it is a vigorous example in miniature of the Romanesque Revival, one strand of the Gothic Revival that predominated as the architecture of choice for ecclesiastical and college buildings in the mid-nineteenth century.[5] There is nothing exceptional in the architecture of the porch-entrance, therefore, except that it looks out of place. It would look much better in the Kildare Street Club, which was soon to be built by Deane and Woodward, the architects of the engineering building of Trinity College, or in Dawson Street, in the neighbourhood of the façade of St Anne's Church.[6] Our porch – in itself an item of joy – is a sore thumb in the context of the Palladianism of its neighbours.

The covered space to which the porch gives access is an unplanned addition, necessitated by the need to prop up the wall of the neighbouring house, and it has no architectural or liturgical function (Plate 2).[7] On entering the rectangular space concluded by a domed apse that is the church proper, the visitor is obliged to tread through a set of half-size columns supporting the gallery at the back – an introduc-

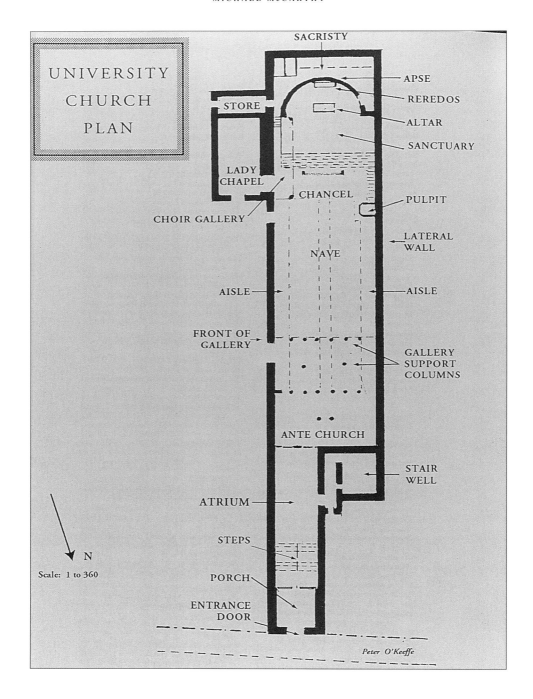

2 – Plan of University Church
(Peter O'Keeffe; courtesy J.A. Gaughan, NEWMAN'S UNIVERSITY CHURCH (Dublin 1997))

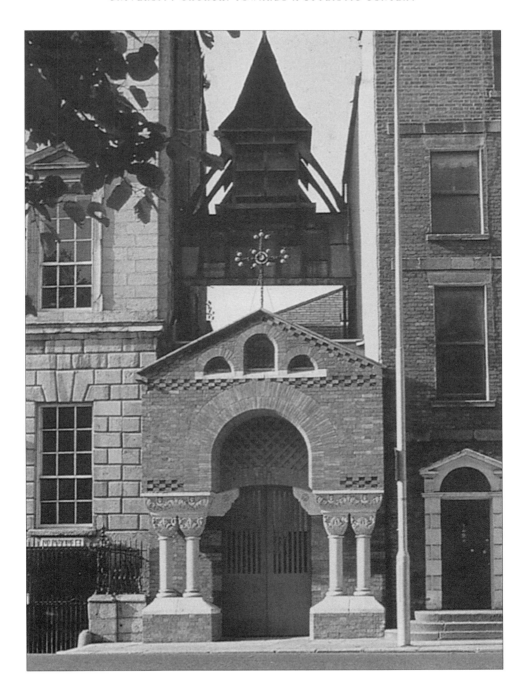

3 – Entrance to University Church
(photo Jacqueline O'Brien; courtesy J.A. Gaughan, NEWMAN'S UNIVERSITY CHURCH (Dublin 1997))

4 – Julius Schnorr von Carolsfeld
LUDWIG I SUMMONS THE GERMAN ARTISTS IN ROME TO MUNICH, 1850
(from H.F. Nohbauer, MUNICH: CITY OF ART (Munich 1994))

*5, 6 – Basilica of St Boniface, Munich, 1828-50, and a design for the wall decoration by
G.F. Ziebland and H. von Hess (from H.F. Nohbauer, MUNICH: CITY OF ART (Munich 1994))*

tion that serves to heighten by contrast the light and space of the hall of the church (Plate 1). Its dimensions and its lighting were in fact determined by the site, which was the garden area to the rear of No. 87 St Stephen's Green. The windows are above the house levels and are comparable, therefore, to the clerestory of a cathedral. Their being made of bottle-glass to give a suffused light makes them directly comparable to contemporary practice in the furnishing and fitting of the early Christian basilicas.

This was a topic of lively discussion in the period, mostly because of the decision to rebuild the basilica of S. Paolo fuori le Mura in Rome in accordance with its original design and decoration, a process that lasted from 1823 (the year of the catastrophic fire) to 1854, when the reconsecration was attended by international interest and major publications.[8] These were eagerly studied for architectural and decorative motifs by contemporary artists visiting Rome, notably by the German group known as Nazarenes, whose closest parallel in England were the Pre-Raphaelites, most closely associated with the University of Oxford. The architects of the engineering building at Trinity College in Dublin, Thomas Deane and Benjamin Woodward, had been brought to Oxford to build its new museum, and later the Debating Room of the Oxford Union Society,[9] all to be decorated by the Pre-Raphaelites.

John Hungerford Pollen was curate at St Peter-le-Bailey in Oxford in 1845, the date of his first recorded ecclesiastical work – the painting of the ceiling of that church. A fellow of Merton College, he was also its dean and bursar when, in 1850, he executed his more notable work, the painting of the ceiling of the college chapel. He was introduced to Dante Gabriel Rossetti and the Pre-Raphaelite Brotherhood by Benjamin Woodward, whom he had probably met in Dublin in 1854, and he was to work with the Pre-Raphaelite Brotherhood on the frescoes of the Oxford Union Debating Society in 1857/58. His friendship with Benjamin Woodward was very close, and Pollen was to provide extensive decorative schemes, unexecuted, for Woodward's buildings in Oxford and London, as well as for Kilkenny Castle Gallery, recently restored, and domestic commissions for the firm of Deane and Woodward.[10]

C.P. Curran has noted the closeness of the relationship between these two artist-architects in that decade, and the same author has stressed the importance of John Hungerford Pollen's visit to Munich in 1847, where three instances of the revival of the early Christian basilica for modern church architecture were rising under the guidance of the Nazarene painters, who had been summoned back from Rome to guide the construction of the northern extension to the city inaugurated by King Ludwig I of Bavaria (Plate 4). Of these, the most important to Pollen was the Basilica of St Boniface, praised by the young artist as 'altogether a most gratifying work for the present day' (Plates 5, 6).[11]

The context in architectural theory of the basilican revival in Munich in the first half of the nineteenth century lies in the design movement *Rundbogenstil* (Round Arch style), which rose as a questioning of the appropriateness of the Greek post-and-lintel structural system as a model for contemporary architecture.[12] This found formulation principally in the writings of Heinrich Hübsch, especially the treatise of 1828, *In What Style Ought We Build?*. His reasoning was structural rather than historicist or associative, and he found many disciples throughout Germany in the following decades, perhaps as much from the historicist and associative connections of the arch with German Romanesque architecture as for its purported structural advantages. The style reached its culmination in the church-building programme of Ludwig I in Munich, when John Hungerford Pollen was there, and Curran reminds us that he was not the only enthusiast for the basilican style espoused by Ludwig's architects, quoting a fervent wish for the adoption of the style published by Cardinal Wiseman in *The Dublin Review* of 1847.[13]

At that time the unique instance of basilican revival in church planning in England, St Mary and St Nicholas in Wilton, Wiltshire, had just been completed to the designs of T.H. Wyatt and David Brandon.[14] Neither architect was to build in that style again, though they each enjoyed very active careers as church architects, so the patron of the church must be credited with the choice of style.[15] The enthusiasm for the style expressed by Wiseman and Pollen in 1847 was to be reflected in the taste of John Henry Newman when he commissioned a building for the Oratory in Birmingham four years later. Roderick O'Donnell has published a set of drawings – plan, elevation, a section in longitude and two transverse sections – of a proposal dated 1851 for that oratory. The drawings are signed by Louis Duc, a Parisian architect who never again designed a church. Understandably, Newman's editors had confused him with the leader of the Gothic Revival in France, the well-known Viollet le Duc, and we must be grateful to have the confusion sorted.[16] These proposals are basilican throughout, and Newman kept them by him, though they were not executed.

It is possible that the basilican church at Wilton affected Cardinal Wiseman's enthusiasm for the use of the style in Munich and consequently, or coincidentally, the leanings of Pollen and Newman towards the basilican style in structural and decorative terms. Of the three Munich buildings, the All Saints Court church has been restored in structure, but without any attempt at restoration of its decoration. The same is true of St Boniface's, though it is only half the size it was before the war, and it has lost any pretension to basilican plan and scale, as well as to the rich decoration of Georg Friedrick Ziebland and Heinrich von Hess, so admired by Pollen (Plates 5, 6). Only the Ludwigskirche, built by Friedrich von Gartner from 1829 to 1845, can be seen in its original plan and with its original decoration – frescoes by

8 – Pulpit of University Church, Dublin
(photo K.J. Romanowski; courtesy J.A. Gaughan, NEWMAN'S UNIVERSITY CHURCH (Dublin 1997))
opposite
7 – Peter von Cornelius, THE LAST JUDGEMENT (1836-40), St Ludwig's Church, Munich
(from H.F. Nohbauer, MUNICH: CITY OF ART (Munich 1994))

Peter von Cornelius, principally *The Last Judgement*, the second largest version of that theme after Michelangelo's Sistine painting (Plate 7). The Sistine Chapel is also, of course, the source of the oil paintings executed for Newman and Pollen in Rome to be hung in the new church in Dublin.[17]

A larger factor that has not been brought into discussion to date is that the Ludwigskirche, besides serving as a parish church, was designed as the new church for the Ludwig-Maximilians-Universität. The university, consisting of eighty professors and 1,500 students, had been transferred from Landshut to Munich by King

Ludwig I in 1826, and the buildings of the Ludwigstrasse were designed to accommodate it. The overall plan had been the work of Leo von Klenze, who had also planned the museum district to the south, presided over by St Boniface's, into which the king introduced the Benedictines to demonstrate the linking of religion with the arts and the natural sciences – links which were to be cultivated at the university.[18] The Catholic authorities in Dublin contemplating the establishment of a new university were bound to be heavily influenced by the example of the King of Bavaria in the preceding decades (Plate 8).

Dr O'Donnell has demonstrated that Newman was predisposed towards the style before coming to Dublin. He found a fellow-enthusiast in John Hungerford Pollen, and he was warm in his appreciation of the basilican University Church that the artist-architect provided for him. Amid the grandiosities of the classical revivals and the strident polemics of the Gothic revivals (especially that of Pugin) predominant in post-emancipation Ireland, the basilican style is a still small voice in ecclesiastical architecture. We can be grateful that it found expression in the creation of Newman and Pollen, which we enjoy as an oasis of prayer and reflection in the tumult of the city centre.

———

ACKNOWLEDGEMENTS

Particular thanks are due to Fr Pearse Walsh for the invitation to address this topic at a seminar in the church on 12 May 2003, and to my colleague Dr Joseph McDonnell for introducing me to Fr Walsh and for having read an early version of the text. David Griffin also offered corrections to the draft text, and Dr Christine Casey was also a reader and discussant of the paper.

ENDNOTES

[1]   J. Lever (ed.), *Catalogue of the Drawings Collection of the RIBA*, vol. O-R (London 1974) 83.
[2]   J.A. Gaughan, *Newman's University Church* (Dublin 1997); E. Kane, 'John Henry Newman's Catholic University Church in Dublin', *Studies*, summer-autumn 1977, 1-19; C.P. Curran, *Newman House and University Church* (Dublin 1945).
[3]   Gaughan, *Newman's University Church*, 27, where the design of the porch-entrance is also attributed to J.H. Pollen.
[4]   F. O'Dwyer, *The Architecture of Deane and Woodward* (Cork 1997).
[5]   S. Muthesius, *The High Victorian Movement in Architecture, 1850-1870* (London 1972).
[6]   O'Dwyer, *Deane and Woodward*, 132-51, 328-40, 388.
[7]   Kane, 'University Church', 17.
[8]   G. Giacoletti, *La rinnovata Basilica di S. Paolo sulla via Ostiense* (Rome 1845).

[9]   O'Dwyer, *Deane and Woodward*, ch. 5.

[10] *ibid.*, 357-9.

[11] Curran, *Newman House and University Church*, 49-50.

[12] N. Pevsner, *Some Architectural Writers of the Nineteenth Century* (London 1972) ch. 9.

[13] Curran, *Newman House and University Church*, 50-1.

[14] N. Pevsner, *Buildings of England: Wiltshire* (London 1963) 514-15.

[15] B.F.L. Clarke, 'The production of a powerful and ingenious idiosyncrasy', *Church Builders of the Nineteenth Century* (London 1969) 107.

[16] R. O'Donnell, 'Louis Joseph Duc in Birmingham, a "Style Latin" Church for Cardinal Newman, 1851', *Gazette des Beaux-Arts*, NS 5, xcviii, 1981, 37-44.

[17] Remarks on the churches in Munich are from personal observation on a recent visit. For the copies from Raphael in University Church, see Kane, 'University Church', 6-8.

[18] H.F. Nohbauer, 'Ludwig I and Munich Classicism', *Munich: City of Art* (Munich 1994) 51-8.

———

1 – Unknown artist, JOHN THOMAS TROY O.P. (1739-1823), AS BISHOP-ELECT OF OSSORY, c.1777,
oil on canvas, 97 x 73 cm (S. Clemente, Rome; all photos by the author unless otherwise stated)

Friends, Roman bindings, and Dr Troy

JOSEPH McDONNELL

T HE CAREER OF JOHN THOMAS TROY (1739-1823), ARCHBISHOP OF DUBLIN, IS one of the most remarkable, if controversial, of any Irish eighteenth-century Catholic clergyman (Plate 1). Born in Porterstown, near Dublin, in 1739, Troy's ancestors came to Ireland from Britain in the seventeenth century as part of the Cromwellian settlements, and by the eighteenth century the family had both a Protestant and Catholic line.[1] Educated as a priest of the Dominican order in Rome in the convent of S. Clemente, which he entered in 1756, Troy returned to his native country in 1777 as 'Rome's man in Ireland', first as Bishop of Ossory, and from 1786 till his death in 1823, as Archbishop of Dublin.[2]

Troy, the first effective national leader of the Catholic Church, was possessed of boundless energy, and displayed constant enthusiasm for his pastoral duties and an eagerness to impose Roman discipline and practice on the Irish Church; his enormous correspondence reveals his influence in English, Canadian and American ecclesiastical affairs.[3] As Bishop of Ossory he made his mark early on with his outspoken support for law and order, which attracted the approval of members of the government such as the Chief Secretary, Thomas Orde, and the Viceroy, Lord Rutland.[4] On the American War of Independence, the bishop commented in a pastoral letter that 'our American fellow-subjects [were] seduced by specious notions of liberty and other elusive expectations of soverignty' and opposed the spread of revolutionary principles in Ireland, preaching the need for deference and obedience to the Crown and the authorities.[5] Later as Archbishop of Dublin, Troy earned the undying hatred of many of the United Irishmen – Wolfe Tone called him a great scoundrel – when he issued a sentence of excommunication in 1798 against all those of his flock who would join the rebellion. He also actively supported the Act of Union, believing that it would advance full Catholic emancipation. Daniel O'Connell (1775-1847), on the other hand, declared that he would rather have the

Penal Laws back in all their severity than lose the parliament on College Green.[6]

Most nationalist historians in the nineteenth century dismissed Troy as a reactionary 'steady loyalist',[7] and a recent commentator has declared that the archbishop was among the 'supreme practioners of the traditional and, ineffectual, strategy of supplication' for the repeal of the Penal Laws.[8] Yet R.B. McDowell offered a more sympathetic assessment of the prelate's predicament when he wrote 'that by training, temperament, conviction and status, Troy was a conservative, and although "the powers that be" crown and parliament, were Protestant, since they were striving to preserve social order and defend the country against invasion, they received his loyal and unflinching support'.[9]

Troy's dedication to the reform and advancement of the Catholic church in Ireland is probably most visible in his acts of patronage, such as the founding of the seminary at Kilkenny, and his leading role in the establishment of the Royal College of Maynooth in 1795. In addition, the many churches erected or decorated testify to his zeal, and, above all, the building of the Pro-Cathedral in Dublin in the Greek Revival style,[10] one of the most noteworthy buildings to grace the capital since the days of Gandon's Custom House and Four Courts.

Having spent his formative years in Rome where he was imbued with the architectural splendour of the city and the decorum of the church ceremonies, Troy was naturally anxious to import Roman discipline on his return to Ireland in 1777. We obtain an insight into his attitude to the importance of church furnishings and ritual in the very precise and detailed inventories he drew up of the episcopal plate, vestments, and decorations in his Kilkenny church before he departed for the see of Dublin in 1787. There can be few Irish bishops, before or since, who took such a keen interest in, or rendered such precise inventories of, liturgical objects, from the description of the textiles down to the smallest item of lace.[11] This was in marked contrast to the minimalist account, consisting of just under five lines, accorded by Archbishop Carpenter (1770-1786) in his inventory of 'Ornaments' belonging to the archdiocese of Dublin in 1770.[12]

Among the recorded items described by Troy in the inventory of 30 January 1787 is an 'Ordo & Canon *pro Missa Pontificali* elegantly bound with Dr. Burke's arms on the cover – The gift of Dr. Troy'.[13] By great good fortune, this altar missal, as richly bound as anything the Pope might receive, survives, though now quite worn, in a private collection, where it has remained unidentified until now (Plate 5).[14] It was probably given by Troy, when he was a professor at S. Clemente, to Bishop Thomas Burke (De Burgo) of Ossory (1759-76) (Plate 2), author of the celebrated *Hibernia Dominicana* (discussed presently), during his *ad limina* visit to Rome in 1769.[15] Troy's gift of the deluxe folio missal, printed in Rome in 1729, and one of the most sumptuously produced liturgical works of the century, was an

2 – Unknown artist, THOMAS BURKE O.P., BISHOP OF OSSORY (1759-76), oil on canvas, 98 x 76 cm, inscribed 'Fr Thomas De Burgo. O.P. Episc. Ossoriensis. 1759'
(S. Clemente, Rome)

3 – Title page of HIBERNIA DOMINICANA, 230 x 185 mm
(S. Clemente, Rome)

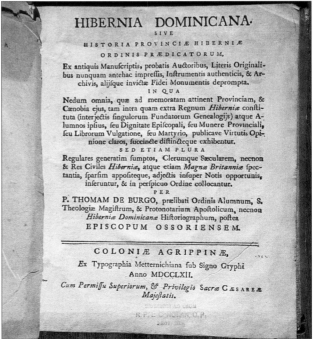

HIBERNIA DOMINICANA.
SIVE
HISTORIA PROVINCIÆ HIBERNIÆ
ORDINIS PRÆDICATORUM,

Ex antiquis Manuſcriptis, probatis Auctoribus, Literis Originali-
bus nunquam antehac impreſſis, Inſtrumentis authenticis, & Ar-
chivis, alijſque invictæ Fidei Monumentis deprompta.
IN QUA
Nedum omnia, quæ ad memoratam attinent Provinciam, &
Cænobia ejus, tam intra quam extra Regnum *Hiberniæ* conſti-
tuta (interjectis ſingulorum Fundatorum Genealogijs) atque A-
lumnos ipſius, ſeu Dignitate Epiſcopali, ſeu Munere Provinciali,
ſeu Librorum Vulgatione, ſeu Martyrio, publicave Virtutis Opi-
nione claros, ſuccinctè diſtinctèque exhibentur.
SED ETIAM PLURA
Regulares generatim ſumptos, Clerumque Sæcularem, necnon
& Res Civiles *Hiberniæ,* atque etiam *Magnæ Britanniæ* ſpec-
tantia, ſparſim appoſiteque, adjectis inſuper Notis opportunis,
inſeruntur, & in perſpicuo Ordine collocantur.
PER
P. THOMAM DE BURGO, prælibati Ordinis Alumnum, S.
Theologiæ Magiſtrum, & Protonotarium Apoſtolicum, necnon
Hiberniæ Dominicanæ Hiſtoriographum, poſtea
EPISCOPUM OSSORIENSEM.

COLONIÆ AGRIPPINÆ,
Ex Typographia Metternichiana ſub Signo Gryphi
Anno MDCCLXII.
Cum Permiſſu Superiorum, & Privilegio Sacræ CÆSAREÆ
Majeſtatis.

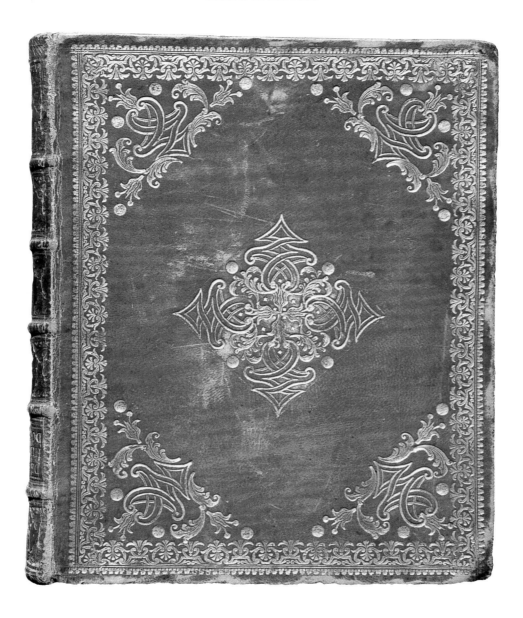

4 – Roman binding on Thomas Burke's HIBERNIA DOMINICANA (Cologne 1762).
Contemporary reddish tan goatskin and tooled in gold, 236 x 190 mm.
(S. Clemente, Rome)

opposite

5 – Roman binding with the arms of Thomas Burke OP, Bishop of Ossory (1759-76), on CANON
MISSAE PONTIFICALIS (Rome 1729). Bound in reddish-tan goatskin and tooled in gold, the gift of
Dr John Thomas Troy OP of S. Clemente, c.1769, 396 x 274 mm. (courtesy Aidan Heavey)

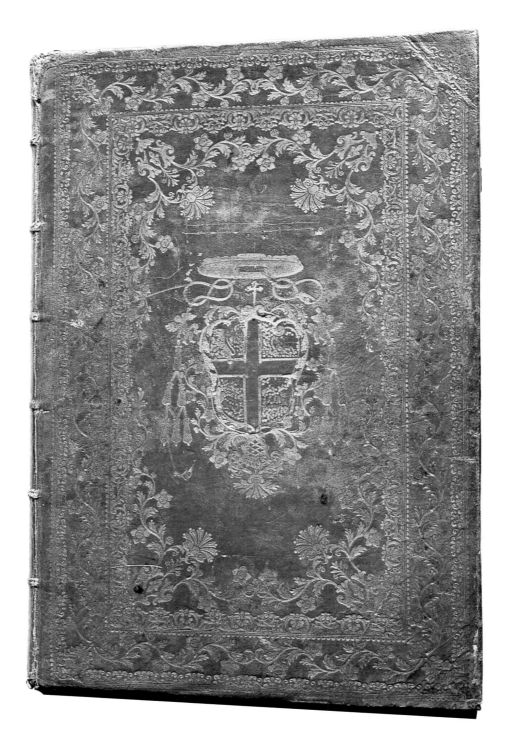

6 – *Agostino Masucci (1690-1769), POPE CLEMENT XII (1730-40), AND HIS NEPHEW CARDINAL NERI CORSINI (1685-1770), SECRETARY OF STATE. He was patron of the architect Alessandro Galilei (1691-1736).*
214 x 146 cm (detail)
(Galleria Corsini, Rome, inv 4565; courtesy Corsini Gallery)

BURKE. HIBERNIA DOMINICANA, 1762.

7 – *Roman binding, tooled in gold with the arms of Cardinal Francesco Carafa (1722-1818), on Thomas Burke's HIBERNIA DOMINICANA. Bound for presentation to the cardinal, almost certainly at the instigation of Dr John Thomas Troy OP, Superior of S. Clemente (whereabouts unknown)*
(reproduced from OLD KILKENNY REVIEW, ii, 1982, 376)

expression of the close friendship which had grown between the energetic young Dominican friar and the scholar-bishop of Ossory (whom Troy was to succeed), and which was to continue with exchanges of letters, almost on a daily basis, until Burke's death in 1776.

After Burke returned to Ireland from Rome in 1770, he immediately busied himself with bringing out a supplementary volume to his *Hibernia Dominicana*, originally published in 1762. His friend Dr Troy, whom he called 'his grandson', was pressed into action, diligently searching the archives of the various religious houses in Rome for new material for the *Supplementum*, which came out in 1772.[16] The project originated in 1748 when the Master General of the Dominicans decreed that each province of the Order should compile its history. In Ireland, Dr Thomas Burke (1710-1776), who had studied for the priesthood in Rome, where he made a good impression on Pope Benedict XIII (1724-1730), was chosen to write the history of the Irish province in 1753, a task completed in four years. The work in Latin came out in 1762 with the title *Hibernia Dominicana* (Plate 3), but the imprint, or place of publication, is given as a Cologne printing house, while it is now generally accepted that it was actually printed in Kilkenny, where Burke was living as bishop of Ossory since 1759, and in any case, some copies have the Kilkenny imprint.[17]

After his work came out, Burke sent fifty copies of it to Rome for distribution and presentation (Plate 4). A previously unpublished list survives in the archives of S. Sabina in Rome, naming the dignitaries, individuals and institutions who received presentation copies (Plate 12),[18] starting with Cardinal Neri Corsini (1685-1770), the nephew of Pope Clement XII (1730-1740) and the head of the powerful Propaganda Fide and 'Protector of Ireland', to whom the volume was dedicated (Plate 6). Corsini's copy, sumptuously bound in red goatskin and tooled in gold with his armorial bearings on each cover, has been located in the library of the Corsini Gallery in Rome (Plate 8).[19] The names of seven other cardinals follow, including the Cardinal Duke of York (1725-1807), son of the Old Pretender, the person to whom Burke probably owed his advancement to the see of Ossory. Also included in the list are various powerful and influential prelates in the church's hierarchy, some of them well known, even today, such as the great patron of the arts Cardinal Albani, and Cardinal Lorenzo Ganganelli, the future Pope Clement XIV, who suppressed the Jesuit Order, a friend of Burke since his Roman days. Their copies of *Hibernia Dominicana* have not been discovered to date, but they must have been bound up in the same style as Corsini's, as was de rigueur for presentation to princes of the Church at this time.

Dr Tom Wall, in an article written some thirty years ago, reproduced a lavishly bound copy of *Hibernia Dominicana* with an unidentified prelate's coat of arms (Plate 7).[20] This can now be identified as belonging to Cardinal Francesco Carafa di

8 – The dedication copy of Thomas Burke's HIBERNIA DOMINICANA *to Cardinal Neri Corsini
(1685-1770) with his arms on the covers, in a contemporary Roman binding of red goatskin
and gold tooled, 240 x 190 mm (courtesy Corsini Library, Rome)*

opposite

9 – Roman binding with the arms of Archbishop John Carpenter of Dublin (1770-86) on
CAEREMONIALE EPISCOPORUM *(Venice 1772), the gift of Bishop Troy, c.1777. Tan goatskin, tooled
in gold, 202 x 115 mm. (courtesy UCD library)*

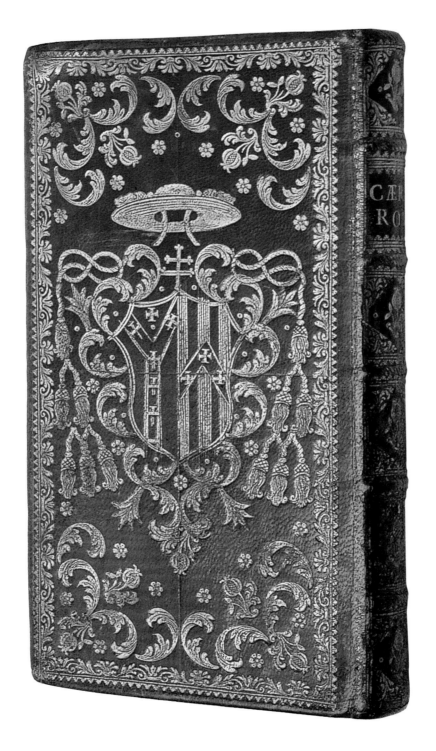

Trajetto of Naples (1722-1818),[21] whose handsome portrait by Anton von Maron (1733-1808) hangs in the Louvre. Carafa's name is not included in Burke's list, referred to above, for the good reason that he was probably unknown to him. Carafa was made a cardinal in 1773, with S. Clemente designated as his titular church, and this was more than likely the reason he received a specially bound copy of *Hibernia Dominicana*, ten years after its publication. Troy, by now the superior of S. Clemente, was surely responsible for this piece of promotion. In Troy's own annotated copy of *Hibernia Dominicana*, bound together with the *Supplementum* of 1772, in the National Library of Ireland, Carafa's name appears twice in the annotations, but not in the printed text.[22] Also, Troy must have been responsible for the elaborately bound copy presented to Pope Pius VI which has been recorded in the literature.

It is ironical that Burke should have put on such a display in Rome, whilst in Ireland he felt obliged to use a fictitious imprint in his book because of the Penal Laws; after all, he narrowly avoided arrest shortly after his return to Ireland in 1743 when he was due to say Mass at a particular location. In the event, another priest who had stepped into his place at the last moment was apprehended and transported to the colonies.[23] However, on this occasion, the only harm to Burke and his tome came not from the government, but from his fellow bishops in Ireland when they ordered that certain pages from *Hibernia Dominicana* be ripped out because of the perceived offence they caused, thus ensuring the book's lasting fame.[24]

Among Troy's last acts as superior of S. Clemente was the acquisition of the library which had belonged to the Irish artist James Forrester (1730-1776), who died in Rome on 31 January 1776.[25] His books, which are still preserved in S. Clemente, remain a lasting memorial to the many Irish artists who worked and lived in Rome in the eighteenth century.

On his return to Ireland from Rome after his appointment as Bishop of Ossory in succession to his old friend Thomas Burke in the summer of 1777, Troy recorded in his diary his purchases of books in Marseilles and Paris.[26] He also recounted how his breviary was soaked during a thunderstorm on a stop outside Marseilles. Doubtless the breviary was expensively bound in Rome, like the companion service books in his baggage such as the *Pontificale Romanum* (Plate 10)[27] and the *Caeremoniale Episcoporum* (Plate 11),[28] which have fortunately survived. Dr Troy's baggage probably also contained a second set of the episcopal service books, similarly bound, for presentation to Archbishop John Carpenter of Dublin, with his armorial bearings on each cover – an apt choice as the prelate was a noted bibliophile whose library contained many finely bound volumes, such as the works of Erasmus, which had belonged to the famous book collector, Jean Grolier (1479?-1565), now preserved in the library of Trinity College Dublin.[29] Troy's gift to Carpenter, of which the *Caeremoniale Episcoporum* (Plate 9) survives in almost mint condition in the library of University College Dublin,[30] was no doubt intended as a token of gratitude for the archbishop's active support, as Dr Troy's appointment to the see of Ossory was not a popular one, especially since he was imposed by Rome in the face of a local candidate put forward by the priests of the diocese.

After Troy's return to Ireland, he continued to receive books from Rome, as the posthumous auction catalogue of his library attests, such as a magnificently bound Roman missal, a present from Pius VI in 1784.[31] A poignant manuscript note at the end of the same catalogue lists a number of liturgical works suitably bound, including an *Officio Defunctorum*, that were sent from Rome at the time of the archbishop's death in May 1823, a fitting tribute to 'Rome's man in Ireland'.

––––––

ACKNOWLEDGEMENTS

I should like to express my gratitude to Dr Hugh Fenning OP for his assistance, especially in identifying many of the names on Bishop Thomas Burke's list of presentation copies of his *Hibernia Dominicana*. I am also grateful to Professor Michael McCarthy for his help and encouragement; Siobhán O'Rafferty at the library of the Royal Irish Academy for helpful assistance; Norma Jessop at the library of University College Dublin for kindly providing the transparency of the binding of Archbishop Carpenter's *Caeremoniale Episcoporum*, reproduced here; the staff of the National Library; Aidan Heavey, the owner of Bishop Burke's missal, reproduced and identified here for the first time; the late Tom Wall for his encouragement and generosity; and the late Fr P.J. Murphy of Robertstown, a generous book collector, and raconteur.

In Rome, my greatest debt is to Fr Denis O'Brien, rector of S. Silvestro in Capite, for his encouragement and generous hospitality. I am grateful to Brother Stephen Buckley, also of S. Silvestro, for his constant help and good humour; Professor Paul Murray OP of the Angelicum for his kind assistance; Fr Seamus Touhy OP of S. Clemente for his patience and generosity; Cathal Duddy and the community of St Isidore for their welcome and hospitality; Fr Ramon Hernandez OP, archivist of S. Sabina for his help and kindness; Monsignor William Sheehan of the Vatican Library for his assistance and advice; Sivigliano Alloisi of the Galleria Corsini for helpful assistance; Michel Wittock for help in various ways; I should also like to thank the staff of the Corsini library, the Casanatense library, the Biblioteca Nazionale, and especially the library of the American Academy in Rome.

ENDNOTES

[1]   Vincent J. McNally, *Reform, Revolution and Reaction: Archbishop John Thomas Troy and the Catholic Church in Ireland 1787-1817* (Lanham 1995) 8-9.
[2]   Hugh Fenning, *The Irish Dominican Province, 1698-1797* (Dublin 1990) 438.
[3]   McNally, *Reform*, 225; Dáire Keogh, '"The pattern of the flock": John Thomas Troy, 1786-

10 – Roman binding, with the arms of John Thomas Troy OP, Bishop of Ossory (1776-87) on
PONTIFICALE ROMANUM *(Venice 1772). Reddish-tan goatskin, tooled in gold, c.1777, 200 x 115 mm.*
(private collection)

11 – Roman binding, with the arms of John Thomas Troy OP, Bishop of Ossory (1776-87) on
CAEREMONIALE EPISCOPORUM (Venice 1772). Tan goatskin, tooled in gold, c.1777, 202 x 115 mm.
(Dominican Priory, Tallaght)

1823', in James Kelly and Dáire Keogh (eds), *History of the Catholic Diocese of Dublin* (Dublin 2000) 215; Fenning, *The Irish Dominican Province*, 439.

[4] McNally, *Reform*, 18.

[5] W. Carrigan, *The History and Antiquities of the Diocese of Ossory* (Dublin 1905), i, 185; McNally, *Reform*, 15.

[6] Cited by Mary Purcell, *Dublin's Pro-Cathedral* (Dublin 1975), unpaginated, n.5.

[7] Keogh, 'The pattern of the flock', 216.

[8] J. Smyth, *The Men of No Property* (London 1992), 54, cited by Keogh, 'The pattern of the flock', 217, n.8.

[9] R.B. McDowell, in a foreword to McNally, *Reform*.

[10] M. McCarthy, 'Dublin's Greek Pro-Cathedral', in James Kelly and Dáire Keogh (eds), *History of the Catholic Diocese of Dublin* (Dublin 2000) 237-46.

[11] Carrigan, *History and Antiquities* (Dublin 1905) i, 195-6:

> Memorandum
>
> During my administration of the parish of St. Canice, Kilkenny, *in commendam*, & which commenced in March, 1777, the following benefactions were made to the parish chapel, besides others of inferior note.
> A flowered silk vestment with yellow lace by Mrs. Dominick Meagher.
> A green sprigged silk vestment & antipendium by Miss Mary Ann Walsh.
> A linen worked cover for the tabernacle by Mrs. Seix.
> A flowered silk vestment with white lace by Mrs. Cormick alias Summerville.
> N.B. the lace purchased & vestments made up for Dr. Troy.
> A plate for the wine and water cruets by Dr. Troy.
> A carpet for the altar steps, a thurible & a genuflectory, all by Dr. Troy.
> A large silver chalice, a black vestment, a fine alb and a small pixis, all by Richard Archer.
> An embroidered chalice veil, by Dr. Troy.
> N.B. It was a present to him from Mr. Magrath of Dublin.
> A rich brocade vestment by Mr. Barnaby Murphy of Cadiz.
> A silk cope with silver lace by ditto.
> An humeral or veil for the Benediction of the B. Sacrament, ditto.
> Silver cruets with plate of the same, ditto.
> A flowered purple silk vestment by Mrs. Chantillion of Cadiz, mother-in-law of ditto.
> N.B. The lace was purchased & vestment made up by Dr. Troy.
> Six silver candlesticks, cross & altar charts, by Joseph Loughnan.
> Artificial Italian flowers for solemnities & Holy Week, by Dr. Troy.
> A crimson damask cope with lace, by ditto.
> N.B. It was a present to him from Mrs. Luke Meagher.
> Two altar cloths with lace, ditto.
> Many corporals and purifiers, by Dr. Troy.
> Purple covers for the altar in Holy Week & ornaments for the Sepulchre, by ditto.
> Cover for the branch, a small alb & surplice, by ditto.
> N.B. The new floor of the chapel, the gilded ordinary candlesticks & late third Confessional were made by subscription of the parish.
> A large alb & amice, by Dr. Troy.
> N.B. It was a present to him from Mrs. Luke Meagher.
> A new carpet for the altar steps, by Dr. Troy.
>
> Witness my hand. Kilkenny 3rd Feb., 1787.
> F. Joh. Thomas Troy, Epus. Ossorien. Electus Dubliniensis.

[12] M.W. O'R[iordan], 'Inventory of the Ornaments &c. belonging to the Archbishop of Dublin', *Reportorium Novum*, i, no. 2, 1956, 501.

[13] Carrigan, *History and Antiquities*, i, 196:

> Memorandum
>
> On Tuesday, January 30th, 1787, I delivered to the Rev Patrick Molloy, Dean, John Dunne, John Byrne & Richard O'Donel, prebendaries of the Chapter of Ossory the following articles belonging to the Catholic Bishop of Ossory for the time being.
> One rich embroidered mitre wth. The arms of the Holy See.
> Another inferior, ditto.
> Both were cleaned and lined at Dr. Troy's expense.
> One gold pectoral cross.
> Another silver. Ditto, washed wth. gold.
> One topaz ring.
> One ruby, ditto.
> Another inferior ruby, ditto.
> An old fashioned large useless ring.
> An elegant folio edition of the Pontificale Romanum – the bequest of Dr. Burke.
> Ordo & Canon pro Missa Pontificali in folio, elegantly bound with Dr. Burke's arms on the cover. – The gift of Dr. Troy.
> An octavo edition of the Roman pontifical.
> A silver oilstock wth. Dr. Burke's arms. – The gift of Dr. Troy.
> A Dalmatic & Tunicelle. – Bequest of Dr. Burke.
> Two clumsy pair of Pontifical gloves.
> A small clerical cap. – The gift of Dr. Troy.
> An ebony crozier, tipped in silver, bequeathed by Dr. Burke.
> A crimson velvet case for the Breads, ditto.
> A small silver Remonstrance for the Visitations with a case, made by subscription of the Diocesan Clergy.
> The cruets for the holy oils wth. a mahogany case. – The gift of Dr. Troy.
> An oak box, bequeathed by Dr. Burke; with other trifling articles.
>
> John Thomas Troy, Ossory.
>
> N.B. At the same time I delivered to the above mentioned gentlemen some diocesan papers & a Registry of the Diocess commenced by Dr. Burke and continued by me till my departure from the Diocess.
>
> John Thomas, Ossory

[14] *Canon Missae pontificalis ad usum Episcoporum ac Praelatorum Solemniter, vel privatè celebrantium. Sub auspiciis SS. Domini Nostri Benedicti Decimi Tertii Pont. Max. Romae, Ex Typographia Vaticana. Apud Jo: Mariam Salvioni* (Rome 1729) size: 396 x 274 mm. Bound in Rome in a reddish-tan goatskin, and tooled in gold with the arms of Bishop Thomas Burke (1710-1776) on the upper cover, the lower revealing the Pignatelli arms (the family of Pope Innocent XII, 1691-1700), where the overlaid arms of Burke have worn off.

Provenance: as stated in note 13, the volume is listed in the 1787 inventory drawn up by Bishop Troy: 'Ordo & Canon *pro Missa Pontificali* in folio, elegantly bound with Dr. Burke's arms on the cover – The gift of Dr. Troy'. An inscription on the half-title reads: 'St. Mary's Cathedral Kilkenny'. Sold at Mealy's auction in Castlecomer, 11-12 December 1970, lot 932a. 'Canon Missae Pontificalis, folio Rome 1729. Engr. Frontis. Red and black title with vignette. Full page engravings. Full calf armorial (Cardinal). Two tooled floral borders, gilt with arms in centre'; Museum Bookshop, 35 Kildare Street, Dublin, Catalogue 3, August 1972, no. 11. 'Canon Missae Pontificalis ad Usum Episcoporum ac Praelatorum ... Benedicti ... Pont. Max. Embellished with full page copper plt. engs. & tail pieces. engd. t/p. Full light brown mor. tooled gilt. Folio. Ex. Typographia Vaticana Romae Apud Joannes Mariam Salvioni. 1729. £50. Very fine Bishop Armorial binding with a highly ornate glt. Floral surround & border on both covers. 6 bands'; acquired by Aidan Heavey from the Museum Bookshop. It was while examining the above volume recently in Aidan Heavey's library that it occurred to me that the armorial bearings on the cover were not Italian, but of the Burke family. This hunch was later confirmed when I came across Troy's description (as noted above) which matched the present volume. Literature: the shop which produced the binding of the *Canon Missae pontificalis*, one of the foremost in Rome, was associated with the Salvioni firm, the publishers of this volume; see A.R.A. Hobson, *French and Italian collectors and their bindings* (Oxford 1953) 160. Other bindings on which some of the same tools are found, include the 20-volume set of the works of Piranesi, De Rossi, etc, which came from the library of the Russian Imperial family at Tsarskoe Selo and sold at auction on 20-21 June 1933 (Gilhofer & Ranschburg, Lucerne) lot 437 (plate 37). Ten volumes of this set, minus the Piranesi works, were later in the library of F.H. Kissner and sold by Christie's in Rome on 3-5 October 1990, lot 447 (with illustration). A similarly tooled folio volume of De Rossi, *Studio D'Architettura Civile* (Rome 1702), is in the Royal Library at Windsor (R.R. Holmes, *Specimens of Royal, Fine and Historical Bookbinding selected from the Royal Library, Windsor Castle*, 1893, plate 134), while another similar unpublished binding is in the Chester Beatty Library.

[15] Burke's arrival in Italy was noted in the *Gazzetta Toscana*, when he was entertained in Leghorn on 13 September 1769 by Richard Cosgrave, a Catholic merchant, and left for Florence where he christened the son of Thomas Lyttelton of Hagley on 31 March 1770; see John Ingamells, *A Dictionary of British and Irish Travellers in Italy 1701-1800* (New Haven and London 1997) 289, cited under DeBorgh (sic.).

[16] Fenning, *The Irish Dominican Province*, 420-1; an extract from a letter in the Dublin Diocesan Archives from Bishop Thomas Burke of Ossory to Troy in Rome throws light on their close collaboration: 'Kilkenny, 5 April 1773, A hundred supplements nailed in a box are waiting in Dublin for the first ship to Leghorn' (DDA Hib. Dom 1/a, folder 2). According to Fr Fenning, to whom I am obliged for this reference, Burke's letter details his plan for a second edition to be printed (by implication) at Dublin.

[17] 'A sketch of the Life and Writings of Doctor Thomas Burke, later Roman Catholic Bishop of Ossory', *Anthologia Hibernia*, i, February 1793, 93-4; A. Coleman, 'Thomas De Burgo: Author of the "Hibernia Dominicana", and Bishop of Ossory', *Irish Ecclesiastical Record*, 3rd series, xiii, July-November 1892, 587-600, 707-19, 828-41, 1010-25; *Irish Book Lover*, ix, nos 11 and 12, June-July 1918, 121-3; Thomas Wall, *Introduction to the Gregg reprint of Hibernia Dominicana*, 1970, i-iv. For an illustration of *Hibernia Dominicana* with the Kilkenny imprint see J. McDonnell, *500 Years of the Art of the Book in Ireland* (Dublin and London 1997) cat. 56.

[18] Referred to in Hugh Fenning, *The Undoing of the Friars of Ireland* (Louvain 1972) 265, n.4. The list is in the general archives of the Order of Preachers (Dominicans), Santa Sabina, Rome, filed under XIII.69164 (Prov. Hiberniae Addenda). The single sheet of paper, of Roman manufacture, is watermarked with an anchor in a circle with the initials G and N, surmounted by a star and the letter F beneath; see E. Heawood, *Watermarks* (Hilversum 1950) pl. 1.

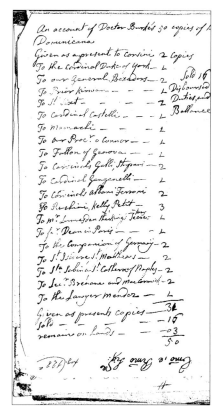

An account of Doctor Burke's 50 copies of his Hibernia Dominicana

Given as a present to Corsini [a]	2 copies
To the Cardinal Duke of York [b]	1
To our General Boxadors [c]	2
To Prior Kirwan [d]	1
To St. Sixt. [e]	2
To Cardinal Castelli [f]	1
To Mamachi [g]	1
To our Proc. O Connor [h]	1
To Fallon of Genova [i]	1
To Cardinals Galli, [j] Stopani [k]	2
To Cardinal Ganganelli [l]	1
To Cardinals Albani [m] Ferroni [n]	2
To Richini [o], Kelly [p], Petit [q]	3
To Mr. Lumesden [r] the kings Secretary	1
To far. Dean in Paris [s]	1
To the Companion of Germany [t]	2
To St. Isidore [u] St. Matthews [v]	2
To Sta. Sabina [w] St. Cathern of Naples [x]	2
To Secr. Brenane and MacCormick [y]	2
To the Lawyer Mendez [z]	1

Given as presents copies	31
Sold	16
Remain on hands	03

	50

	s	b
Sold 16 copies for	16:	77
Disbursed for freight		
Duties, and bindings	12:	76
	------- ----------	
Balance	4: ~~97~~	
	4:	01

12 – 'An account of Doctor Burke's 50 copies of his Hibernia Dominicana': an undated sheet, c.1763 (?), recording the names of 31 individuals and institutions who received copies of HIBERNIA DOMINICANA, together with an account of the remaining copies and expenses incurred. (S. Sabina Archives, Rome, XIII. 69164)

Names identified from the above list

a   Corsini, Neri (1685-1770), created a cardinal by his uncle Pope Clement XII in 1730 and held several positions in the papal curia. He was made Cardinal Protector of Ireland in 1763 until his death. The cardinal was the founder of the famous Corsini library and art gallery in Rome; see Sivigliano Alliosi, *Personaggi e Interpreti Ritratti della Collezione Corsini*, exhibition catalogue (Rome 2001); G. Moroni, *Dizionario di Erudizione Storico-Ecclesiastica*, xvii (Venice 1840-1861) 286; Fenning, *The Undoing of the Friars of Ireland*, 120 and *passim*. For an assessment of his career and patronage, see his entry in J. Turner (ed.), *The Grove Dictionary of Art*, 7 (London 1996), 897-8

b   Henry Stuart, Cardinal Duke of York (1725-1807), son of James III, the Old Pretender. He was created a cardinal in 1747 and founded a library at Frascati (now in the Vatican), which is celebrated not least for its rich collection of eighteenth-century Roman bindings. *Libraries, Guests of the Vatican During the Second World War* (Vatican City 1945) 17-18, 32-4, 51-4; Ion S. Monro, 'Books and Henry Stuart, Cardinal Duke of York', *The Book Handbook*, i, 1 (London 1949) 191-205; A. Shield, *Henry Stuart, Cardinal of York, and his times* (London 1908). J. Lees-Milne, *The Last Stuarts* (London 1983).

c   Boxadores, Juan T. de (1703-1780), General of the Dominican Order, created a cardinal by Pope Pius VI in 1775. Moroni, *Dizionario*, vi, 82-3.

d   Kirwan, Patrick OP., Prior of S. Clemente, deposed in 1766; Fenning, *The Irish Dominican Province*, 357 and *passim*.

e   St Sixtus, Irish Dominican College in Rome. H. Fenning, 'SS. Sisto e Clemente, 1677-1797', in L. Boyle, *San Clemente Miscellany I* (Rome 1977), ch. 2.

f   Castelli, Cardinal Giuseppe (1705-1780), Prefect of Propaganda (1763-1780). The congregation of the Propaganda, one of the most powerful offices in the Church, was in charge of ecclesiastical affairs in 'Missionary' countries such as Ireland at this period. For Castelli's extensive dealing with Ireland, see Fenning, *The Undoing of the Friars of Ireland*; *The Irish Dominican Province, 1698-1797*, *passim*; C. Eubel, *Hierarchia Catholica*, iii, 13, and vi, 21; Moroni, *Dizionario*, x, 211.

g   Mamachi, Thomas OP (1792), author of *Annales Ordinis Praedicatorum*, theologian of the Casanatense library from 1749. The copy of *Hibernia Dominicana* in the Casanatense library, which is bound in white vellum, is located in the MSS department: Z.XV.17, whilst the *Supplementum* has the call no. AA.XI.153; neither volume has any indication of provenance apart from the library stamp.

h   O'Connor, Dominic OP, procurator general of the Irish province, resident in Madrid 1760-70 where he died. Fenning, *The Irish Dominican Province, passim*.

i   Fallon, Thomas OP (died 1774), a parish priest in Genoa by 1753.

j   Galli, Antonio (1697-1767), made a cardinal in 1753, was prefect of the Index. Eubel, *Hierarchia Catholica*, ii, 17; Moroni, *Dizionario*, xxviii, 122-3.

k   Stopani (Stoppani), Giovanni Francesco (1695-1774), diplomat, created a cardinal in 1753. Moroni, *Dizionario*, lxx, 93-5; Eubel, *Hierarchia Catholica*, ii, 40. The Palazzo Stopani (later Vidoni) in Rome was engraved by Piranesi, see J. Wilton-Ely, *The Mind and Art of Giovanni Battista Piranesi* (London 1978) pl. 128; Stopani owned a splendid table service from the Doccia porcelain factory with his coat of arms boldly painted on each piece; two beakers from the service were sold at Christie's in London in December 1978.

l   Ganganelli, Cardinal Lorenzo: as Pope Clement XIV (1769-1774) he ordered the supression of the Jesuits. Troy was friendly with Ganganelli during his years in Rome. L. von Pastor, *The History of the Popes*, xxxvi-xxxviii (London 1950-51) *passim*; Coleman 'Thomas de Burgo', *passim*.

m   This could refer to either of the two Albani cardinals: Albani, Alessandro (1692-1779), the eminent patron of the arts, was a nephew of Pope Clement XI (1700-1721). He also held the post of Vatican Librarian and was Cardinal Protector of the Dominican Order. Moroni, *Dizionario*, i, 180; Eubel, *Hierarchia Catholica*, vi, 22; A. Blunt, *Guide to Baroque Rome* (London 1982) 208. See his entry in Turner (ed.), *The Grove Dictionary of Art*. Albani, Giovanni Francesco (d.1808), titular cardinal of S. Clemente, transferred to the Dominican convent of S. Sabina in 1760. He was, like his uncle, a patron of the arts and a book collector. Moroni, *Dizionario*, i, 180-1 Eubel, *Hierarchia Catholica*, ii, 34.

n Ferroni (Feroni) Giuseppe (1693-1767): of a wealthy Florentine family and an eminent collector, Feroni was created a cardinal by Pope Benedict XIV in 1753. He held the position of prefect of the Congregation of Sacred Rites and Ceremonies. Moroni, *Dizionario*, xxiv, 41. Eubel, *Hierarchia Catholica*, ii, 38; Catrina Caneva, *La collezione Feroni* (Florence 1998).

o Richini, Thomas Augustine OP, Master of the Sacred Palace (1759-1778), mentioned in *Hibernia Dominicana*, 53, note; Fenning, *The Irish Dominican Province*, 254.

p Kelly, most likely Charles Kelly OP, theologian of the Casanatense Dominican Library and house of studies (1756-1793). Roman agent and a great associate of Thomas Burke, the author of *Hibernia Dominicana*, and a father figure of John Thomas Troy; Fenning, *The Irish Dominican Province, passim*.

q Petit, Francis OFM, a Roman agent in 1766. Fenning, *The Undoing of the Friars of Ireland* 274.

r Lumisden, Andrew (1720-1801), private secretary to the Old Pretender, James III from 1762. J. Ingamells, *A Dictionary of British and Irish Travellers in Italy 1701-1800* (New Haven and London 1997) 616-17; Michael McCarthy, 'Andrew Lumisden and Giovanni Battista Piranesi', in Clare Hornsby (ed.), *The Impact of Italy: The Grand Tour and Beyond, The British School at Rome* (London 2000) 65-81; Fenning, *Irish Dominican Province*, 357-8.

s Dean, John (also Deane) OP, resident at the Dominican 'Novitiate General' in Paris from 1745 until his death on 12 May 1780 aged 80.

t Companion of Germany, i.e. Emerich Langenwatter, assistant General of the Dominican Order for Germany (and Ireland too); see *Hibernia Dominicana*, ix; Fenning, *The Irish Dominican Province*, 254.

u St Isidore's college of the Irish Franciscans in Rome was founded by Luke Wadding in the seventeenth century. The church contains sculptures by Bernini. A. Daly, *S. Isidoro* (Rome 1971); P. Conlon, *St. Isidore's College Rome* (Rome 1982).

v St Mathew's, the old church of S. Matteo in the via Merulana belonged to the Irish Augustinians in the eighteenth century. R. Anderson, *Roman Churches of Special Interest for English-Speaking People* (Vatican City 1982) ch. 8.

w S. Sabina, the basilica of Santa Sabina dates from the early fifth century and belongs to the Dominican Order. E. Male, *The Early Churches of Rome*, translated by D. Buxton (London 1960) chapter 3.

x St Cathern of Naples: the Dominican convent of Santa Caterina di Formello in Naples. See Fenning, *The Irish Dominican Province*, 419 for a charming account of a visit to the Naples convent by Michael Kelly, the famous Irish singer and actor; originally published in M. Kelly, *Reminiscences* i (London 1826) 26.

y McCormick, Andrew OP, resident of the Irish Dominican convent of S. Sisto in Rome 1762-1768.

z Mendez, Giovanni, a Roman lawyer; Fenning, *The Undoing of the Friars in Ireland*, 258, 265.

[19] Thomas Burke (De Burgo), *Hibernia Dominicana* (Coloniae Agrippinae 1762). Bound in Rome in bright red goatskin and tooled in gold with the arms of Cardinal Neri Corsini (1685-1770), to whom the volume was dedicated, on both covers; all edges gilt; size: 240 x 190 mm. Recorded in the list (as note 18 above) of 31 copies sent to Rome for presentation: 'Given as a present to Corsini – 2 copies'; perhaps only this copy was elaborately bound. Corsini Library Rome, shelf no. 210, F8.

[20] Thomas Wall, 'Two Episcopal Bookcovers from Ossory', in *Old Kilkenny Review*, 2, 4, 1982,

373-7. The present whereabouts of Carafa's volume is unknown.

[21] Pompeo Litta, *Famiglie Celebri Italiane* (seconda serie II) (Turin 1910), Stemme dei Carafa del ramo 'della Spina', tavola xiv (della tavola ix). Moroni, *Dizionario*, ix, 249.

[22] National Library of Ireland, L.O.1,160. *Hibernia Dominicana*, 1762, and *Supplementum*, 1772, bound together in vellum and inscribed on the flyleaf: 'Ad usum habet F. Johannes Thomas Troy O.P., Anno 1763, Supplementa adjunctum anno 1773'. Armorial bookplate of Troy as Bishop of Ossory on the front pastedown. The *Supplementum* incribed: 'Ex Dono Authoris anno 1773'. Troy's annotated references to Cardinal Carafa occur on pp 415, 853. For Troy's different bookplates, see Brian North Lee, *British Bookplates, A Pictorial History* (North Pomfret Vermont 1979), 62-4, no. 64; Gerald Slevin, 'The Heraldic Practice of the Archbishops of Dublin', in *Reportorium Novum*, i, 2, 1956, 471.

[23] Daphne Pochin Mould, *The Irish Dominicans* (Dublin 1957), 171.

[24] Wall, *Introduction to Hibernia Dominicana* (reprint 1970).

[25] H. Fenning, 'SS. Sisto e Clemente, 1677-1797', in Boyle, *San Clemente Miscellany I*, 50.

[26] Mary Purcell, 'Letters of Dr. Troy', *Studies*, Autumn 1979, 208.

[27] *Pontificale Romanum*, N. Pezzana (Venice 1772), size: 200 x 115 mm. Bound in Rome in a reddish-brown goatskin (now faded to a tan colour), gold tooled with the arms of Bishop Troy on both covers; the spine has five raised bands; edges of the boards decorated with a diagonally hatched roll; edges of the leaves gilt with gauffering line; endbands consist of green and white silk threads; red sponged paper pastedowns. Provenance: Troy's signature on the flyleaf. Sold at Mealy's auction of Fr P.J. Murphy's library in Robertstown Hotel, county Kildare, 20 May 1977, lot 179A; private collection. Literature: previously unpublished. For an account of the shop which produced this binding, see Hobson, *French and Italian collectors and their bindings*, 160.

[28] *Caeremoniale Episcoporum*, N. Pezzana (Venice 1772), size: 202 x 115mm. Bound in Rome in a reddish-brown goatskin (now faded to a dark tan), blue-green endbands; gauffered edges of the leaves, gilt. Provenance: signature of 'J. Th. Troy' on the flyleaf. An inscription at the foot of the title page reads: 'St. Mary's Cathedral, Kilkenny'; ex libris of F.X. Dixon on the front pastedown, and later book-label of Tom Wall, 1984; Dominican Priory archives, Tallaght, county Dublin. Literature: T. Wall, 'Two Episcopal Bookcovers from Ossory', in *Old Kilkenny Review*, 2, 4, 1982, 373, illustration 376 (incorrectly described as Irish bindings). For an account of the shop which produced this binding, see Hobson, *French and Italian collectors and their bindings*, 160.

[29] Howard Nixon, *Bookbindings from the Library of Jean Grolier*, (London 1965) no. 30; V. Morrow, 'Bibliotheca Quiniana', in P. Fox (ed.), *Treasures of the Library, Trinity College Dublin* (Dublin 1986), 186-8 (Quin 114).

[30] *Caeremoniale Episcoporum*, N. Pezzana (Venice 1772), size: 202 x 115mm. Bound in Rome in a dark red goatskin and tooled in gold with the arms of Archbishop Carpenter on both covers, all edges gilt. Spine has five raised bands, with the second panel lettered directly on the spine; the endbands are blue, white and black plait with bead; edges of the boards gilt with a hatched roll; turn-ins plain; edges of the leaves gauffered and gilt; endpapers are mottled red and white. Provenance: an inscription on the flyleaf reads: 'J. Carpenter, Ex dono F. John Thomae Troy Epi Ossoriensis, postea Archp. Dublinensis'. The bookplate of Archbishop Carpenter, dated 1770, is found on the verso of the title page with an inscription in Irish; Library of University College Dublin 41.R.30. Literature: Colm Ó Lochlainn, *Irish Book Lover*, 42, 3, May-June 1934, 57; T. Wall, *The Sign of Dr. Hay's Head* (Dublin 1958), illus-

trated 109; T. Wall, 'Two Episcopal bookcovers from Ossory', in *Old Kilkenny Reivew*, 2, 4, 1982, 373 (incorrectly described as Irish bindings); J. McDonnell, *Ecclesiastical Art of the Penal Era* (Maynooth 1995) no. 76, 48. For an account of the shop which produced this binding, see Hobson, *French and Italian collectors and their bindings*, 160.

[31] The auction catalogue of Archbishop Troy's books is in the library of the Royal Irish Academy: C.19:

> A Catalogue of the very choice and valuable Library of the late Most Rev Doctor Troy, Roman Catholic Archbishop of Dublin, embracing an collection of the best works in divinity and Ecclesiastical History (including the Writings of the Primitive Fathers, many of them of the best Continental Editions;) an excellent body of Irish History, some particularly rare and curious. The French, Italian, and Latin branches of literature are also well selected. The miscellaneous part consists of works of general perusal, and are well chosen. There are also a few prints, books of prints, and some very good mahogany bookcases. To be sold by order of the executors, on Wednesday, June 25, 1823 and following day at the Rotunda (entrance Cavendish-Row).
>
> Charles Sharpe, Auctioneer, 33, Anglesea Street, Dublin.

The sale consisted of just under 1,100 lots, including the following:

> 60. *Caeremoniale Missae*, 12mo. Rome 1762
> Archbishop Carpenter's copy.'

> 65. *Esercizj di Pietà*, splendidly bound in red morocco, Rome 1771

> 84. *Canon Missae Pontificalis*, splendidly printed, illustrated with the most exquisite fine engravings, magnificently bound, red morocco, large folio Rome 1784. This superb copy was sent to Dr. Troy, as a present by His Holiness. [For examples of Pius VI's bindings, see M. Tocci, *Legatura Papali da Eugenio IV a Paolo VI* (Vatican City 1977), pl. cxci-cxcv.]

> 149. *Caeremoniale Episcoporum* – Benedicti Papae XIV, red morocco, gilt leaves Venice 1794 [date incorrect, possibly 1772]

> 566. *Supplementum Hiberniae Dominicanae a Thomae De Burgo*, an interleaved copy. 1772.

> 913. DOUAY BIBLE, 5 vols. Elegantly bound, Dublin, Coyne 1811

> 952. Sermons by MURPHY (Fr) 2 vols. Elegantly bound in morocco, gilt Dublin 1808

> 976. HOLY BIBLE (DOWAY) (quarto), very neat Dublin, Coyne 1816

> 977. —— handsomely bound, gilt leaves, Dublin Cross 1719 [should read 1791]

> The foregoing Works have within these few days arrived from Rome, as a present to Archbishop Troy.

> 385. Missale Romanum, 4to. Morocco, gilt

> 386. Aliud exemplar
> Officium Defunctorum.

———

1 – Cut-glass celery vase, c.1830, with fan-like scalloped rim and panels divided by split bands. Celery vases such as this one were made at the Waterford glassworks.
(courtesy National Museum of Ireland, registration no. 1956.76)

Selling Waterford glass
in early nineteenth-century Ireland

ANNA MORAN

A COLLECTION OF BUSINESS RECORDS AND CORRESPONDENCE ASSOCIATED WITH the Waterford glassworks has shed new light on the inner workings of this well-known glasshouse. Analysis of these records, held by the National Museum of Ireland, provides a detailed insight into the design, production and sale of glass at the Waterford glasshouse during the early nineteenth century. They also facilitate a re-evaluation of traditionally nurtured views which present the Waterford glasshouse as predominantly a producer of highly sought-after luxury cut glass, which it successfully made and sold until excessive excise duties levied by the British government brought about its demise.[1] This study, which focuses on how they sold their wares, highlights the difficulties they faced in selling their luxury cut glass, forcing them to rely on the sale of their plainer and cheaper goods. The ways in which the glasshouse sought to increase its sales at a time of severe economic hardship reveals a picture which is more complex than that commonly presented.

HISTORY AND SOURCES

The Waterford glassworks was in operation between the years 1783 and 1851. It was set up by the Quaker merchants George and William Penrose, who, like other entrepreneurs at the time, benefited from the premiums which were available to Irish glassmakers. Premiums came in the form of grants awarded by the Irish parliament through the Dublin Society, 'for the encouragement of manufactures, particularly glass manufacture'.[2] The year 1780 saw the removal of restrictions on the exportation of glass from Ireland, which had been in place since 1746. Further encouragement was provided by the Act of 1781-82, which removed the duty imposed on coal when used in glass manufacture.[3] George and William Penrose, with the assistance of John Hill and a team of glassmakers from Stourbridge invited over to work for them, established the glasshouse on the quay in Waterford.[4] During the 1780s, the Waterford glasshouse was one of seven glassworks manufacturing flint glass in Ireland. By 1833 it was one of eight concerns in Ireland, each of them sited close to a port from where they could export their goods.[5]

Following the death of William Penrose in 1799, ownership passed into the hands of a partnership comprised of Jonathan Gatchell, Ambrose Barcroft and James Ramsey. Upon the dissolution of this partnership in 1811, Jonathan Gatchell became the full owner. Following the death of Gatchell in 1823, as the instructions of his will set out, the glassworks was placed in the hands of a partnership until 1835, when George Gatchell, Jonathan's youngest son, came of age. While the exact composition of the partnership changed over the period, it principally comprised members of Jonathan Gatchell's immediate family: his daughter Elizabeth Walpole, and her husband Joseph Walpole, together with Jonathan's brother-in-law Nehemiah Wright, who acted as trustee for the partnership, as well as Nehemiah's son Jonathan who managed the glasshouse between 1831 and 1835.

The name of Waterford is synonymous with heavy, richly cut glass, and resonates with luxury associations and a design identity which has come to symbolise the highest degree of traditional Irish skill and craftsmanship. The perception of the Waterford glasshouse is so prominent that vast amounts of early nineteenth-century cut glass are attributed to the Waterford glassworks when in fact only a fraction of it could possibly have been made in Waterford. This was commented upon in 1920 by M.S.D. Westropp (1868-1954) in his seminal publication on Irish glassmaking.[6] Similarly, the glass scholar Hugh Wakefield was keen to point out that early nineteenth-century Ireland, as home to a very small number of glasshouses, only ever produced a small proportion of the total amount of cut glass produced in the British Isles.[7] In spite of Wakefield's research – supported by other glass scholars of authority – the tendency to describe all cut glass indiscriminately as Irish or even as 'Waterford' persists to this day.[8]

The surviving records, which comprise a collection of letters, account books and patterns, were sourced in the early years of the twentieth century by M.S.D. Westropp.[9] The majority of the letters, known as the Gatchell Letters, date to the early decades of the nineteenth century and were principally written between various members of the Gatchell, Walpole and Wright families, who together ran the glassworks.[10] The drawings, done in the 1820s and 1830s, are thought to have been executed by Samuel Miller, foreman of the glasscutters at the Waterford glassworks.[11] The drawings give an insight into the assortment of objects produced, which included a wide range of decanters, goblets, celery vases and sugar bowls (Plates 1-4).[12] The designs also act as evidence that the Waterford glassworks was producing glass in the same richly cut style dominant in the products of all the major glasshouses in the British Isles. The innumerable permutations of lines cut at different angles, leaving protrusions of varying relief, was made possible through use of a steam engine which powered the lathes at a faster and more even rate than had been possible with hand-turned lathes. The use of steam power in glass cutting was first introduced during the last decade of the eighteenth century.[13] While somewhat later than other glasshouses, the managers of the Waterford glassworks did invest in a steam engine in the mid-1820s, ensuring that they would be able to produce glass equal to that made elsewhere.[14] Evidence that their designs compared favourably with those of others is provided by the fact that they were awarded silver medals at both the 1835 and 1836 exhibitions of manufactures at the Royal Dublin Society.[15]

The surviving account ledgers, also dating to the 1820s and 1830s, facilitate analysis of the business organisation which sustained their manufacturing activities.[16] Outgoing payments for materials, labour, equipment and fuel, combined with incoming revenue from the many retailers who purchased glass on a wholesale basis, facilitate analysis of the complex and geographically wide networks of supply and distribution on which the business was based. Also present within the accounts are the regular payments made in accordance with the excise duty. It is this duty which has been blamed for the decline of the Irish glass industry.

THE DECLINE OF THE IRISH GLASS INDUSTRY DURING THE EARLY NINETEENTH CENTURY

Contrary to traditional thinking, the economic impact of the Act of Union of 1800 was not quite as immediately deleterious as previously claimed.[17] As pointed out by David Dickson, Dublin enjoyed a period of wartime prosperity, and the 'prophesised exodus' of peers and upper-class families was not quite as sudden as expected.[18] Any rise in gentry absenteeism was compensated for by an increased military presence, and high prices for agricultural produce benefited farmers and landlords.[19] Research on the assay records of the Dublin Assay Office reveals that the volume of silver produced in the city in 1810 remained substantial.[20] Similarly, the cabinet maker John Mack, later a partner in the firm of Mack, Williams & Gibton, received many significant institutional commissions during the early years of the nineteenth century and during this period his business expanded.[21]

Economic decline did, however, set in at the end of the Napoleonic wars, and the period 1816 to 1818 witnessed food shortages not just in Ireland, but also in Britain and Europe.[22] The economic gloom which presided saw a drop in the prices of manufactured goods, setting the scene for further decline during the 1820s and

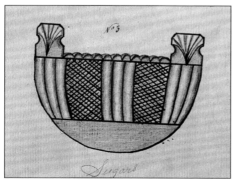

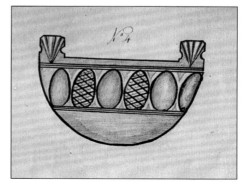

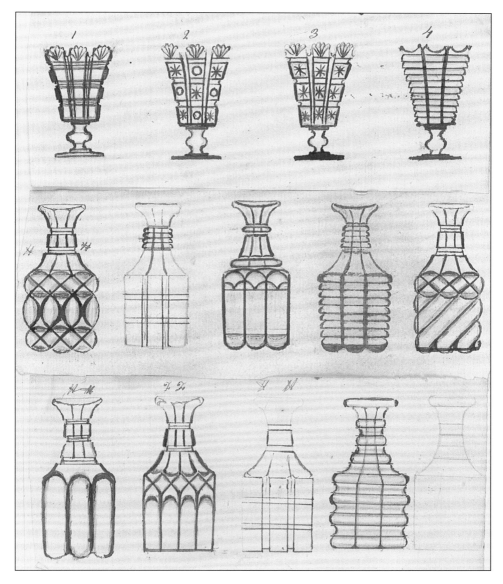

4 – One of the Samuel Miller drawings, said to have been used at the Waterford glasshouse during the 1820s and 1830s. This sheet featuring designs for celery vases in the top row and decanters in the two rows below (courtesy NMI)

opposite

2 – Cut-glass sugar bowl and stand: the heavy style of cutting dates this piece to the late 1820s or early 1830s. Sugar bowls and stands of this design were made at the Waterford glassworks. (courtesy NMI, registration nos 1886.60 and 1886.61)

3 – Samuel Miller drawings of two sugar bowl designs (courtesy NMI)

1830s.[23] During this period of recession, glassmakers in Ireland felt particularly aggrieved. Without a native source of coal which could fire their furnaces to the correct degree, the Irish glassmakers were forced to import their fuel. High transportation costs saw the price of coal quadrupling between the coal mine and the Irish coast.[24] Sand, lead, saltpetre and potash, together with clay for making pots to contain the molten glass in the furnace, had to be imported by the Irish glassmakers. This resulted in much higher production costs than those incurred by their English counterparts.

Hopes of compensating for high production costs through trade with Britain were somewhat hampered by increasing duties on glass exported between England and Ireland.[25] Glass exported from Ireland was subject to a 10% duty, together with countervailing duties equivalent to the excise duty paid on glass manufactured in England. Whereas English glassmakers were eligible to receive a bounty known as a 'drawback' on glass exported, Irish glassmakers were not.[26] Their pleas to be allowed this bounty are recorded in the *Appendix to Twelfth Report of Commissioners of Inquiry into the Revenue arising in Ireland, Scotland &c.*[27] During the years 1825-26, the excise duty was extended to Ireland. This came about partly due to the pressure exerted by the Irish glassmakers. It also represented an attempt to eradicate illicit glasshouses in Ireland known to be making substandard glass which was then smuggled into England and Scotland.[28]

Unfortunately, the extension of the excise duty to Ireland did not have the desired effect, and a parliamentary report of 1835 records the despairing requests to have the duty removed.[29] The repeal of the duty in 1845 did little to revive the industry, which had suffered greatly in the face of intense competition from Belgian and Bohemian glasshouses. The Waterford glassworks closed in 1851, and by 1852, of the eight flint glasshouses at work in Ireland in 1833, only two survived – one in Belfast and one in Dublin. In attempting to account for this decline and to apportion blame, many writers have taken a patriotic stance. Writing in 1984, Ida Grehan wholeheartedly blamed the taxes imposed by the British government:

> The Waterford glasshouse had come to a peak of perfection with international recognition when the Act of Union and heavy taxes levied to pay for England's overseas battles destroyed the glass industry. The furnaces which had transformed Waterford from the name of a city port on the river Suir to an Irish myth were quenched, and the glass-blowers and engravers sadly scattered.[30]

While the excise duties did have a restrictive and damaging effect on the Irish glass industry, its decline cannot be wholly attributed to the extension of the excise duty. Moreover, an approach not determined by national pride, but rather one which takes account of the broader social and economic context, reveals that the duties were part of a wider, more complex set of interrelated social and economic factors which impacted on the glass industry. One crucial factor which must be addressed is the nature of the Irish market during the early nineteenth century.

THE MARKET FOR IRISH GLASS
IN EARLY NINETEENTH-CENTURY IRELAND

In 1833, the Dublin glassmaker Martin Crean stated in his plea to the commissioners of the *Thirteenth Report of Excise Inquiry*, 'the duty is much felt on the low priced articles which the Irish manufacturers make, for generally speaking all the rich cut goods come from England'.[31] Irish glassmakers found that the excise duty payable on each piece of glass manufactured increased the retail price they needed to charge in order to make a profit. This left them unable to compete effectively with the cheaper British glass which flooded the Irish market. The impression gained from the evidence presented is that cheaper, plainer articles provided the bulk of their trade. This was accounted for by the apparent preference of Irish consumers of the more expensive objects for imported rather than Irish glass. The Ronayne brothers, proprietors of the Terrace Glassworks in Cork, echoed the testimony of Martin Crean:

> We make, at present moment, but half what we made before the duty was imposed. There being, generally speaking, no opulence amongst us, the great demand was for ordinary glass: the duty has so enhanced the price, that the great bulk of the people have substituted common English ware, and tin articles of all descriptions ... Here then a great class of consumers are swept away from the manufacturer; the few consumers of a better description of glass being, for the greater number; an impoverished gentry, who still reside amongst us, are supplied from England and Scotland, where capital is so assisted by cheaper fuel, and all other materials in the manufacture.[32]

It must be acknowledged that such sentiments were presented in a legislative and official context where testimonies may have been embellished in the hope of having the duty removed. Nevertheless, the study of newspapers, inventories and diaries of Irish consumers reveal that a preference for imported over native-made goods was an established characteristic within the buying patterns of those purchasing luxury goods in eighteenth-century Ireland.[33] Clearly, the dictates of choice for such consumers were fashion and novelty, while consumers of cheaper utilitarian goods shopped with economy and function in mind.

Irish consumers of the more expensive goods were discerning in their choice, ensuring that their wares would communicate the correct messages. Out of necessi-

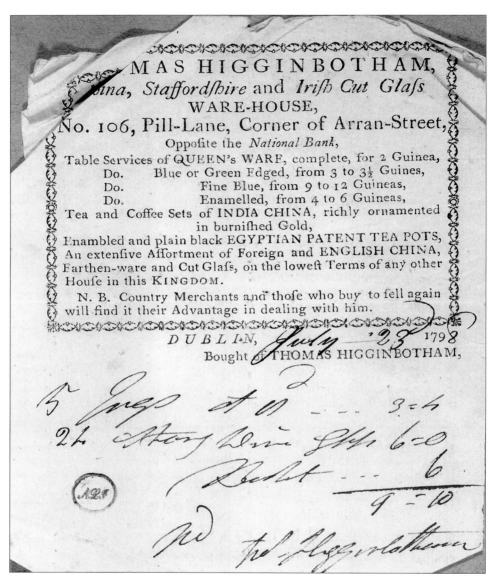

THO̶MAS HIGGINBOTHAM,
ina, *Staffordſhire* and *Iriſh Cut Glaſs*
WARE-HOUSE,
No. 106, Pill-Lane, Corner of Arran-Street,
Oppoſite the *National Bank*,
Table Services of QUEEN's WARE, complete, for 2 Guinea,
   Do.   Blue or Green Edged, from 3 to 3½ Guines,
   Do.   Fine Blue, from 9 to 12 Guineas,
   Do.   Enamelled, from 4 to 6 Guineas,
Tea and Coffee Sets of INDIA CHINA, richly ornamented
in burniſhed Gold,
Enambled and plain black EGYPTIAN PATENT TEA POTS,
An extenſive Aſſortment of Foreign and ENGLISH CHINA,
Earthen-ware and Cut Glaſs, on the loweſt Terms of any other
Houſe in this KINGDOM.
   N. B. Country Merchants and thoſe who buy to ſell again
will find it their Advantage in dealing with him.

DUBLIN, *July* 23 1798
Bought of THOMAS HIGGINBOTHAM,

*5 – Bill for jugs and 'strong wine glasses' bought by the Earl Fingall on 23 July 1798 from
Thomas Higginbotham's China, Staffordshire and Irish Cut Glass Warehouse (courtesy NLI)*

opposite
*6 – Page from an account ledger listing various retailers and the quantities of glass purchased by
each of them from the Waterford glassworks on 1 January 1823 (courtesy NMI)*

7 – Billhead of William Jackson, The Kings China Warehouse, dating to 1831 (courtesy NLI)

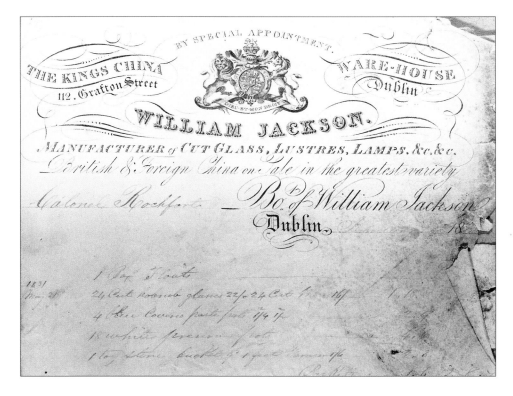

ty, retailers provided as wide a variety of goods as possible. A bill for goods bought by the Earl of Fingall on 23 July 1798 from Higginbotham's China, Staffordshire and Irish Cut Glass Warehouse illustrates this point (Plate 5).[34] Their billhead details the fact that they sold not only Irish glass, but also 'an extensive assortment of foreign and ENGLISH CHINA, Earthenware and Cut glass'.[35] Clearly, Irish glass was sold alongside the products of the more ideally sited English glasshouses, and in awareness of their competition, Irish glassmakers sought to convince their consumers that their variety of glass was 'for excellence of quality ... equal to any made in England'.[36] As pointed out by Edward Wakefield in 1812, the use of British glass was 'prevalent in Ireland' despite the fact that it was often more expensive.[37]

In an advertisement placed in June 1808, the Dublin-based John Kennedy, 'agent to the Waterford glassworks', was keen to point out that he would also be selling Derby china at his next auction.[38] For the purpose of the advertisement he goes as far as changing the name of his warehouse to the Waterford Glass and Derby China Warehouse.[39] William Jackson of 112 Grafton Street also bought glass on a regular basis from the Waterford glassworks (Plate 6).[40] However, a billhead dating to 1831 indicates that William Jackson also offered 'British and Foreign China on sale in the greatest variety', showing that he also sought to meet the demand for imported wares (Plate 7).[41]

Industry became increasingly focused in Ulster, and in a bid to improve the industrial potential of the rest of the country, initiatives were taken to improve communication. In this aim, the Dublin and Liverpool Steam Navigation Company was established with Irish Quaker capital in 1824.[42] However, in the short term this only acted in facilitating the import of a greater quantity of British goods at a faster pace. Efforts to promote the consumption of Irish manufacture, which had begun in the eighteenth century, were stepped up in the 1840s with the formation of the Irish manufacture movement.[43] Such developments, however, which tended to focus on textile industries, did not create a new demand for Irish glass.

The impression gained from the primary sources is that during the early nineteenth century, the market for glass made at Waterford did not radically exceed that for glass from any other Irish glasshouse. That said, while there is no indication from the Gatchell Letters that the proprietors believed their produce was considered superior or to be in any greater demand than that of their rivals, the Quakers who owned and ran the Waterford glassworks were proud of their reputation as honest traders, good employers and manufacturers who had the ability to produce glass equal to any other. As Quakers, they were able to avail of a wide network of contacts in England and Ireland. The latest patterns being used in England and Scotland were sourced with speed, and news of any change in the prices being charged by rival glasshouses quickly reached Waterford.

Evidence that the problems experienced by the glassmakers who testified to the commissioners of the *Thirteenth Report of Excise Inquiry* were also experienced by those at the Waterford glasshouse is apparent upon reading the Gatchell Letters. In a letter to his father, dated 9 September 1832, Jonathan Wright, manager of the glasshouse between 1831 and 1835, despaired at the current state of the business:

> the present prospects of the business are indeed by no means encouraging except two good orders last week one from Jason Penistan, Kilkenny and the other per Walsh of Wexford there has been very little doing either at the shop or the glasshouse and still there is the weekly accumulation of cut goods.[44]

Concerns regarding the cut glass which was accumulating in their stockrooms are noted repeatedly in the letters which were exchanged between various members of the Wright and Walpole families, who together managed the glasshouse. Following capital investment in a steam engine to power the cutting lathes, and the employment of Samuel Miller, a foreman of the glass cutters, the glasshouse managers were loathe to decrease production before the steam engine had paid for itself. While the letters testify to the great difficulties faced, also apparent is a paternal responsibility for their employees. This is combined with an optimistic hope that the economy would improve, that the duty would be reduced or eliminated, that sales would increase, and their financial position would recover.

Ensuring that one's product, in terms of quality and price, was able to compete against that of others in the free market was not enough to guarantee that the Waterford glassworks would survive longer than the other glasshouses, forced to cease production during the 1830s and 1840s. Particular selling strategies, such as advertising, marketing, tactical stock management and the provision of a pleasurable environment in which to shop, were utilised and developed.

The sources reveal that the glass was sold in a variety of ways. These included the sale of glass direct to retailers and merchants in Ireland and England, and further afield in locations such as Newfoundland, Philadelphia and New York. Of no less importance was their salesman, George Saunders, who travelled the country loaded with baskets and casks of glass.[45] However, the primary focus here is on their retail establishment, known as the ware room, run in conjunction with the glassworks, and their particular use of the tactical strategies of selling mentioned above.[46]

THE WATERFORD GLASS WARE ROOM

During the second half of the eighteenth century, the city of Waterford witnessed significant development. A growth in agricultural activity had led to a burgeoning provisions trade with Newfoundland, making the port of Waterford the third busiest in the country.[47] With the aid of both mercantile and corporation funds, successive building projects were begun in 1705 and the quay was lengthened beyond the constricting medieval town walls, allowing the city to expand. The quay, compared in 1834 by the English traveller and social commentator Henry D. Inglis to the quay of the Saône at Lyons, featured a wide gas-lit promenade ideal for strolling shoppers.[48] The ware room is listed as No. 14 Merchants' Quay; however, it is worth noting that the quay was home not to one, but three shops from which glass could be bought.[49] Further competition was provided by the so-called Temple of Fancy, also on the quay. This last-mentioned concern, housed at Sharpe's Large Lounge Rooms, was a temporary outlet for Monsieur Ely when he arrived from Bristol in the summer of 1835 with a shipment of 'fancy goods' from Paris and Geneva.[50] French goods were often seen as more fashionable than English goods. This is hinted at in the description of one Dublin heiress as 'smoking hot with fashion and elegance from Paris'.[51]

Commentators writing in the 1820s and 1830s, including Thomas Wyse, who wrote specifically in relation to the Waterford region, wrote angrily about the lack of support for native industry.[52] Other writers wrote of the squalor which hid behind the beauty of the quay, and in 1835, Robert Graham, a Scottish Whig touring Ireland, wrote that in Waterford city, 'they seem to have scarcely any manufacture or establishment for employing the people, except those concerned with the sale of corn and cattle'.[53] However, two days later, on 15 June, he went to survey a glass-works which he described as 'almost the only manufacture in Waterford'. [54]

With very little manufacturing in the town, the presence of the glasshouse, which in 1839 employed seventy people, was important to the industrial profile of Waterford city.[55] A range of imported goods – from the very cheap goods off-loaded as dead stock through auction, to the more expensive wares desirable in their foreignness – provided intense competition for those at the Waterford glass retail establishment. The ways in which the glasshouse managers responded to the challenge will now be addressed.

ADVERTISING AND MARKETING

In comparison with retailers of other products, such as textiles, ceramic and glass retailers advertised in newspapers less frequently. Nevertheless, newspapers provide a very important source of information about the glass trade. Samuel Alker, the Dublin-based retailer of 'China, Glass, Japan and Plated ware', advertised on 6 January 1808 in *Saunders' Newsletter and Daily Advertiser*.[56] He emphasised his ability, through contacts in England, to provide a vast assortment of goods at the lowest prices, boast-

8 – Billhead used at the Waterford Glassworks between 1830 and 1835
(courtesy NMI)

ing of 'having almost every pattern in the United Kingdom' at his warehouse and gal-leries. While the rhetoric suggests the possibility of extensive credit and a pleasurable environment in which to shop, the most important piece of information of which Alker informs his public is his change of address for his wholesale customers.

It is likely that ceramic and glass retailers also relied on the familiar tech-niques of the distribution of trade cards and circulars. The survival of a trade card and trade circular provides evidence that managers of the Waterford glassworks were engaged in what was at the time a common business practice. While these items of ephemera do not illustrate pieces of glass, a surviving billhead does illus-trate their logo during the 1830-35 period (Plate 8). Hand-distribution of trade circu-lars facilitated not only the personal communication, which was so important during this period, but also allowed the salesman to collect invaluable information on the nature of the market.

Referring to glass which had been sent to Dublin to be sold through his father's linen shop, Jonathan Wright wrote to his brother who worked in the Dublin shop: 'I have often wished to know how you get on – how the goods have been answered & what progress they make in selling.' [57] Later in the same year Jonathan Wright emphasised that 'it seems now necessary more than ever that an active and stirring canvas should be kept up as well as to ascertain the circumstances of cus-tomers as to learn the terms other houses sell at'.[58] By keeping a close eye on how their goods were selling in Dublin, they were able to make informed decisions regarding the choice and price of the objects they sold, both on a wholesale basis and through their retail ware room in Waterford.

As referred to above, expertise and personal communication were crucial to the sales service required by eighteenth- and early nineteenth-century consumers. Consumers visiting the retail ware room at Waterford would have been attended to by trained staff – implied by a reference which is made to training George Gatchell for work in the ware room.[59] Perhaps he was being trained in the 'Art of Selling', referred to by William Johnstone, the sales assistant of the glass retail shop in Liverpool, in a letter dated 26 February 1856,

> I have been grinding away at the goods in the endeavouring to fix them in my memory rather than refer to a book which I carry in my pocket. I have managed that part of it now very well ... what I have to learn now is the Art of Selling which I have yet to acquire.[60]

The Waterford ware room advertised that it sold on a ready-money basis, which meant that every object should have had a price for the sales assistant to memorise, just as William Johnstone was being forced to do. This reduced the need to haggle over prices, and possibly made it more accessible to a wider range of clientele. However, if customers were ordering large quantities or a bespoke service, for example, price negotiations might have taken place in the 'back parlour' with food and/or drinks. In 1835 Jonathan Wright wrote angrily to his brother saying that their shop assistant had 'the effrontery to send a note saying she was entitled [to recompense] on account of entertaining customers and as a customer to two services of glass these might amount to £30'.[61] The 'back parlour' was specifically mentioned as being part of the shop in the dissolution of the partnership, and was evidently an important area.[62]

Advertising and marketing were vital interrelated components of the selling experience, both very dependent on personal communication and word of mouth. An ever-present element within the rhetoric of many retailer's advertisements was the elegance of their establishment over all others, acknowledging the attention paid to design in the creation of a space in which consumers would enjoy making their selection. Clearly, the appearance, both the exterior and interior, was of considerable importance in terms of catching the attention of passing shoppers, and was thus crucial to the formation of a strong business identity.

SHOP DESIGN AND BUSINESS IDENTITY

> I suppose thou art now enjoying the delightful sea breezes at some of the fashionable watering places, sailing in a fishing boat or some other new interesting occupation whilst I am nailed to the counter striving to catch all the

lasses that are not gone to Donnybrook, so much for comparison.[63]

These are the despairing words of Jonathan Wright, writing in 1824 to his brother who was on his holidays from the Dublin shop on Skinner Row where they both worked at this time. His comments regarding his plight prompt consideration of exactly which tactics the Wrights used to catch the attention of the female shoppers to which he refers.[64] A letter written by Jonathan Wright of 1830 shows that he was eager to create as pleasurable a shopping environment as possible: 'The alteration is now nearly complete on the Quay and they have the finest shop in Waterford – a door in the centre and the two windows 10 feet in length.'[65] The emphasis on window space is indicative of the large size of the outlet, but also of an awareness of the advantages of using window area as display space. From the early eighteenth century, London shopkeepers were taking advantage of the improvements in glass manufacture, moving away from the shuttered windows and replacing them with panes of glass through which passers-by could view goods. However, as Cox points out, many retailers were slow to make the change, and as late as the second half of the nineteenth century some retailers' windows were still unglazed.[66] Some shop-owners, it seems, had the facility to display goods in the window but did not use it to full advantage. This was highlighted by John Fannin, Wedgwood's travelling agent in Ireland, in a letter written by him in Leitrim in 1809. In reference to country shopkeepers, he wrote:

> I am certain that if they lay out their shop tastefully our ware will go off fast but they [retailers] have no idea whatever as to disposing to advantage and unless you make it your business to go into their shops and look well about you may pass without knowing they sell such articles. I have endeavoured to point out the advantages arising from the contrary mode and hope they will adopt it. I sold some hedgehogs – medallions, and richly cut gilt jugs to place in a conspicuous part of their shops in order to make a beginning in that way.[67]

In contrast to the country shopkeepers portrayed so unfavourably by Fannin, who was eager to prove his worth as a salesman, Jonathan Wright was clearly aware of the benefits of window display. The same could be said for the retailer known as Savage, agent to the Cork glasshouse (Plate 9).[68] Savage placed an item in front of every window pane, following the example of large-scale shops in London which would have led in the use of ambitious display techniques. Johanna Schopenhauer, a young German tourist travelling in the 1790s, commented on the elegant shop windows she saw in London. In particular, she noted the 'fairy glitter of the crystal shops' and the apothecaries' windows which gleamed 'like an Aladins cave'.[69] Moreover, within the shop itself, retailers would have been eager to display the

glass to its best advantage. In reference to 'new furnishings' at the Edinburgh glasshouse, the manager was keen to point out to the owner of the glasshouse that not only had a new boiler for the engine been purchased, but also some 'fine red material on the desk to display the goods'.[70]

At a time when goods were of a non-standardised nature and of variable quality, the consumer relied on the retailer for guidance.[71] Impressing the consumer was paramount, and the appearance of the retailer's shop acted as the external manifestation of the business.[72] This was a necessity of which Savage was aware, evidenced by the fact that he chose to illustrate his elegant shopfront on his billhead.[73]

Equally aware of the need to establish a strong business identity was James Donovan, a china merchant and glass manufacturer of George's Quay, Dublin. Donovan was known for importing English ceramics, having them painted in his workshop and then impressing or signing 'Donovan's Irish Manufacture' on the underside.[74] The fact that Donovan was successful in his aim is shown in an inventory of 1821 found amongst the Clements Papers. A new purchase is recorded in the 'List of China' as '1 Donovan C & S' [cup and saucer].[75] An account book within a set of papers pertaining to the same family records the payment of 'Carter's bill for glass'.[76] It is tempting to suggest that 'Carter' might refer to the concern of Mary Carter & Son of Grafton Street.[77] Mary Carter was one of a select group of retailers

10 – Moulded base of a glass decanter which has been impressed with the name of Penrose Waterford, 1783-99
(courtesy NMI)

opposite
9 – Billhead used by John Savage of the Cork Cut Glass Warehouse,
48 Lower Sackville Street, Dublin, dated 19 May 1827
(collection Cork Archives Institute; reproduced from M.S.D. Westropp, IRISH GLASS (London and Dublin (1920) 1978)

and manufacturers who sold pieces of moulded glass bearing their names impressed on the base.[78]

Objects made using the moulding method of manufacture include decanters, jugs, wine coolers, butter coolers, and, to a lesser degree, dishes – essentially any object which could be made by depressing the blown gather of glass into a ribbed mould which had the name impressed into the base of the mould. While under ownership of the Penrose family (1783-99), moulds impressed with Penrose Waterford were used at Waterford, and several examples of Penrose-marked pieces survive (Plate 10).[79] However, there are no known examples marked with the Gatchell name. Often, objects with moulded bases bearing impressed marks were of thinner glass and were cheaper than the very heavy elaborate cut-glass objects made during the 1820s and 1830s. As such objects were generally not moulded, it was not possible to leave an impressed mark on their bases.

A significant element in the overall appearance of the shop was the overall impression given by the plethora of objects which would have been displayed in the shop. Providing an assortment of objects from which the consumer could choose was an abiding priority for the retailer. In order to do this – in other words, to meet the demands of the market – it was necessary for the managers of the Waterford glass ware room to stock goods other than those made in the glassworks.

RANGE AND DIVERSIFICATION

While the Samuel Miller drawings testify to the fact that extremely fine tableware was manufactured at the Waterford glasshouse, it is worth noting that they present only a selection of the goods actually produced (Plates 3, 4). The Gatchell Letters and Waterford glasshouse account ledgers make it apparent that the manufacture of apothecary wares and other plain wares, such as street lamps, comprised a significant portion of their trade, and as these objects do not feature in the Samuel Miller drawings, the importance of these objects to the survival of the glasshouse is commonly forgotten. When submitting evidence to the 1835 report of the commissioners, those running the Waterford glassworks wrote in their request:

> We are manufacturers of flint and phial glass; in the latter, we may say, our trade has been completely superseded by the manufacturers of black bottle metal, they being allowed to make precisely the same quality as common phial, under the denomination of black bottle metal.[80]

It was 'to this cause' that they attributed 'the loss on this branch of our trade, and which we consider a grievance'. Evidently, the sale of phial glass, used mainly by apothecaries, was an important aspect of their trade.

With regard to the more luxury end of their production, when sporadic references from the letters and accounts are seen in tandem with the other surviving sources, one can attempt to give an insight into the range of objects and various patterns which might have faced the consumer on entering the ware room on the quay in Waterford. For example, the only known surviving receipt from the Waterford glassworks' ware room details the fact that in October 1804, Joseph Grubb bought both 'plain' and 'fluted and fingered' decanters, together with both 'plain' and 'fluted stem' wine glasses (Plate 11).[81] The decanters, with what would have been shallow cutting of fluting and fingering, were double the price of the plain decanters, revealing that whether an object was 'cut' or not was a distinction worth making. Similarly, a rare example of an order for some glass in the Gatchell Letters includes both 'best and most fashionable' wines and 'middling wines', together with 'decanters not too high priced'.[82]

While the per capita consumption of wine in Ireland decreased over the course of the eighteenth century, this was compensated for by the increased consumption of locally distilled spirits.[83] Accordingly, the variety of receptacles in demand increased – a need readily met by glass manufacturers. Equally, the fashion for hot beverages was met, and a variety of tea caddies, jugs, caddie spoons and sugar bowls became available (Plate 2). As one individual noted in a letter to the manager of the Midlothian Glasshouse in Edinburgh, 'the highest taste and newest

11 – Account for Joseph Grubb in respect of glass items supplied by
Ramsey, Gatchell & Co., Waterford Ware Room, 1804 (courtesy NLI)

fashion' was to 'have all table, thea [tea], and other services [utensils] of crystal rather than porcelain'.[84]

Also among the objects purchased by Joseph Grubb were '1 cayenne and 1 catsup [ketchup] labelled' for which he only paid 1s 10d, making these among the cheapest items on his shopping list.[85] They are mentioned as being labelled, which probably implies an engraved label as opposed to a silver label which would hang around the neck. When catsup, or ketchup, was introduced in the late seventeenth century, it was considered a luxury; however, by the early nineteenth century, it was more commonplace. Accordingly, its receptacles were clearly available at a range of prices.

The Samuel Miller drawings should not be seen solely as indicators of product range; the way in which they were actually utilised is also of interest.[86] Comparative analysis of these drawings can assist in determining the context in which they were used. In being quite naively hand-drawn in pencil and then black ink, they differ starkly when compared with certain highly finished patterns seen in the archive of the Richardson's glasshouse in Stourbridge, which were clearly used for presentation purposes.[87] The fact that they do not feature extremely detailed measurements, like those seen in some of the patterns in the archive of the Edinburgh glasshouse, lessens the chances that they acted as a guide in manufacture.[88] Instead, it is plausible that these drawings served as an office copy, and remembering that George Saunders was their travelling salesman, it is possible that patterns of a different nature might have existed, as implied by references to 'George's box of patterns'.

Another factor to be borne in mind when considering the range of goods sold by the glasshouse is that the sources indicate that in order to provide an adequate range of goods from which consumers could choose, the glasshouse managers imported glass from Birmingham which they sold alongside their own products. In a letter written in December 1830 to his father Nehemiah, in Dublin, Jonathan Wright informed him of a decision made by those directly in charge of the ware room: 'they are also getting in some coloured glass and other Birmingham goods, this John has been advised to by GS [George Saunders] and myself which we conceive will tend to increase their trade and keep out auctions'.[89]

The pressure to diversify further is seen when the glasshouse managers consider entering into the earthenware business. Such a move is not so surprising since certain similarities exist between the two industries in terms of production and consumption, together with the marketing strategies of their producers. Most retailers of glass also sold ceramics, and in 1811, when Wedgwood's agent in Ireland considered closing the concern, he looked into alternatives. In a letter to Wedgwood, the Dublin-based agent refers to a possible partnership with Peter Chebsey, a man who is 'exclusively in the glass line who has Proposed a partnership as Glass and Earthenware facilitate the sale of each other'.[90]

Various indications that the Waterford glassworks also stocked ceramics in their ware room are provided in the Gatchell Letters. A letter written by their salesman George Saunders, while in Quebec on a sales venture in June 1826, mentions that he had sold a service of 'E Ware' [earthenware]. In reference to this, he mentioned that it was a business of which he had a 'tolerable knowledge'.[91] Two years later, in a letter to John Wright, manager of the ware room, Jonathan Wright stated that he was considering an offer made by Isaac Warren of forming a partnership in the earthenware line.[92] Warren, proprietor of a china and earthenware warehouse at Essex Bridge in Dublin, was one of their more important wholesale contacts, and a diary kept by Jonathan Wright's wife records the number of nights on which Warren stayed with them in Waterford.[93] Jonathan Wright was clearly interested in Warren's offer, writing:

> In addition, too the opposition in the glass business must be felt – I have sometimes been sorry something had not been adapted earlier that would put down such an opposition ... it certainly would be well to consider about it so nearly is it connected with both interests.[94]

Whether or not those running the Waterford glassworks actually entered into a partnership in the earthenware line is uncertain. However, on the subject of diversification, Jonathan Wright asserted:

> In the glass retail shop I urge John to do the same, and I think I could if thou were inclined for it, get the name of a few of the Best Manufacturers of Umbrella mounting in Birmingham from Ostler, a nice kind of man in the Drops Business.[95]

The accounts for the glasshouse show they were also trading in wood, worsted, fish, wax, clover seed and pearl ashes, to name just a selection. The *New Commercial Directory for the cities of Waterford and Kilkenny* of 1839 lists the Gatchells as ship owners. This, combined with a wide network of fellow Quakers around Ireland and Britain, not to mention Montreal and Philadelphia, implied they were in a position to fill their ware room with a wide assortment of goods if they so chose.

While ceramics and glass clearly complement each other, it was not unusual for retailers to sell a very diverse range of goods under one roof. At Esau Clarke's Dublin establishment, Wedgwood's products were sold alongside trumpets and French horns, while Luffingham's, which also sold Wedgwood, was known to have sold groceries as well.[96] Yet there is evidence to show that there were retailers who specialised in the sale of ceramics and glass – for example, James Donovan china merchant and glass manufacturer, mentioned earlier.[97] Analysis of the Waterford account books reveals that Donovan, despite having his own glasshouse making fine table goods, was buying glass from the Waterford glassworks. However, we also know that glass made in Waterford was sold alongside ginghams and worsted cloth in Nehemiah Wright's shop in Skinner Row.

Certainly, the model to which such retailers probably aspired was that of a large specialist shop such as Blade's of Ludgate Hill in London. Against the background provided by such specialised London retailers, who had a very substantial consumer base, the manner in which ceramics and glass were sold in Ireland may appear, in part, arbitrary and unfocused. Cox asserts that the same range of shops was to be found in the English provinces as in London. However, she points out that those shops in the provinces may have been, out of necessity, less specialised, more serviceable, and designed to cater for a more socially mixed clientele.[98] As an important city within the Empire, Dublin was far from provincial. However, the majority of retailers who sold glass, also sold a wide variety of other goods, ranging from earthenware and Japanned wares to plated wares, from expensive display pieces to the very cheap and utilitarian.

If the Waterford glassworks sold not only glass, but also earthenware and umbrellas, they were responding to the challenges of the day and doing what every retailer aimed to do, which was to supply the demands of the market.

CONCLUSION: A DECLINING MARKET

Writing from a temporary sales outlet in Cork which they had hired in the hope of selling some glass, Ambrose Barcroft, a partner in the Waterford glassworks at the time, explained that their lease was about to terminate and he felt it would be pointless to extend it.[99] Referring to the 'lustres and candlesticks', he said: 'I fear neither will go, the former I offered at 40 guineas and the latter at 2/3d [two thirds] selling price or rather under but could not obtain it.'

Upon observing that Barcroft was facing difficulties, the local Cork retailers were quick to take advantage with some managing to secure large discounts. Referring to the Savage family, who were established ceramic and glass retailers in Cork, Barcroft wrote despairingly that the 'Savages were so savage at it that on their taking an £100 worth I promised to find them ... 60 [more] on same terms as they bought which is a sacrifice of about £2 10.' Barcroft also mentions that they have had an order for some cheaper goods, which he refers to as 'tale goods', meaning goods made out of a poorer quality glass.[100] With the 'plain goods selling as fast as they are made', it would appear that the sale of cheaper goods, such as those made using tale glass, was what assisted in sustaining business at the glasshouse.[101]

The practice of providing long periods of credit saw debts accrued in America, which reached into the thousands. In a letter to his brother dated 1 July 1819, Jonathan Gatchell wrote that they had 'about £1100 unsettled in Philadelphia, £760 in New York, £300 in Halifax, nearly £600 in Newfoundland and £150 in Quebec, beside the dead stock on hands at home'. The accounts show that when Jonathan Gatchell died in 1823, there was £2,400 owed to him in debts.[102] Fears were heightened during the 1820s and 1830s as the famine of 1820-22 and concomitant economic decline had resulted in a crisis of confidence in the financial sector. In May of 1820 two banks closed in Cork, and a month later, the death, or possible suicide, of the head of Newport's bank in Waterford left many with useless money instead of financial security.[103] An advertisement in *The Constitution or Cork Advertiser* on 4 March 1826 announced that an auction would take place at the 'office lately occupied by Mrs Graham nearly opposite the Chamber of Commerce, Patrick Street' of 'her splendid assemblage of cut glass which is brought to auction as a consequence of the stoppage of the banks'.[104]

Accounts prepared in August 1835, when George Gatchell came of age and the partnership dissolved, reveal that in 1830 the glassworks had outstanding debts of a colossal £5646 3s 2d, and a sum of £4325 6s 9d which lay in glass and materials.[105] With a weekly accumulation of cut goods, it was necessary to find out exactly which objects were selling well, where they sold, and to whom. In October of 1830, Jonathan wrote to Nathan Wright, their agent in Dublin, asking him to 'send an acct of what salts thou hast sent out, our sale for cut articles is bad & the stock accumulating'.[106] Shortly after this, Jonathan Wright wrote to his father in Dublin asking if there was any money owing to them in Dublin. If there is, he despaired, 'send it here, we have almost nothing towards paying the men next 6th day so let it be before that time'.[107]

As the 1830s progressed, auctions are mentioned with more frequency in the Gatchell Letters. In April 1835 an auction was mentioned in a letter, again from Jonathan Wright to his father. He says the auction will begin with the 'cut goods and rubbish'.[108] Their estimation of the home market in Waterford is seen when they plan an auction of the 'less valuable cut goods, so long as 20 per cent below stock prices are realised'. The more valuable pieces were to be sold in an auction 'exclusively for the trade'. Evidence that members of the trade were also struggling can be observed in an advertisement placed in August 1835 by William Jackson, a client of the Waterford glassworks mentioned earlier. He explained that 'the stock of this establishment, which is one of the most elegant, select and extensive in Dublin, is now selling off at a reduction of from 10 to 30 per cent under former prices'.[109]

Given that all of the fuel used, and a substantial portion of the raw materials needed had to be imported, production costs were high, leaving small profit margins on the cheaper goods. While in part answered by the closure of many glasshouses during this period, the question still remains to be asked: in the face of such difficulties, why did they persist? In his letter to the Commissioners of the Inquiry into Excise, the Dublin glass manufacturer Charles Mulvany pre-empted this enquiry:

> It may be asked of me, why continue in a trade of which by your own showing, you make nothing? The answer is, that from the peculiar locality of my establishment we are much engaged in manufacturing a description of goods for which we can charge a remunerating price, such as the matching of patterns, hurried orders, lamp shades and fittings, apparatus, &c. &c. We are by this enabled to save ourselves; and certainly, we would not remain satisfied with this, but relinquish a trade affording us not only no reasonable profit, but no surplus to meet contingencies, had we not already a large capital invested in buildings, a connexion in trade long formed, and a great number of people dependent on us for support, many who have grown old in our service; and but for the conviction and hope that such a monstrous oppression could not much longer exist.[110]

The London glassmaker Apsley Pellat echoed Mulvany's words in his evidence, stating that 'matching' was a considerable branch of his trade, a factor he attributed to his urban location.[111] Glass by its very nature was easily broken, and a consumer wishing to replace a broken component of a set could have brought a glass object to a retailer or glasshouse to be 'matched'. In fact, the Cork retailer Marsden Haddock, who was trading during the late eighteenth century, boasted on his trade circular that glasses could be 'matched at sight' at his shop.[112] An urban context such as Dublin or London presented a far more substantial market for such a service than could have been accessed on those terms in Waterford. However, perhaps the activity of making copies of patterns explains the nature of the contents of the 'box of patterns' sent by the retailer James Kerr to the Waterford glassworks on 9 September 1832.[113]

In the hands of George Gatchell from 1835 onwards, the Waterford glasshouse continued production until 1851.[114] After submitting an impressive cutglass epergne to the Great Exhibition of 1851 in one last attempt to illustrate their ability to make fine luxury glass, George Gatchell finally admitted that the glasshouse was a losing concern and it was time to close:

> I may mention (in private) that I have quite concluded on giving up the business as soon as I possibly can, as I find it quite useless to strive against adverse circumstances any longer. I have tried several expedients to place the business on a better footing, by getting additional capital, but in vain. There

is a very painful ordeal to pass through and a cheerless future but I have done my best to maintain my ground and I feel less disheartened at the prospect, than I did some time ago.[115]

In his 1916 guide for collectors of English and Irish glass, Yoxall spoke of the charm of old cut glass: 'in cabinets it shines, gleams, glows, and sparkles in a reticent, well-bred way'.[116] The 'common phial', 'tale wines' and 'plain tumblers' which were so important to the story of Waterford glass clearly did not survive to earn a place in Yoxall's cabinet.[117] However, the rare and fortuitous survival of a sample of the Waterford glass business records allows us to look beyond the gleaming surface of the object to reveal a tale of determination in the face of economic upheaval. In providing an insight into the reality of trying to survive as a manufacturer on the eve of the Great Famine, these records encourage us to look at the broader social and economic context to understand the nature of the Irish glass industry. Just like any small manufacturer during the early nineteenth century, those running the Waterford glassworks took every step in the struggle to maintain its consumer base. Amidst accounts of consumer manipulation and tactical manoeuvring by successful figureheads such as Josiah Wedgwood and Mathew Boulton, a valuable case study is provided by the experiences of those running this small, yet legendary manufacturing concern.

———

ACKNOWLEDGEMENTS

I am grateful to the boards of the National Library of Ireland and the National Museum of Ireland for permission to use material in their possession. I would also like to thank my MA thesis supervisors Dr Helen Clifford, Honorary Fellow, Eighteenth Century Studies Centre, University of Warwick, and John Styles, Head of Postgraduate Study at the V&A, for their generous support and encouragement. I would also like to express my gratitude to the Friends of the V&A and Jane Wainwright for financial assistance while completing my Masters degree. For their continuous support I am indebted to Mairead Dunlevy, Keeper Emerita, National Museum of Ireland, and Dr Paul Caffrey, lecturer at the National College of Art & Design. I am also most grateful to Mary Boydell, Alison FitzGerald and Beverly Casebow for their help while doing this research, and to Audrey Whitty and Sandra McElroy, Assistant Keepers in the National Museum of Ireland, for their help in sourcing photographs. Finally, I would like to express my sincere gratitude to the Hon Desmond Guinness and the Irish Georgian Society for awarding me the Desmond Guinness Scholarship for 2003.

ENDNOTES

The following abbreviations are used: NLI   National Library of Ireland
                                          NMI   National Museum of Ireland
                                          PRDS   *Proceedings of the Royal Dublin Society*

Thirteenth Report of Excise Inquiry   *The Thirteenth Report of the Commissioners appointed*
                                          by His Majesty to inquire into the establishment of the
                                          Department of Excise, and into the Management and
                                          Collection of the Excise Revenue in all its branches,
                                          throughout the United Kingdom

[1]   Examples of interpretations written in this vein include: I. Grehan, 'Waterford, an Irish Art', *Irish Arts Review*, i, 2 (Dublin 1984) 20-3, and Phelps Warren, *Irish Glass, The Age of Exuberance* (London (1970) 1981). It should be noted that the Waterford Crystal factory, now owned by Waterford Wedgwood, was set up in 1947 and has no direct connections with the earlier glassworks, which operated between 1783 and 1851.

[2]   *PRDS*, 1784-85: the Society's aim to encourage glass manufacture, in accordance with the parliament's wishes, was discussed at a meeting on 11 August 1785. The sums awarded annually to claimants were proportionate to their annual production to a maximum of 10%. *PRDS*, 1787-88: it was ordered at a meeting on 15 March 1787 that William Penrose of Waterford receive a premium of £160, having proved that flint glass to the value of £1600 had been manufactured at the Waterford glasshouse. Proof of production generally came in the form of an affidavit from both a proprietor and an office clerk from each glasshouse concerned.

[3]   The relevant statute is 21 and 22 George III, c 17, 1781-2. This act declared that additional duty on coal was not to be imposed when used for the manufacture of glass, sugar or salt.

[4]   M.S.D. Westropp, *Irish Glass*, M. Boydell (ed.) (London and Dublin (1920) 1978) 210. Mary Boydell notes that George Penrose (1722-1796) was an uncle of William Penrose (1746-1799), not a brother as previously thought.

[5]   These figures do not take account of glasshouses principally manufacturing bottles.

[6]   Westropp, *Irish Glass*, 1978, 204

[7]   H. Wakefield, *Nineteenth Century Glass* (London 1982, 2nd ed.) 20. Wakefield's views are based upon analysis of the statistics showing the amount of duty paid by glassmakers in England, Scotland and Ireland in 1833. The figures for duty paid on glass of all descriptions are as follows: England: £680,084 1s $8^3/_4$ d; Scotland: £45,491 14s 6d and Ireland: £22,399 19s $0^1/_2$d. These statistics are tabulated in the *Appendix to Thirteenth Report of Commissioners of Excise Inquiry*, xxxi, 1835.

[8]   Both Mary Boydell and Charles Hajdamach have echoed Wakefield's views. M. Boydell, *Irish Glass*, Heritage Series no. 5 (Dublin 1976); C.R. Hajdamach, *British Glass 1800-1914* (London 1991) 127.

[9]   These sources are in the NMI, Art & Industry Archive. Westropp was first employed in 1899 as a curator by the NMI, later being appointed Keeper of the Art & Industry Division in 1930, in which capacity he worked until his retirement in 1936.

[10] NMI, Art & Industry Archive, Gatchell Letters, vols 1 and 2, registration no. 1956.154.

[11] NMI, Art & Industry Archive, registration no. 1927.102. Samuel Miller is first mentioned in

the Gatchell Letters in December 1828 in which he is described as 'foreman of the glasscutters', Gatchell Letters, document 25, 9 December 1828. He is mentioned again in 1831 and also in 1832, Gatchell Letters, document 49, 11 August 1831, and document 55, 10 June 1832 respectively.

[12] NLI, Westropp Papers, MS 24,936. M.S.D. Westropp was alerted to the existence of the 'Miller Drawings' in a memorandum to him from the Cork historian and medal dealer Robert Day, dated 28 November 1910. The drawings were bequeathed to the NMI by Ms Anne Miller, daughter of Samuel Miller, in 1927.

[13] Hajdamach, *British Glass 1800-1914*, 39.

[14] The earliest reference to a steam engine in the surviving documentary sources for the Waterford glasshouse dates to 25 July 1827, NMI, Art & Industry Archive, account ledger, registration no. 1956.138.

[15] Westropp, *Irish Glass*, 82; *PRDS*, 1834-35, appendix xii, 'Adjudication of Premiums at the Second annual exhibition of Irish Manufactures, Productions, and inventions, at the Royal Dublin Society's house, May 1835'. Gatchell, Walpole & Company, Waterford, were awarded a large silver medal for their submission of 'A Rich Cut Flower Vase & Dish'.

[16] NMI, Art & Industry Archive, registration nos 1956.132-52. In addition, various items of ephemera associated with the glasshouse also survive – for example, a billhead which was used between 1830 and 1835 (Art & Industry Archive, box 114, reference 749). These account ledgers, together with the Gatchell Letters and other records pertaining to the Waterford glassworks, were acquired by M.S.D. Westropp from Samuel Hudson Wright in December 1917 for the sum of £8. The NMI acquired these records at the sale of Westropp's estate at a Sotheby's sale on 25 June 1956.

[17] D. Dickson, 'Death of a capital? Dublin beyond the Union' in P. Clark and R. Gillespie (eds), *Two Capitals: London and Dublin, 1500-1840* (Oxford 2002) 124.

[18] *ibid.*

[19] C. Ó Gráda, *Ireland, A New Economic History, 1780-1939* (Oxford 1995) 46.

[20] A. FitzGerald and C. O'Brien 'The production of silver in late-Georgian Dublin', *Irish Architectural and Decorative Studies: Journal of the Irish Georgian Society*, iv (2001) 28.

[21] A. Alexander 'A firm of Dublin Cabinet-makers Mack, Williams & Gibton', *Irish Arts Review Yearbook*, 11 (Dublin 1995) 142.

[22] Ó Gráda, *Ireland, A New Economic History*, 159.

[23] *ibid.*, 160.

[24] *ibid.*, 316.

[25] C. Ross, 'The Excise Tax and Cut glass in England and Ireland, 1800-1830', *Journal of Glass Studies*, xxiv (1982) 57-64.

[26] *ibid.*, 58.

[27] *Appendix to Twelfth Report of Commissioners of Inquiry into the Revenue arising in Ireland, Scotland &c.*, xiv, 1825, appendix 120, 753-76: 755. Letter from James Roche, secretary to Flint Glass Manufacturers, Ireland, 'praying an uniformity in the Law and Practice for collecting the Duty on Glass in Ireland to that in operation in England'.

[28] In 1825, the duty amounted to £12 10s per 1,000 lbs of glass metal for flint or phial glass. The relevant statute is 6 George IV c 117, 5 July 1825.

[29] *Appendix to Thirteenth Report of Commissioners of Excise Inquiry*, xxxi, 1835.

[30] Grehan, 'Waterford, an Irish Art', 20.

[31] *Appendix to Thirteenth Report of Commissioners of Excise Inquiry*, xxxi, 1835, appendix 45, 152-6.

[32] *ibid.*, appendix 4, 70.

[33] T. Barnard, 'Integration or Separation? Hospitality and Display in Protestant Ireland, 1660-1800', in L. Brockliss and D. Eastwood, *A Union of multiple identities: the British Isles c.1750-c.1850* (Manchester 1997) 128; S. Foster, 'Going Shopping in 18th-Century Dublin' *Things*, iv, 1996, 50.

[34] NLI, Fingall Papers, MS 8029(1). The Higginbothams were important ceramic and glass retailers who ran retailing establishments in Dublin from at least 1784 until 1864. While initially situated at 20 East Arran Street, trade directories list various addresses over this period for T. & W.H. Higginbotham and Edward Higginbotham. They include 1 and 106 Pill Lane, 102 Grafton Street, and also 11 and 12 Wellington Quay. They are known to have sold imported English-made ceramics which were decorated in Ireland and then signed on the underside with the name of Higginbotham.

[35] Another bill for goods bought at a shop owned by the Higginbothams survives and is now in the D. Westropp collection. It dates to 27 June 1817, and the name of the shop is described as T. & W.H. Higginbotham's extensive China and Earthenware Room, Waterford Glass Stores and Cut Glass Manufactory. The Waterford glass account ledgers show that Thomas Higginbotham purchased glass on a wholesale basis from the Waterford glassworks, and their purchases in 1817 (totalling £307 8s 4d) were approximately 50% greater than they had been the previous year (totalling £217 13s 11d). NMI, registration no. 1956.133, account of T. and W. H. Higginbotham.

[36] These are the words used by Thomas Burnett & Co. in charge of the Cork Glass Company between 1783 and 1787, *Hibernian Chronicle*, 6 May 1784, cited in Westropp, *Irish Glass*, 115.

[37] E. Wakefield, *An Account of Ireland Statistical and Political* (London 1812) 755.

[38] *Wilson's Dublin Directory* lists a John Kennedy, agent to the Waterford glasshouse between the years 1789 and 1807, at 50 Stephen Street, and between 1807 and 1811 at 42 Stephen Street, Dublin.

[39] *Saunders' Newsletter and Daily Advertiser*, 4 June 1808.

[40] Throughout the early 1820s, William Jackson regularly bought considerable quantities of glass from the Waterford glassworks. During the first six months of 1823, William Jackson ordered twelve hogsheads and two tierces of glass, totalling £249 18s 8d. During the same six months, William Carter of 84 Grafton Street ordered only three hogsheads and one tierce of glass, totalling £54 9s 7d. NMI, registration no. 1956.138, account ledger. William Carter was the son of Mary Carter who together traded as Mary Carter & Son, glass dealers of 80 Grafton Street between 1779 and 1806. Later, from 1810 to 1830, William Carter alone operated as a 'China and Delf Seller' at 84 Grafton Street.

[41] NLI, Rochfort Papers, MS 8682(4). The bill is for various ceramic and glass items, including '24 Cut Hobnob glasses' costing 22s, and '24 Cut wines' costing 16s, purchased by Colonel Rochfort from William Jackson during May and December 1831.

[42] J. Hill, *From Patriots to Unionists* (Oxford 1997) 290.

[43] For an account of the Buy Irish campaigns of the eighteenth century, see S. Foster 'Buying Irish Consumer Nationalism in Eighteenth Century Dublin', *History Today*, 47, June 1997.

[44] Gatchell Letters, document 62: letter from Jonathan Wright to Nehemiah Wright, 9 September 1832.

[45] *ibid.*, document 42, same to same, 20 January 1831.

[46] The Waterford glass ware room is mentioned in a newspaper advertisement on 12 December 1799, *Ramsey's Waterford Chronicle*, 12 December 1799, cited in Westropp, *Irish Glass*, 73.

[47] J. Mannion, 'The Waterford Merchants and the Irish Newfoundland Provisions trade, 1770-1820', in L.M. Cullen and P. Butel (eds), *Negoce et Industrie en France et en Irlande aux XVIII et XIXe Siecles* (Paris 1978) 27-43.

[48] D. Dowling, *Waterford Streets Past and Present* (Waterford 1998) 162.

[49] *Harvey's Waterford Directory and Almanac for the year 1839* (Waterford 1839).

[50] *Waterford Chronicle*, 29 August 1835.

[51] D. Herbert, *Retrospections of Dorothea Herbert 1770-1806* (Dublin 1988), cited in S. Foster, 'Going Shopping', 43-4.

[52] D. Cowman, 'Trade and Society in Waterford 1800-1840', in W. Nolan and T.P. Power (eds), *Waterford, History and Society* (Dublin 1992) 446.

[53] R. Graham, *A Scottish Whig in Ireland, 1835-1838 – The Irish Journals of Robert Graham of Redgorton* (Dublin 1999) 85.

[54] *ibid.*, 91.

[55] The number of employees fluctuated throughout the period during which the glassworks was in operation. This is attested by the various records consulted. However, the nature of the source of each statistic must be borne in mind when being considered. An advertisement placed by the glassworks in April 1820, announcing an auction of glass, describes the glassworks as an establishment which has 'for the past thirty-six years given daily employment to nearly two hundred persons', *Waterford Mirror*, 5 April 1820, cited in Westropp, *Irish Glass*, 75. *Harvey's Waterford Directory and Almanac* of 1839 refers to 70 people being employed by the glassworks. The 1841 Census of Ireland lists that 38 people were employed in glass manufacture in the city of Waterford, and there was only one glasshouse in Waterford. For more information on the census see appendix 4 in Cowman, 'Trade and Society', 457.

[56] *Saunders' Newsletter and Daily Advertiser*, 6 January 1808.

[57] Gatchell Letters, document 35: letter from Jonathan Wright in Waterford to Nathan Wright, summer 1830.

[58] *ibid.*, document 41: letter from Jonathan Wright to his father Nehemiah Wright, 23 December 1830.

[59] *ibid.*, document 29: letter from John Wright to Nathan Wright, 14 December 1829: 'George is a nice lad ... but I regret my aunt is not better qualified to train him up ... I can't leave really till George is trained.'

[60] Museum of Edinburgh, Ford Ranken Archive of Family Correspondence relating to the Holyrood Glasshouse, Edinburgh; collection of Dr and Mrs Cruickshank. Letter from William Johnstone, 17 Ripy Street, Liverpool, to John Ford Junior, St John Street, Edinburgh, 26 February 1856. Although slightly later than the period concerned, this letter is still worth quoting. I am grateful to Beverly Casebow for allowing me to read transcriptions of these letters.

[61] Gatchell Letters, document 104: letter from Jonathan Wright to Nathan Wright, 18 June 1835.

[62] Upon coming of age in 1835, George Gatchell gained complete ownership of the glassworks. The partnership on that date consisted of Nehemiah Wright, Elizabeth Knott (late Walpole) and Nathan Gatchell. To recompense for the dissolution of the partnership, George Gatchell offered the partners a five-year lease on the retail ware room. In the agreement detailing this proposal, he specified that he would 'give up to thee the Retail Glass Business on the Quay,

with the shop and back parlour, for five years, upon the following terms, thou paying all taxes and a reasonable rent'. Gatchell Letters, document 95: letter from George Gatchell to John Wright, 7 April 1835.

[63] *ibid.*, document 19: letter from Jonathan Wright in Skinner Row, Dublin, to Nathan Wright, 23 August 1824.

[64] This was written in August when the Donnybrook Fair was held every year.

[65] Gatchell Letters, document 41: letter from Jonathan Wright to Nehemiah Wright, 23 December 1830. Westropp, *Irish Glass*, 93.

[66] N. Cox, *The Complete Tradesman: A Study of Retailing 1550-1820* (England 2000) 98.

[67] Letter from John Fannin, travelling agent for Wedgwood, written while in Manorhamilton, county Leitrim on 6 October 1809, to Joseph Randall, manager of Dublin's Wedgwood shop. M. Reynolds, 'Wedgwood's Man', *Heart of Breifne* (Cavan 1982) 12.

[68] Cork Archives Institute, Ryan Purcell Papers, U139. This bill was for '3 doz + 6 Lemonade Cans Fluted' costing £2 3s 9d, bought by a member of the Purcell family. John Savage, agent to the Waterloo Glasshouse, Cork, is listed in the Dublin street directories at 48 Lower Sackville Street in 1824. From 1826 to 1828 he is listed at the same address as an agent to Foley and O'Connell of the Cork Glass Company, and in 1829 John Savage is listed at the same address as proprietor of a 'China and Glass Warerooms', indicating no direct association with any one glasshouse.

[69] J. Schopenhauer, *A Lady's Travels: journeys in England and Scotland from the diaries of Johanna Schopenhauer*, translated and edited by R. Michaelis-Jena and W. Mearson (London 1988) 138-9, cited in Cox, *Complete Tradesman*, 97.

[70] Museum of Edinburgh, Ford Ranken Archive, letter from George Roy to John Ford, manager of the Midlothian Glasshouse (later trading under the name Holyrood Glasshouse), 20 February 1820.

[71] C. Walshe, 'Shop Design and the Display of Goods in Eighteenth Century London', *Journal of Design History*, viii, 3, (Oxford 1995) 158.

[72] *ibid.*

[73] In an advertisement placed by Savage notifying the public of an auction to be held in Waterford on 13 February 1823 of 'Richly Cut Glass from the Cork Glass Works', he emphasises that the glass being auctioned was 'exactly similar to the elegant [selection] in the proprietor's newly formed splendid establishment at No. 48 Lower Sackville Street, Dublin', *Ramsey's Waterford Chronicle*, 13 February 1823.

[74] In this context, the term 'manufacturer' should be taken to mean organiser or co-ordinator as opposed to producer.

[75] Trinity College Dublin, Clements Papers, MS 7277, item 16. I would like to thank Alison FitzGerald for pointing me towards this collection of papers.

[76] NLI, Clements Papers, MS 9625, 31 December 1805.

[77] Mary Carter's business was carried on by William Carter; see note 40 above.

[78] It should be noted that it is unlikely that all pieces of moulded glass sold by these retailers would have borne their names impressed on the base. However, retailers who are known to have sold pieces marked with the names of their concerns include Francis Collins, Dublin; James Armstrong, Ormond Quay; J.D. Ayckbowm, Dublin, and Mary Carter, 80 Grafton Street. While Ayckbowm did operate as a glass manufacturer for a short period between 1799 and 1802, and James Armstrong was a glass-cutter by trade, the retailers mentioned would

have had to commission particular glasshouses to make the glass using specific moulds, and it is not clear which glasshouses supplied which retailers. Indeed, as Westropp points out in relation to James Armstrong, the glass itself may have been of English origin. Westropp, *Irish Glass*, 199.

[79] Other glasshouses, which also maintained this practice, include the Waterloo glasshouse, county Cork; the Cork Glass Company; Charles Mulvany and Company, Dublin; and B. Edwards, Belfast. In a similar manner to the retailers referred to in note 78 above, not every piece of moulded glass produced by the glasshouse would have borne an impressed name on the base.

[80] The managers of the Waterford glassworks explained in their statement that as flint and phial manufacturers they paid 56 shillings per hundredweight of glass. However, the black bottle makers only paid 5 shillings per hundred weight of glass, enabling the latter to dispose of them at an even lower price than the duty alone came to on the former. *Appendix to Thirteenth Report of Commissioners of Excise Inquiry*, xxxi, 1835, appendix 6, 73.

[81] NLI, MS 17390. Account for Joseph Grubb in respect of glass items bought from the Waterford Glass Ware Room, 23 October 1804.

[82] Gatchell Letters, document 12: letter from Martha Barnes in Edenderry to her uncle Jonathan Gatchell in Waterford, 8 December 1799.

[83] Barnard, 'Integration or Separation?', 137.

[84] Museum of Edinburgh, Ford Ranken Archive, cited in G. McFarlan, 'Early nineteenth-century patterns from the Ford Ranken Archive', *Journal of the Glass Association*, 4 (1992) 8, letter from J.H. Koch to John Ford, manager of the Midlothian Glasshouse (later trading under the name Holyrood Glasshouse), 26 April 1823.

[85] NLI, MS 17390.

[86] Also of vital importance is the issue of the role of patterns in the transmission of design. This subject is considered in the author's MA thesis. A. Moran, *Manufacturing Mythology? Waterford glass in the early nineteenth century*, unpublished V&A/RCA MA thesis, 2002.

[87] Collection of the Broadfield House Glass Museum, England, placed on loan to Dudley Library Services, Webb Richardson pattern books. The Webb Richardson pattern books are those which were used at the glasshouse owned by the partnership of William and Benjamin Richardson and Thomas Webb, situated in Wordsley in Stourbridge, England. The pattern books studied date from 1829, when the partnership was formed, into the late 1830s.

[88] Museum of Edinburgh, Ford Ranken Archive. The pattern books studied are those which were used at the Edinburgh glasshouse, which was variously named the Caledonian (*c*.1798-1819), the Midlothian (1819-35), the Holyrood (1835-98), and the Royal Holyrood Flint Glassworks (1898-1904). The pattern book 'FR9', which bears the date of 27 August 1826 on the inside cover, includes patterns which provide very precise and detailed dimensions for each part of the piece of glass. Clearly such patterns were intended to be used as guides during the production process. For further information on the Ford Ranken Archive, see McFarlan, 'Early nineteenth-century patterns'.

[89] Gatchell Letters, document 41: letter from Jonathan Wright to Nehemiah Wright, 23 December 1830. Westropp, *Irish Glass*, 93.

[90] University of Keele, Wedgwood Manuscripts, 2407-3: letter from J. Randall, Capel Street, Dublin, to Josiah Wedgwood, 7 June 1811. I am grateful to Mairead Dunlevy for this reference.

[91] Gatchell Letters, document 22: letter from George Saunders in Quebec to John Wright, 20 June 1826.

[92] The Gatchell Letters testify to a close business relationship shared between the Waterford glassworks and Isaac Warren, and it is clear that when George Gatchell came of age and took over the running of the glassworks, Warren offered the Wrights financial backing if they wished to buy the glassworks from George Gatchell. The Dublin street directories list an Isaac Warren as the proprietor of a glass warehouse at 31 Essex Street from 1824 to 1837. Another glass warehouse is listed, at 21 Essex Street, under the name of Warren & Company, from 1829 to 1841. From 1838 until 1856, Isaac Warren is listed as a china merchant at 7 Adelaide Road and 21 Essex Street. Additional members of the Warren family also feature in the street directories, each working in the business of ceramics and glass retailing.

[93] Dublin, Religious Society of Friends Archive, portfolio 35, item vii: the diary of Jonathan Wright's wife, covering the years between 1832 and 1835.

[94] Religious Society of Friends Archive, portfolio 34, item vi, April 1828.

[95] Gatchell Letters, document 54: letter from Jonathan Wright to Nathan, 6 April 1832.

[96] Esau Clarke was described as a French horn and trumpet maker in *PRDS*, 27 June 1771, 190, but later featured in a 1787 Dublin street directory as a delft merchant. M. Reynolds, 'Wedgwood in Dublin, 1772-1777', *Irish Arts Review*, i, 2 (Dublin 1984). In a personal account book of the Rt Hon Richard Jackson and his wife Anne Jackson, 1767-1778, the following entry is noted: 'Paid Luffingham for Cheshire Cheese, Dozen of Beer and a China Mug', 24 March 1768; TCD, MS 9218, 7, cited in Foster, 'Going Shopping', 50.

[97] M. Reynolds, 'James Donovan "The Emperor of China"', *Irish Arts Review*, i, 3 (Dublin 1985) 28-36. Donovan had a brass establishment for making lamps and other articles; however, as brass was used in glass lamps, it was consequently a logical extension of production.

[98] Cox, *Complete Tradesman*, 114.

[99] Gatchell Letters, document 14: letter from A. Barcroft in Cork to Jonathan Gatchell in Waterford, 24 April 1805. Between 1799 and 1811, the glass works was owned by three partners – Jonathan Gatchell, Ambrose Barcroft and John Ramsey.

[100] A notebook dated 1828, containing recipes used at the Waterford glassworks, includes 'Instructions to fill a pot with Tale'. The book instructs the user to 'Fill the tray with skimmings or chert metal or washed tale and put in about eight shovels full of batch. Put in a pinch of manganese at the bottom and likewise ... about 8 or 10 pinches managanese and so to fill it up.' The recipes are in the D. Westropp collection, and I would like to thank Mary Boydell for making her copy of this notebook accessible to me.

[101] Gatchell Letters, document 48: letter from Jonathan Wright to Nathan Wright, 28 July 1831.

[102] *ibid.*, document 20b: 'Debts due to the estate of Jonathan Gatchell', 19 November 1825.

[103] NLI, MS 3288. *Enquiry into the Poor in Waterford* (1834) 96-7, the 'Extract from the Annual Statement furnished by the trustees of the Waterford Savings Bank', 20 November 1833, reveals that in 1820 the 'amount of deposits remaining' reduced from £10,662 6s 10d to £6577 18s 5d. This reduction was explained by the recorder: 'In the month of June 1820, Newports Bank failed and the distress and panic consequent thereon explains the cause of the reduction in this year'. These figures also reveal that 1,218 of the 2,714 depositors had a figure not exceeding £20 in the bank, and only 16 of the 2,714 depositors had between £150 and £200 lodged. Enquiry carried out by Patrick Francis Johnston and Edmond Moylan.

[104] I would like to thank Mairead Dunlevy for this reference.

[105] Excise duty had to be paid regardless of whether the glass sold or not. Therefore, duty had to be paid on the glass which sat in store rooms, later to be sold at a great loss. With this in mind,

one should be cautious when interpreting statistics pertaining to duty paid on glass retained for home use. *Returns relating to Glass Retained for Home Use, and Quantities Exported, Duty Charged, and Drawback paid on each description, in the United Kingdom, from 1814 to 1841* (England 1841) 160.

[106] Gatchell Letters, document 36: letter from Jonathan Wright to Nathan, 15 October 1830.

[107] *ibid.*, document 33: letter from Jonathan Wright in Waterford to Nehemiah in Dublin, 27 June 1830.

[108] *ibid.*, document 99: same to same, 23 April 1835.

[109] *Saunders' Newsletter and Daily Advertiser*, 11 August 1835.

[110] *Appendix to Thirteenth Report of Commissioners of Excise Inquiry*, xxxi, 1835, appendix no. 44, vol. 31, 148.

[111] *ibid.*, appendix no. 31, vol. 31, 122.

[112] The full verse which features on Marsden Haddock's trade circular is quoted in R. Day, 'Eighteenth Century Trade Circulars and Invoices of Cork Traders', *Journal of the Cork Historical and Archaeological Society*, vii, 1901, 170.

[113] Gatchell Letters, document 62: letter from John Wright to Nehemiah Wright, 9 September 1832.

[114] Between 1836 and 1848, a partnership existed between George Gatchell and George Saunders, who had, up to that time, been an employee of the glasshouse.

[115] Waterford Crystal Museum, Letter from George Gatchell to 'Jonathan', 21 April 1851.

[116] J.H. Yoxall, *Collecting Old Glass English and Irish* (New York 1916) 1.

[117] Gatchell Letters, document 97: letter from Jonathan Wright to Nathan Wright, 7 May 1835. 'Tale wines' are included in a list of objects, with associated prices, intended to be passed to Isaac Warren. Plain tumblers are mentioned in a letter from Jonathan Wright to Nathan Wright: 'I should like to know what articles of glass you might be wanting most – perhaps a few wines rumours good plain tumblers carofts', Gatchell Letters, document 108: letter, 10 August 1835.

———

1 – THE FRONT OF ST WARBURGHS CHURCH
2 – THE FRONT OF ST ANNS CHURCH
from Charles Brooking, MAP OF THE CITY & SUBURBS OF DUBLIN (1728)
(courtesy Irish Architectural Archive)

A reluctant observer:
Swift and architecture

JOSEPH McMINN

L ATE SEVENTEENTH-CENTURY DUBLIN, COMPARED TO LONDON, OFFERED VERY little to distinguish it as a metropolis shaped and dramatised by architecture of a high imaginative order. To a great extent, this comparative poverty was the effect of a political and colonial settlement which put its resources and energies into defence rather than celebration, into building rather than architecture. As Edward McParland points out, the priority for seventeenth-century settlers in Ireland was to protect and consolidate their position in the country:

> It was not simply its defences that needed to be established on a new foot-
> ing, but also its representative buildings (there was no great library building
> in Ireland in 1700, and no great royal palace or government building), and
> its infrastructure of communications, industry, education, philanthropy, and
> religion.[1]

In 1667, the year in which Swift was born, there was still only one bridge across the River Liffey. Ships had to dock beyond the city at Ringsend, from where their cargo had to be transferred up river, and the city walls continued to suggest a medieval centre rather than an expansive city. Maurice Craig characterises Swift's Dublin at this time as a place 'squalid and constricted'.[2] With a population of approximately 50,000, the city was concentrated on the south side of the river, its skyline dominated by two cathedrals – St Patrick's and Christchurch. Dublin Castle, the centre of the English administration in Ireland, and a vice-regal residence, was largely a dilapidated site. As a result of a series of fires in the late seventeenth century, the most destructive of which broke out in 1684, the Castle resembled a medieval ruin, and remained in that state for most of Swift's lifetime.[3] Bernard de Gomme's map of 1673, which was commissioned by the English government for military and strate-gic reasons, shows how the urban landscape is beginning to expand from its earlier

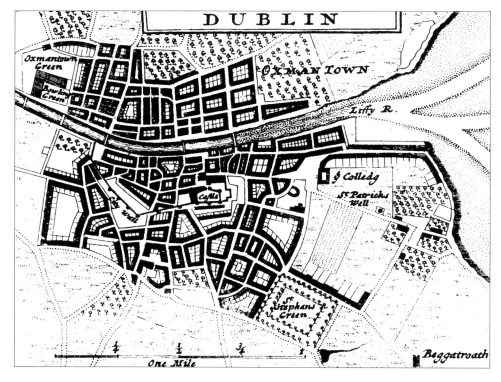

3 – Dublin by Henry Pratt, 1708, based on maps by Bernard de Gomme and Thomas Phillips,
reproduced from Herman Moll, A NEW MAP OF IRELAND (London 1714)
(reproduced with permission of the Council of Trustees of the National Library of Ireland)

concentration in the south-west to areas closer to Trinity College, Chichester House and St Stephen's Green in the south-east (Plate 3).[4] In the same year in which de Gomme produced his map, the young Swift was sent from Dublin to Kilkenny School, returning ten years later to enter Trinity College. Nearly a hundred years old when Swift began his undergraduate studies, Trinity College still retained its largely Elizabethan design; the development and expansion of Ireland's only university began after Swift had graduated.[5]

During Swift's time as a student at Trinity College, James Butler, 1st Duke of Ormonde, consolidated plans for what was to become one of Dublin's greatest architectural achievements, the Royal Hospital, Kilmainham, which Maurice Craig refers to as the 'earliest secular public building in the country'.[6] The architect was William Robinson, Surveyor General, who was responding to the government's concern over the large number of sick and invalided soldiers in the country who needed a settled and protected home. Based on Les Invalides in Paris (and later copied at Chelsea Hospital in London), Kilmainham was, in McParland's words, 'the earliest large-scale exercise in architectural classicism in the country',[7] a monumental design which would eventually set the classical standard for Georgian Dublin. The Royal Hospital opened in 1687, shortly before the onset of yet another period of war in Ireland, a period in which there was no significant architectural activity.[8]

The political and military crisis of the final decade of the seventeenth century saw Swift leaving Dublin for the relative security of England, and for a career outside the provincialism of Ireland. Any attempt to understand Swift's views on, and responses to, architecture should work within the context of a culture shaped, and usually divided, by sectarian and political loyalties. As part of the Protestant settlement, Swift usually associated Ireland with barbarism, and looked to England for models of refinement and superior taste. After leaving Trinity in 1689, he spent most of the next decade in England, where he worked as secretary to Sir William Temple at Moor Park in Surrey. During these years he took his MA from Hart Hall in Oxford, and almost certainly made his first visits to London. His work for Temple was interrupted, briefly, by his decision to take Holy Orders, and to become a priest in the Church of Ireland. Swift's earliest experiences as a clergyman in Ireland were associated with ruin and decay, and there is no sense that anything in the Irish landscape, urban or rural, attracted his visual sense. His first living, the prebend of Kilroot, in county Antrim, just ten miles north of Belfast, had neither rectory nor glebe, not even a church.[9] In 1699 he was granted the vicarage of Laracor, in county Meath, about twenty miles north of Dublin, but once again in a parish without a rectory. Over the course of the next few years, while supervising the building of a small cottage for himself, complete with landscaped garden, he rented rooms in nearby Trim, a town dominated by the ruins of its Norman castle, having been besieged by Cromwellian forces in 1649. While the area was much more congenial to Swift than county Antrim had been, it was still, as Ehrenpreis suggests, a precarious living, with the town of Trim as 'the commercial centre of a busy and important Protestant island in a sea of Roman Catholicism'.[10] The eventual satisfaction which Swift enjoyed with his first real home at Laracor could not have contradicted his sense that he was serving an impoverished Church in an impoverished land. After the deprivation and provincialism of these years, Swift was more determined than ever to try his luck again in England. Within ten years he would be a resident of London, an intimate of ministers, and a regular visitor to the homes of the artistocracy and royalty.

Swift made several journeys to London in the first decade of the new century, initially as chaplain and secretary to the Earl of Berkeley, and later as negotiator for the remission of taxes upon the Church of Ireland. His literary career begins in these same years, with the anonymous publication in London of *A Tale of a Tub* (1704), and various tracts and pamphlets on Church and State. His fifth visit of these years, in August 1710, resulted in a three-year stay, during which time he served as chief propagandist for the new Tory administration, notably as writer of the Tory *Examiner*, a paper in which he defended government policy and attacked the Whig opposition. These are some of the best documented years of Swift's life and literary activity. His regular correspondence with friends in England and Ireland, but especially his *Journal to Stella*, give us a detailed and dramatic account of Swift's new social life in London, the places he lived in and visited, how he travelled about the great city, and his impressions of the capital's great buildings. Only a decade beforehand, Swift was employing his own builders to construct a modest cabin for his vicarage at Laracor: now he was to become a regular visitor to Whitehall and Windsor.

London stood in monumental contrast to Dublin. Its population at the turn of the century was close to three-quarters of a million, more than ten times that of Swift's birthplace.[11] The shape and style of the city had been transformed by the twin catastrophes of the previous century, the plague of 1665, and the Great Fire of the following year.[12] Over 100,000 people died in the plague, while the Great Fire destroyed over 400 acres, levelling most of the city's public buildings. A single architect – Sir Christopher Wren – took over the job of rebuilding London's churches, nearly all of which had been reduced to ashes.[13] His major project was the redesign and reconstruction of St Paul's cathedral, the city's greatest achievement in Renaissance architecture, comparable at the time to the work of Bramante and Michelangelo in St Peter's in Rome.[14] Work on St Paul's began in 1675 and was completed in 1710, the year in which Swift returned to London. Only a month after his arrival he was taken by friends to see this architectural wonder, the pride of a rebuilt London: 'Today I was all about St Paul's, and up at the top like a fool, with Sir Andrew Fountain [sic] and two more; and spent seven shillings for my dinner like a puppy...'[15]

Standing on top of a cathedral (instead of praying inside one) struck Swift as absurd, and he registers no appreciation whatsoever of the aesthetic or religious character of the place. Sir Andrew Fountaine, on the other hand, was a leading connoisseur of the arts, described by Ehrenpreis as 'an exquisite virtuoso'.[16] Mention of his friend's name, and the cost of his dinner, seem typical of so many of his encounters with the landscape of London: he usually preferred people to places, and was obsessed with the cost of dining out. Public architecture, however, cannot be avoided, even though its charms may be dismissed, and this anticlimactic piece of sightseeing does not close the story of Swift's observations upon London.

Architecture interested Swift for its literary and satirical possibilities, and its value was nearly always assessed with reference to his moral and political principles. Whenever he engaged with some famous architect or building, he tended to consider its political symbolism above all else, showing little or no interest in merely formal or technical matters. During his several visits to London in the early years of the eighteenth century, his mind was focused on securing a deal for his church with the Whig administration, and he soon became resigned to long periods of attendance upon courtiers, ministers and potential allies. By the time he returned in the autumn of 1710, he had already become well known in political and literary circles, in London's coffee-houses, and was a regular (and grateful) guest at many dinner-tables of the city's upper classes. In November of that first year he wrote to Stella, telling her of an evening spent in company which included England's greatest living architect, John Vanbrugh, a man who was carrying on the Baroque achievements of his elderly contemporary, Wren:

> I dined today at sir Richard Temple's, with Congreve, Vanburg [sic], lieutenant-general Farrington, &c. Vanburg, I believe I told you, had a long quarrel with me about those Verses on his House; but we were very civil and cold. Lady Marlborough used to teaze him with them, which had made him angry, though he be a good natured fellow.[17]

Swift had come face to face with the architect he had satirised in two poems, one of which, 'The History of Vanbrug's House', had been published in London only a few months before this social encounter.[18] Closely associated with the Whig interest, Vanbrugh had designed Castle Howard in Yorkshire in 1701, and had started work in 1705 on Blenheim Palace, outside Oxford, the future home of the Duke of Marlborough (Plate 4).[19] The satirical verses alluded to in his letter to Stella, however, referred to a very different project, one which had provoked Swift's outrage many years previously, giving us a decisive picture of his interpretation of grandiose architectural projects carried out by 'modern' virtuosi like Vanbrugh. 'The History of Vanbrug's House', written in 1706, refers to a house which the architect had built for himself on the site of Whitehall Palace, which had been destroyed by fire in January 1698. First Wren, then Vanbrugh, was commissioned to restore Whitehall. Vanbrugh's temporary residence on the building site, the so-called 'Goose-Pie House', was ridiculed by Swift as one whose design was plagiarised from games which children play, constructing 'houses' from cards and mud.[20] For Swift, knowing that Vanbrugh began life as a dramatist, the architectural project is a farce, its author a charlatan, someone without training, experience or education – 'Van's genius, without thought or lecture, / Is hugely turned to architecture'.[21] The poem also mocks those who would equate and confuse classical and contemporary architects, flattering themselves into the illusion that imitation of the ancient world somehow proves their good taste:

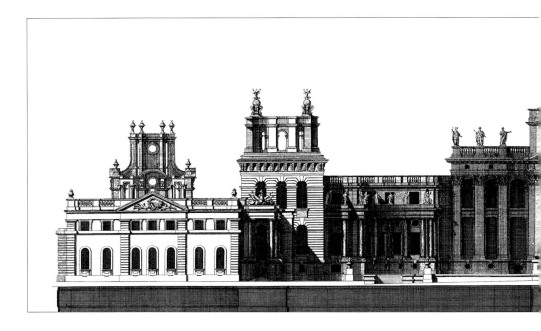

From such deep rudiments as these
Van is become by due degrees
For building famed, and justly reckoned
At court, Vitruvius the second.
No wonder, since wise authors show,
That best foundations must be low.
And now the Duke has wisely taken him
To be his architect at Blenheim.[22]

Trying, with little success, to make his own way at court, it must have been pretty galling for Swift to watch someone he considered an illusionist, quickly becoming an intimate of the Whig aristocracy. We have no evidence that Swift actually saw Vanbrugh's house, but he is more interested here in reputation than reality, in political advancement than artistic ability. Vanbrugh was what Swift hoped to become, a court favourite, something he was to achieve over the next couple of years.

Swift had first exercised his contempt for Vanbrugh in an earlier poem, 'Vanbrugh's House', in a draft version written in 1703 and in a revised, extended version written in 1708, which was eventually published in 1711 in *Miscellanies*.[23] This poem rehearses Swift's caricature of Vanbrugh as virtuoso, a man who could switch from writing plays to building palaces, as if it were merely a matter of inspi-

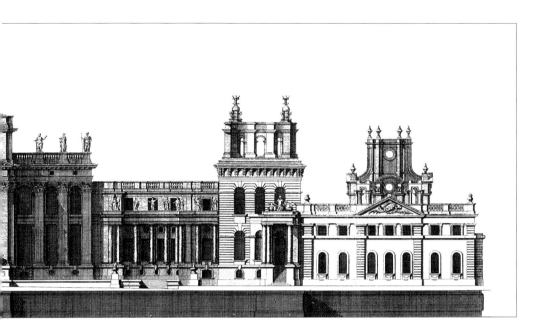

4 – Blenheim Castle, from Colen Campbell, VITRUVIUS BRITANNICUS (London 1725)
(courtesy Irish Architectural Archive)

ration, and not training.[24] Structured around his favourite conceit of a battle between Ancients and Moderns, between authentic classical achievement and superficial contemporary fashion, Swift damns Vanbrugh both as artist and architect, a modern who can only plunder the ruins of the past. To complete his satire on the ignorance of contemporary admiration for Vanbrugh, Swift allows an observer to sing ironic praises of the modern artist:

> So modern rhymes wisely blast
> The poetry of ages past,
> Which after they have overthrown,
> They from its ruins build their own.[25]

Dining together must have been rather uncomfortable, more for Vanbrugh than for Swift, who scarcely knew the man he had satirised so mercilessly.[26] The figure and the reputation of Vanbrugh interested and irritated Swift, who saw them in a political and cultural context of his own imaginative construction. For some, Vanbrugh's ability to move with ease between the sister-arts confirmed his versatility; for Swift, such an ability only confirmed the man's superficiality. Undoubtedly, the poems on Vanbrugh tell us more about Swift's cultural values and preferences, inflexible and conservative, than about the architect's rightful claim to fame.

These two poems on Vanbrugh were originally prompted by, and amplified, a poem which Swift had written a few years earlier while working at Moor Park, 'On the Burning of Whitehall in 1698', the first poem he ever wrote on an architectural topic.[27] One of Swift's earliest poems, written when he was thirty, it shows a deeply political and religious reading of the disaster, seeing the conflagration as a form of divine retribution on a place whose past was corrupt and shameful. Reviewing the history of what he calls 'This pile', Swift lists all those monarchs, from Henry VIII to James II, who had lived there, and who had betrayed their God as well as their nation. The destruction of this den of iniquity is presented as an apocalyptic drama:

> Heaven takes the cure in hand, celestial ire
> Applies the oft-tried remedy of fire;
> The purging flames were better far employed,
> Than when old Sodom was, or Troynovant destroyed.
> The nest obscene of every pampered vice,
> Sinks down of this infernal paradise,
> Down come the lofty roofs, the cedar burns,
> The blended metal to a torrent turns.[28]

Biblical and historical analogies – with Sodom and its gross immorality, with 'Troynovant' and its allusion to ancient London founded by the survivors of Troy (but also to the Great Fire of 1666) – give the poem a severe, judgemental perspective without any sense of a noble building lost to the nation. And yet, in its final lines, Swift sees God's hand at work in the miraculous and symbolic survival of Inigo Jones' great Banqueting House:

> But mark how providence with watchful care,
> Did Inigo's famed building spare,
> That theatre produced an action truly great,
> On which eternal acclamations wait,
> Of kings deposed, most faithful annals tell,
> And slaughtered monarchs would a volume swell.
> Our happy chronicle can show alone
> On this day tyrants executed – one.[29]

The defiant allusion here is to King Charles I, who was executed outside the Banqueting House, a sacred site preserved by Divine justice, a memorial ground for those, like Swift, who championed his role as a virtuous monarch murdered by an uncouth horde of illiterate Dissenters, a martyr to a sacred institution (Plate 5).[30] This poem shows, amongst other things, how Swift cannot look at a building without looking at its owner, how he brings his political and religious principles to the

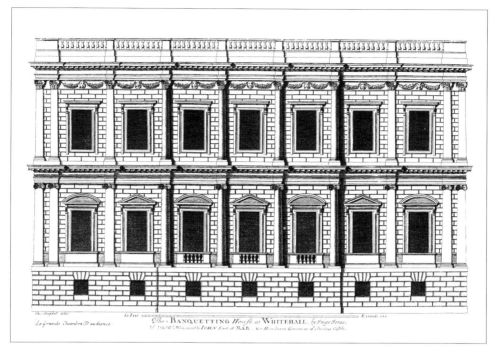

5 – THE BANQUETTING HOUSE AT WHITEHALL from VITRUVIUS BRITANNICUS
(courtesy Irish Architectural Archive)

fore when assessing the value and integrity of a site such as Whitehall, a place which, in his view, deserved to burn. Some of these considerations may help explain Swift's rush to judge Vanbrugh, who would presume to restore a monument which embodied a history of shame.[31] More than twenty years after he had first attacked Vanbrugh, Swift seemed to repent of his personalised satire, and in the jointly signed introduction to *Miscellanies in Prose and Verse* (1727), Pope and Swift named both Vanbrugh and Addison as two innocent victims of unfair poetic abuse. The apology (published a year after Vanbrugh's death), sounds like it came much more from Pope than from Swift.[32]

As a clergyman and willing servant of the Tory and High Church interest, one might expect that Swift would be interested in ecclesiastical, if not secular, architecture, in monuments to God and not those to passing political interests. Yet there seems to have been only one occasion on which Swift used his position as Tory propagandist to voice his opinions on the state of the city's churches, and that was in his capacity as the pseudonymous *Examiner*. In May 1711 he wrote a piece about a new government proposal to build fifty new churches in the capital, a project approved by Queen Anne, showing the government's determination to prove itself as the traditional and continuing friend of the Established Church. After two decades of Whig power, it was now the turn of the Tories to celebrate their return, and to do so through a reaffirmation of High Church triumphalism.[33] In his piece for the *Examiner*, Swift applauds the proposal, and at first suggests that the proposal is a necessary and inevitable part of the changing demographic character of London since the Restoration:

> Since that Time, the Encrease of Trade, the Frequency of Parliaments, the Desire of living in the Metropolis, together with that Genius for Building, which began after the *Fire*, and hath ever since continued; have prodigiously enlarged this Town on all sides, where it was capable of Encrease.[34]

Yet it becomes immediately clear that Swift wants to use the proposal as a pretext for attacking the Whigs, and specifically their support of the Duke of Marlborough and the continuing war in Europe. A monstrous and offensive symbol of Whig godlessness and war-lust, he argues, is the home presently being built for the Duke, Blenheim Palace, an architectural extravaganza which the Duke does not deserve and which the nation cannot afford. Swift contrasts this disproportionate and excessive expenditure with the practice of the ancient Romans when paying just and reasonable tribute to their best generals:

> The *Romans*, upon a great Victory, or Escape from publick Danger, frequently built a Temple in Honour of some God, to whose peculiar Favour they imputed their Success or Delivery; And sometimes the *General* did the like, *at his own Expense*, to acquit himself of some pious Vow he had made. How little of any Thing resembling this hath been done by us after all our Victories![35]

The cost of this admirable and virtuous project for fifty new churches, it is calculated, would be well below what is being spent on the Duke of Marlborough's palatial home, a monument to Mammon and Vanity. Apart from a few token gestures towards the poor state of many churches in the city, 'those ancient *Gothick* structures',[36] Swift's polemic shows little or no interest in, or understanding of, ecclesiastical buildings in the city, and fails to even mention Wren's work over the previous decades. Blenheim, like Whitehall, was a symbol of modern decadence, and deserved no support from a God-fearing and virtuous people. Swift's friend, Alexander Pope, a leading virtuoso of the age, would later agree with this severe judgement of Blenheim and Marlborough, but in terms which included a clear and learned appreciation of architectural styles.[37] If Swift was ever to approve of a building or home, he would have to approve of the patriotism and virtue of its owner.

In all his years in and around London, Swift visited or was introduced to many outstanding places and homes, including Hampton Court and Windsor. Only a few weeks after his arrival in London in September 1710, he tells Stella of his first visit to Hampton Court, noting the distinguished nature of his company:

> Lord Halifax was at Hampton-court at his lodgings, and I dined with him there with Methuen, and Delaval, and the late attorney-general. I went to the drawing room before dinner (for the queen was at Hampton-court) and expected to see *nobody*; but I met acquaintance enough. I walked in the gardens, saw the cartons of Raphael, and other things, and with great difficulty got from Lord Halifax, who would have kept me tomorrow to shew me his house and park, and improvements.[38]

Strolling around the rooms of this famous Tudor palace, extensively redesigned and rebuilt by Wren for William and Mary, Swift sounds like an intruder who finds little worthy of comment, even the drawings by Raphael, located in the King's Gallery.

Swift never records another visit to Hampton Court.[39] His favourite place during these years was Windsor Palace, where he was a regular and willing visitor, usually in the company of ministers. The setting, rather than the architecture, impressed and delighted him. He seems to have made his first visit there in July 1711, telling Stella, 'Windsor is a delicious place', but adding that he had passed through it, very briefly, seventeen years previously, when he would have been with Temple at Moor Park.[40] He soon began to see Windsor not so much as an architectural monument, but as a kind of health farm, where he could cure his aches and pains by walking regularly in the splendid grounds: 'I take all opportunities of walking; and we have a delicious park here just joining to the castle, and an avenue in the great park very wide and two miles long, set with a double row of elms on each side.'[41]

His lodgings at Windsor overlooked the Thames, and he regularly rode in company around the grounds, once going as far as Ascot to see the newly planned racecourse to be opened by Queen Anne.[42] Windsor becomes a kind of pastoral retreat from London, 'a most delightful Place', as he tells Stella, where he can enjoy the good life, and which, most importantly, 'abounds in Dinners'.[43]

In his correspondence, especially that with Stella, there is a clear sense of Swift cultivating the image of a man with important connections, and living in a metropolis rich with historical and cultural monuments, a world which those in Ireland can only imagine, and which is now his daily milieu. At the same time, he cannot help sounding like an outsider, a visiting tourist seeing great sights for the first time. On several occasions he undertakes sightseeing tours of the city, and records visits to Westminster Abbey (to see the tombs), the Tower of London, and the newly built Buckingham House (now Buckingham Palace).[44] He was regularly invited to some of the great houses outside the city, such as Wimbledon House, an

6 – Altar-table by Jacques Tarbary, from the chapel at the Royal Hospital Kilmainham
(courtesy Irish Architectural Archive)

Elizabethan mansion which Swift tells Stella 'is much the finest place about this Town'.[45] Of the many districts in which he lodged in and around the capital, his favourite was Chelsea, where he lived for more than a year, and from where he enjoyed the walk, or the riverboat, into town to meet friends.[46] Dr John Arbuthnot, the Queen's physician, with whom Swift had made friends, also lived at Chelsea, where he worked at the Royal Hospital, yet another creation of Wren, completed in 1689. Writing to Stella, in a rare moment of comparative observation in matters of design, Swift notes a similarity between the Dublin and the London hospitals: 'I dined with Dr Arbuthnot (one of my Brothers) at his Lodgings in Chelsea, and was there at Chappel, and the Altar put me in mind of Tisdal's outlandish would at your Hospital for the Soldiers.'[47]

Despite the orthographical distraction of 'would' for 'wood', and the presence of a mysterious 'Tisdal', this is clearly an allusion to the elaborate woodcarving in the chapel at Kilmainham, carried out by Jacques Tarbary, a French Huguenot who had settled in Dublin (Plate 6).[48] Swift, then, must have visited Kilmainham, but we cannot date that visit with any certainty. Dating aside, Swift's remark about 'outlandish would' does not suggest an appreciative response.

Further down the Thames from Chelsea, at Twickenham, lived Alexander Pope, whose riverside house and gardens were one of the literary landmarks of Georgian London (Plate 7).[49] In March 1726, Swift returned to London with the manuscript of *Gulliver's Travels*, staying for several weeks at Twickenham, from where he undertook many visits and tours in the company of old friends, including Gay, Congreve and Arbuthnot.[50] These outings included visits to several great stately homes, including Lord Bolingbroke's estate at Dawley, near Uxbridge, and Lord Bathurst's residence at Richings Park, near Colnbrook.[51] Pope and Swift also visited the home of Lord Burlington, 4th Earl of Cork, the leading figure in English Palladianism, and a close friend of Pope. During this visit, Burlington presented the Dean with a copy of Fréart's *Parallèle de l'Architecture Antique et de la Moderne* (1702), with the following mock-honorary inscription: 'I give this Book to Dr. Jonathan Swift, Dean of St. Patrick's Dublin; in order to constitute him the Director of Architecture in Ireland, especially upon my own Estate in that Kingdom.'[52]

Swift was becoming one of the major social attractions of Pope's London circle, with many of the leading figures in politics and the arts keen to meet or resume friendship with the legendary dean. His many invitations included those from the Princess of Wales and Prime Minister Walpole. The one person he had hoped to see

7 – An Exact Draught and View of Mr Pope's House at Twickenham (1735),
an engraving by Peter Rysbrack

again, the Earl of Oxford, was too busy to resume acquaintance, leaving Swift with the poor alternative of exchanging letters with him. Before Swift left to return home to Ireland, he asked the Earl to return a valuable book he had earlier lent him, Humphrey Prideaux's *Marmora Oxoniensia*, in a 1676 folio edition.[53] This was a rare volume on the antiquities of Oxford, one which the Earl borrowed on a later occasion and failed to return.[54] Swift's other great ministerial friend from these years, Viscount Bolingbroke, presented him with a 29-volume set of *Graevius and Gronovius*, an encyclopaedic account of ancient Greece and Rome, with particular volumes dedicated to the architecture of the classical world. This magnificent collection remained the pride and joy of Swift's personal library.[55] After five months at the heart of the social, political and cultural scene in London, Swift packed his belongings, and returned to the deanery in mid-August.

Once back home in Dublin, Swift could not resist depressing comparisons between the two countries, telling Pope, 'Going to England is a very good thing, if it were not attended with an ugly circumstance of returning to Ireland'.[56] He had written to Vanessa in the same morose vein over a decade earlier, recalling her visit to see him at Windsor. Having recently settled in Celbridge, county Kildare, she must be struck, Swift insists, by the depressing contrast:

> Does not Dublin look very dirty to You, and the Country very miserable. Is Kildrohod [Celbridge] as beautiful as Windsr [sic], and as agreeable to You as the Prebends Lodgings there; is there any walk about You as pleasant as the Avenue, and the Marlborough Lodge.[57]

Like Lemuel Gulliver, Swift discovers that travel and the discovery of new landscapes can become a deeply depressing as well as liberating experience, one by which 'home' is increasingly seen through the comparative imagery and memory of other, idealised places. Provincial Ireland is seen and judged through the images of royal England, and the cultivation of England is remembered alongside the wretchedness of the Irish landscape.

Apart from his short, savage poetic reflections upon a few landmarks in London, which were provoked by political rather than aesthetic impulses, Swift remained largely unresponsive to and underwhelmed by the architecture of the capital. In his study of Grub Street culture in London during the early eighteenth century, Pat Rogers may provide us with a reason for this seeming indifference. He agrees that Swift 'moved among great men', but argues that his real passion lay among 'the underlings of the world of letters', a world he had so richly satirised in *A Tale of a Tub*.[58] If Swift does not seem that interested in 'high' art, he was certainly fascinated, even obsessed, with low-life, with 'the life of the streets', a topic which Rogers believes was handled by Swift with 'vivid and graphic immediacy'.[59]

If architecture is a form which requires the spectator to gaze upwards often in wonder and curiosity, then we might say that Swift usually looked in the opposite direction, keeping his eyes more clearly focused on the gutters of London. His most vivid poems about London's landscape, 'Description of the Morning' and 'A City Shower', seem to confirm this reading of Swift's perverse perspective on the ugliness, and not the beauty of the city.[60]

Swift loved London, its majesty as well as its horrors, its wealth as well as its poverty, but above all for the fictional opportunities it helped him imagine. In the end, however, it seems that Wren's London, static and impersonal, was of less interest to him than the social world of high and low company, of dining rooms and taverns, promenades and visits. As Ian Campbell Ross has argued, Swift would always retain an Irish colonist's nostalgia for the 'home country', and for 'English metropolitian culture', those sources of an imagined and complex identity which became deeply involved in his role as 'Hibernian Patriot'.[61]

In May 1713, while preparing to make his way home to Ireland to take up his new position as Dean of St Patrick's (Plate 8), Swift had received a letter from the

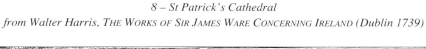

8 – St Patrick's Cathedral
from Walter Harris, THE WORKS OF SIR JAMES WARE CONCERNING IRELAND (Dublin 1739)

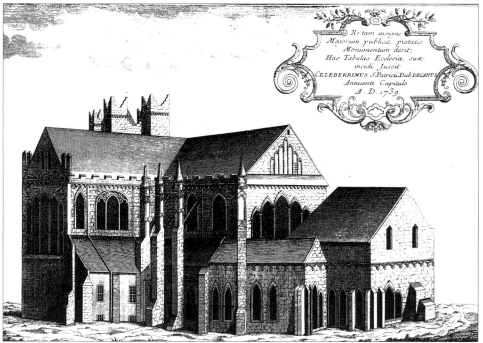

Archbishop of Dublin, William King, extending a formal welcome to the parish. In this letter, King reminds Swift that building work on the cathedral, commenced by the outgoing dean, John Stearne, will be an ongoing responsibility, and gives him a detailed outline of the work to be done:

> Your Predecessor in St. Patrick's did a great deal to his church and house but there is still work for you, he designed a spire for the steeple, which kind of ornament is much wanting in Dublin, he has left your Oeconomy clear and 200ll in bank for this purpose. The Steeple is 120 feet high, 21 feet in the clear wide where the spire is to stand, the design was to build it of brick, 120 feet high, the scaffolding we reckoned to be the principall cost, which yet is pretty cheap in Dublin, the brick and Lime are good and cheap. But we have no workman that understands any thing of the matter. I believe you may be acquainted with several that are conversant with such kind of work, and if you would discourse some of them, and push on the work as soon as settled, it might be of use to you, and give the people there an advantageous notion of you...[62]

This lecture on building management and economy was scarcely the warm embrace Swift might have hoped for or imagined. In his reply of the following week, he tried to sound as courteous as possible, but respectfully queried his superior's judgement:

> As to the Spire to be erected on St. Patrick's Steeple, I am apt to think it will cost more than is imagined; and, I am confident, that no Bricks made in that Part of Ireland, will bear being exposed so much to the Air: However, I shall enquire among some Architects here.[63]

King replied immediately, and at the end of a brief letter about diocesan matters, he added a curt reminder of his original prescription, saying, 'Our Irish brick will do very well for the steeple, and five or six thousand will finish it'.[64] Nothing in these refrigerated exchanges touches upon matters of style or design. King's recommendations are utilitarian and financial, while Swift's anxieties are characteristically economic. Laying out this kind of money on an 'ornament' to his new cathedral was not Swift's priority, and the spire was not erected in his lifetime.[65] In fact, over the three decades in which he served as Dean, Swift preserved, but never improved the rather ruinous state of his cathedral.[66]

These exchanges are, however, best appreciated and understood in the wider context of King's work over many years to increase the number, if not the quality, of churches in Dublin, a project which was possibly inspired by the similar one in London only a few years previously. Edward McParland emphasises King's industry in church-building, while acknowledging his insensitivity to 'the symbolical value of great architecture'.[67] The best example of King's limited influence in these matters concerned plans, drawn up by the commissioners in Dublin, for redesigning and rebuilding St Werburgh's church, just around the corner from St Patrick's cathedral (Plate 1). Viscount Robert Molesworth, the Irish Whig statesman, had offered to employ the services of the Italian architect Alessandro Galilei, but King seems to have persuaded the commissioners that Thomas Burgh, Robinson's successor as Surveyor-General, should be entrusted with the task, largely because King was averse to a Roman Catholic shaping the design of the church, preferring instead the solid if dull effort of a loyal soldier.[68] In letters to Molesworth, written in the summer of 1716, thanking him for his public-spirited gesture, King tries to reflect on the reasons for Ireland's architectural poverty:

> I believe we are as backward in Ireland as to Architecture and indeed as to all arts and Sciences as most Cuntries in Europe, nor is it any Wonder it Shou'd be So, considering we are a Depending Province and Depend on those (as it universally happens in such cases) who make it their business to hinder all improvements which in my opinion is a weak and foolish piece of Policie.[69]

Blaming England for Ireland being 'a Depending Province', thereby blocking all forms of progress, was an interpretation which would later unite King and Swift, one which the Dean would make central to the rhetoric of his *Drapier's Letters* ten years later:

> Whereas a *Depending Kingdom* is a *Modern Term of Art*, unknown, as I have heard, to all antient *Civilians*, and *Writers upon Government*; and *Ireland* is on the contrary called in some Statutes an *Imperial Crown*, as held only from God; which is as High a Style as any Kingdom is capable of receiving.[70]

King also shared his belief with Molesworth that the uncouth settlers of the Cromwellian age were largely responsible for the ruinous state of the country's buildings:

> 'Tis no wonder that we are backward in Architecture in Ireland, considering that it is not 600 years Since we had any building of Stone and lime in it, and ever Since we have bin in Continual warres the only [way] we cou'd have any prospect of improving in it, was on the Settlement after '41, and then the persons that had the Estates, were generally a parcel of ruff Soldiers, that had so little taste of fine Building, that it was their principle to pull Down the best they found Standing, and wanting everything, they were for taking up with anything, that wou'd cover them from the rain. Since that we have bin So unsettled that men have thought themselves Happy if they cou'd Secure the

necessarys of living and have not bin much solicitous about the ornaments of it. At present the generalitie of men of fortunes and imployments living out of the kingdom, and the little relish and prospect any have of living at home are insuperable discouragements to expensive buildings. In So much that I see little hope of a valuable Architects either finding employment or Subsistence in Ireland and this is the reason I dare not venture to invite Senor Galile into Ireland least he shou'd Starve there.[71]

Much of this is a plausible historical explanation, yet some of it seems distinctly disingenuous. A country dominated by political and military insecurity will very probably favour the defensive and the utilitarian in matters of design, but King suggests that it was the lower-class Protestants of the seventeenth-century settlement whose influence proved stronger that that of King's own ruling class of the Church of Ireland establishment – that, in fact, the tastelessness of the former class blocked the imagination of the latter. (Swift shared many of these facile prejudices about the divisive and ruinous influence of Dissenters and nonconformists in Ireland, making them the scapegoat for many of the country's barbarous divisions, ignoring the fact, as did King, that he was very much part of the cultural 'establishment' of colonial Ireland).[72] The disagreements over St Werburgh's had an ironic conclusion, since, as McParland points out, Burgh's design was eventually as 'Roman' as Galilei's might have been, as was his other church, St Ann's in Dawson Street, both examples of what he calls 'canonical Italianate classicism' (Plate 2).[73]

Molesworth, usually assigned to the footnotes of Swift's career, stands out as one of the very few figures of this period who tried to advance Irish design and architecture through contacts with the continent. His patronage of Galilei resulted in the Italian's designs for Castletown House in Kildare, the most splendid classical country home of the century, built in the 1720s for Speaker Conolly.[74] But Molesworth was exceptional, not typical, and lamented the state of the arts in Ireland, writing to Galilei in 1719, 'We have no tast in this Country of what is excellent in any of ye Fine Arts. & I doubt shall not have for severall years to come.'[75] Swift was an admirer of Molesworth, and of his improvements at the family home at Breckdenstown, outside Swords, county Dublin,[76] addressing the fifth of his *Drapier's Letters* to the patriotic Viscount,[77] but that admiration did not extend to matters architectural, and most certainly did not endorse the supposed benefits of an Italian influence in art or religion.[78]

In the opening decades of the eighteenth century, and certainly by the time Swift had settled into the deanery of St Patrick's, the architectural landscape of Dublin had seen several major changes and additions which heralded the end of its medieval design and the emergence of a classical style in its metropolitan ambi-

9 – THE COLLEGE LIBRARY
from Charles Brooking, MAP OF THE CITY & SUBURBS OF DUBLIN (1728)
(courtesy Irish Architectural Archive)

tions. As military engineer and later as Surveyor-General, Thomas Burgh was sin-gle-handedly responsible for most of these changes to the monumental elements in the city's changing character. He was responsible for the Royal (now Collins) Barracks opposite Kilmainham (1704), a new custom house on Essex Quay (1707), and, most dramatically, the new library for Trinity College (Plate 9). Narcissus Marsh, who had been provost of Trinity when Swift had been a student there, was one of several clergymen who tried to develop and improve the cultural and archi-tectural character of Dublin.[79] In the opening years of the eighteenth century, he had employed William Robinson to design and build Marsh's library alongside St Patrick's cathedral. If Dublin was ever to present itself as a city of culture and learn-ing, its only university demanded a library in keeping with such an aspiration. Burgh's work on the library began in 1712, while Swift was still in London, and was completed in 1732, resulting in one of the city's most impressive statements of classical order, one which Maurice Craig sees as marked by a 'puritanical severity characteristic of Irish architecture'.[80] We have no record of Swift's view of the great addition to his alma mater, but plans to construct a new parliament building directly opposite Trinity College on College Green resulted in one of his most notorious, occasional satires, giving us a rare and powerful sense of how he interpreted this addition to the architectural symbolism of Georgian Dublin.

New buildings in Dublin were an important part of Ireland's growing confi-dence and assertiveness in relation to political and cultural domination by London. If the expansion of Trinity College was a statement of educational determination, then the plans to replace the dilapidated parliamentary buildings on College Green with something majestic and elevated were part of a changed political landscape, one which Swift himself had helped to shape in the mid-1720s through his

Drapier's Letters, which had famously asserted Ireland's parliamentary sovereignty. While Thomas Burgh was expected to obtain the commission for the new building, it went instead to the young and ambitious Edward Lovett Pearce (a cousin of Vanbrugh),[81] who was well-versed in Italianate architecture, and who had visited John Molesworth in Turin and Alessandro Galilei in Florence.[82] Work began in 1729 (the year in which Swift published *A Modest Proposal*, a nightmarish vision of the Irish human economy), and the parliament, both Commons and Lords, was able to hold its first sitting in October 1731, while work continued until 1739, six years after Pearce's death. Most architectural historians of this period see Pearce's building as the greatest achievement in the rebirth of Dublin. McParland views it as 'a rare moment in Irish, indeed in European, architecture',[83] while Craig sees it 'as one of the chief glories of Dublin'.[84] Here, finally, was a symbol of pride in Irish politics, a monument of order and reason in keeping with the dignity and civility of its proprietors (Plate 10).

Swift viewed this addition to the city landscape rather differently. No lover of politicians of any kind, but especially not of the Irish landlord class he had savaged in *A Modest Proposal*, he was finally provoked into poetic and satirical action by the parliament's plans to reduce the Church of Ireland's income from tithes.[85] In the spring of 1736, 'A Character, Panegyric, and Description of the Legion Club' was published in a London miscellany, Swift having decided not to publish such an inflammatory and risky poem in Dublin.[86] For Swift, as the allusion behind the phrase 'Legion Club' suggests, the inmates of the new parliament house, in their scandalous attempt to deprive the Church Established by Law of its rightful dues,

10 – THE PARLIAMENT HOUSE, from Robert Pool and John Cash, VIEWS OF THE MOST REMARKABLE PUBLIC BUILDINGS, MONUMENTS AND OTHER EDIFICES IN THE CITY OF DUBLIN (1780) (courtesy Irish Architectural Archive)

were comparable to a horde of unclean devils, whose house, a vast 'pile', suggested not a site of order, but a new Bedlam. In the opening lines of this ferocious satire, the speaker presents us with a sharp appreciation of an architectural irony unintended by the city planners:

> As I stroll the city, oft I
> Spy a building large and lofty,
> Not a bow-shot from the College,
> Half a globe from sense and knowledge.
> By the prudent architect
> Placed against the church direct;
> Making good my grandam's jest,
> *Near the church* – you know the rest.[87]

Swift refuses to look at Pearce's building either in isolation or in simply formal terms. Instead, he looks at it in relation to those buildings around it, and laughs bitterly at the incongruity of the neighbouring symbolism. The insistently ideological 'reading' of this architecture (as relentless as the rhyming couplets of the poem's 242 lines), sees something outrageous about a monument to political vanity being placed opposite and alongside a centre of learning and a house of prayer. Mindful of his own plans to leave money in his will for charitable purposes, such as a home for 'lunatics and fools', Swift pictures the new Houses of Parliament as an accidental Bedlam, where the undeserving mad are in charge of a nation's fortunes:

> Let them, when they once get in
> Sell the nation for a pin;
> While they sit a-picking straws
> Let them rave of making laws;
> While they never hold their Tongue,
> Let them dabble in their dung;
> Let them form a grand committee,
> How to plague and starve the city;
> Let them stare and storm and frown,
> When they see a clergy-gown.
> Let them, 'ere they crack a louse,
> Call for the orders of the House;
> Let them with their gosling quills,
> Scribble senseless heads of bills;
> We may, while they strain their throats,
> Wipe our arses with their votes.[88]

The poem identifies many of the MPs and Lords by name (including the family of the architect John Allen, who had worked on Howth Castle),[89] and creates a phantasmagoric landscape similar to that of Dante's *Inferno*, a hell almost beyond imagining, but one inhabited by earthly familiars. Only Hogarth, the poem concludes, could do justice to such an image.

The one figure who escapes from this sustained invective is, oddly, Pearce the architect, the man responsible for this monument to madness, and himself an Irish MP for Ratoath in county Meath. In the poems on Whitehall, as we have seen earlier, Swift's contempt is very much *ad hominem*, and the person of Vanbrugh is fundamental to the poem's design. Swift may have exempted Pearce from the collective charge of venality because the Dean and the architect seem to have enjoyed a certain kind of friendship. While working with Thomas Sheridan on the short-lived paper *The Intelligencer* at the very time when Pearce was beginning the construction of the Parliament House, Swift drew up a list of 'hints' for possible features and articles, including one which reads, 'Building, and praise of Pearce'.[90] In their analysis of the original manuscript of these notes by Swift, Ehrenpreis and Clifford record the fact that in 1730, not long after building work had begun on his project, Pearce actually presented the Dean with a copy of the collected anecdotes of Valerius Maximus from the first century AD, in a folio edition of 1505 printed in Venice.[91] As James Woolley points out, Pearce gave Swift three other gifts of works by classical authors, folio editions of Ovid, Cicero and Lactantius, each inscribed 'The gift of Edw. Pearce Esq. 1730'.[92] How Swift and Pearce came to know each other is not known, but it is not difficult to imagine that the two men, one entrusted with building a most important public monument in the city, the other the most famous clergyman in the city, might have met in the relatively small circle of Dublin society. Yet why would Pearce give the Dean not one, but four expensive gifts, perfectly suited to Swift's classical tastes? Would it have had something to do with his knowledge that Swift had satirised his cousin, Vanbrugh, all those years beforehand? Was Pearce trying to avoid a similar satirical fate by ingratiating himself with Dublin's most daring and subversive pen? It may simply have been the case that the two men shared a love of the classics. Edward McParland notes that Pearce had 'a bookish side', and that he was 'an uncommonly sensitive, learned and discriminating scholar', whose interest in Palladianism was as much academic and historical as it was practical and contemporary.[93] Whatever the answer, Pearce escaped Swift's wrath in a poem which systematically named many of the leading figures involved with the new Houses of Parliament. Reversing his earlier strategy with the poems on Vanbrugh, Swift ignored the builder, and focused exclusively on the owners.

The fact that nearly all of Swift's books relating to architecture were gifts rather than acquisitions confirms his rather passive relationship with that discipline and art. Such a tentative conclusion, however, has the unintended manner of a judicial reprimand, suggesting that Swift should have had a more active interest in architecture, but that he somehow failed to exercise it. Nothing in Swift's education or his Irish cultural background disposed him towards architecture, and from what we know of the artistic scene in Ireland through the remarks of leading figures such as Robert Molesworth, such seeming indifference was common rather than exceptional, and had a great deal to do with the unsettled and undeveloped state of the country in the first decades of the eighteenth century. The contrast with Pope and England is perhaps one important way of appreciating Swift and Ireland in relation to the rise of the virtuoso and a culture which was beginning to embrace the Renaissance ideal of the unity of the arts. As Ian Campbell Ross argues, there was nothing in Swift's Dublin to compare with the literary and artistic circle within which Pope moved, a circle which included so many wealthy and powerful men of taste, who were actively and enthusiastically engaged in debate and practice about appropriate style and form in architecture.[94] On the individual level, Pope's interest in the subject was complex and refined; Swift, by contrast, would not have known his architrave from his arris, and would not have cared. Architectural theory and experimentation held only a passing satirical interest for him, as we see with his representation of Lord Munodi in Part III of *Gulliver's Travels*, a distinguished Lord who has been banished to his country estate for failing to adapt to the new learning and science. Munodi invites Gulliver to his home, a building now under threat from the architectural revolution underway in Balnibarbi: 'We came at length to the House, which was indeed a noble Structure, built according to the best Rules of ancient Architecture. The Fountains, Gardens, Walks, Avenues, and Groves were all disposed with exact Judgement and Taste.'[95] An innocent victim of architectural fashion and chaotic experimentation, Munodi's loyalty to tradition is part of Swift's favourite satirical design which sets the Ancients against the Moderns, a design which was also used to calumniate Vanbrugh.

Swift's 'reading' of architecture and architects searches for expressions and distortions of power, and it deconstructs designs in order to expose signs of tyranny and pride. It is, essentially, a moralistic and political way of viewing great buildings, a perspective not easily seduced by scale or beauty, by those outwards forms which try to conceal the political impulse which sponsors so much of public and private architecture. Above all, Swift dislikes monumental architecture, such as Marlborough's Blenheim, seeing it as a gross expression of the ego and pride of those who commission, as well as build, such extravagances. If we could attribute an architectural ideal to Swift, one which might come closest to his political and moral standards, then we might detect it in the opening lines of a poem which he wrote towards the end of his service to the Tories:

I often wished that I had clear
For life, six hundred pounds a year,
A handsome house to lodge a friend,
A river at my garden's end,
A terrace walk, and half a rood
Of land, set out to plant a wood.[96]

Declaring, or affecting, a complete weariness with the scale and intensity of political life at the English court, Swift proclaims his faith in pastoral retreat, the final refuge of an honest man in a corrupt world. The detail of these lines suggests a return to the modest and homely scale of his vicarage at Laracor, county Meath, a reversion to rural sociability and friendship.[97] Mark Blackwell has shown how deeply attracted Swift eventually became to 'country-house ideology' (going so far as to plan the building of a rural retreat in county Armagh, a project he soon abandoned), an ideology which represented a seeming stability and security which neither politics nor writing offered.[98] If we can trust the declared intent behind these versions of a pastoral utopia, then we might conclude that Swift's experience of architecture only served to reinforce his remote and distrustful relation with the Modern age. He remains, at heart, a primitivist whose imagination is both offended and overwhelmed by the pride and ambition of urban architecture.

———

ACKNOWLEDGEMENTS

Several people have helped me in researching this article, on matters small and large, and I hope I have thanked them all at the appropriate points. In addition, I would like to express my gratitude and thanks to Edward McParland and Ian Campbell Ross, who kindly agreed to read early drafts of this work, and who gave me detailed and comprehensive advice on many matters relating to Swift and eighteenth-century architecture. Anyone venturing into this kind of interdisciplinary field feels all the more secure when assisted by such supportive and generous virtuosi. Finally, I would like to thank David Griffin and his staff at the Irish Architectural Archive, Jane Devine-Mejia of the University of Notre Dame, as well as Gerard Lyne, Joanna Finegan and Elizabeth Kirwan at the National Library of Ireland for their advice and assistance.

ENDNOTES

1   Edward McParland, *Public Architecture in Ireland, 1680-1760* (New Haven and London 2001) 14.

2   Maurice Craig, *Dublin 1660-1860* (Dublin 1980) 6. Much of the information following is taken from Craig.

3   McParland, *Public Architecture*, 91-121.

4   See Noel Kissane, *Historic Dublin Maps* (Dublin 1988). Bernard de Gomme was Engineer in Chief. His map was commissioned for official purposes, and was not published at the time. In 1685 it was used and developed by another engineer, Thomas Phillips, who produced a new map of Dublin for James II, likewise unpublished. Their joint efforts became the basis for a commercial map of Dublin by Henry Pratt, published in 1708 in London. On early eighteenth-century maps of Dublin and Ireland, see J.H. Andrews, *Shapes of Ireland: Maps and their makers* (Dublin 1997) 153-84.

5   McParland, *Public Architecture*, 143-4.

6   Craig, *Dublin*, 59.

7   McParland, *Public Architecture*, 1.

8   Craig, *Dublin*, 71.

9   See his letter of January 1699 to his successor at Kilroot, the Rev John Winder, in which he describes his sermons written there as 'calculated for a Church without Company or a roof, like our [...] at Oxford'. David Woolley (ed.), *The Correspondence of Jonathan Swift, D.D.*, 4 vols, 2 vols published to date (Frankfurt am Main 1999) i, 138.

10 Irvin Ehrenpreis, *Swift: the Man, his Works and the Age*, 3 vols (London and Cambridge, Mass, 1962-83) ii, 95.

11 See John Summerson, *Georgian London* (London 1970) 24.

12 The following details are from Nikolaus Pevsner, *The Cities of London and Westminster*, 2 vols (Harmondsworth 1973), i, 62-8.

13 On Wren's role in redesigning and rebuilding London, see Lisa Jardine, *On a Grander Scale: the outstanding career of Sir Christopher Wren* (London 2002) 247-59.

14 Pevsner, *London*, 74-5.

15 Harold Williams (ed.), *Journal to Stella*, 2 vols (Oxford 1948) i, 53.

16 Ehrenpreis, *Swift*, ii, 179. For a short account of Fountaine's interest in the arts, including his visits to Italy, see Brinsley Ford, 'Sir Andrew Fountaine, one of the keenest virtuosi of his age', *Apollo*, November 1985, 352-8.

17 Williams, *Journal*, i, 83-4. The following day, Swift found himself in Vanbrugh's company once more, while dining at the home of the Portuguese envoy.

18 See Williams, *Journal*, i, 83-4, n.22. The poem had appeared in Curll's unauthorised miscellany, *A Meditation upon a Broomstick, and somewhat beside* (London 1710).

19 For an account of Vanbrugh's achievements in the design of country houses such as Castle Howard and Blenheim, see John Summerson, *Architecture in Britain: 1530-1830* (Harmondsworth 1977), 278-87.

20 For plans and illustrations of 'Goose-Pie House', see Summerson, *Architecture in Britain*, 275-7.

21 Pat Rogers (ed.), *Jonathan Swift: The Complete Poems* (Harmondsworth 1983), 91.

22 *ibid.*, 92.

23 For the textual history of the poem, see Rogers, *Poems*, 629.

[24] Vanbrugh combined both talents when, in 1705, he designed the Queen's Theatre at Haymarket in London. See Summerson, *Architecture in Britain*, 271.

[25] Rogers, *Poems*, 99.

[26] Shortly after this encounter with Vanbrugh, Swift tells Stella that on his first meeting with Henry St John, the Secretary of State told him that 'The History of Vanbrug's House' was 'the best thing he ever read'. Swift did not think so. See Williams, *Journal*, i, 92.

[27] For the text, see Rogers, *Poems*, 80-1. The poem remained unpublished during Swift's life-time, and was first published in Scott's 1814 edition. On the history of the poem's place in the canon, see Rogers, 618.

[28] Rogers, *Poems*, 80-1.

[29] *ibid.*, 81.

[30] King Charles I was one of Swift's 'Great Figures' of history, both ancient and modern. See, for example, Herbert Davis et al (eds), *The Prose Works of Jonathan Swift*, 16 vols (Oxford 1939-68) v, 84. With uncompromising regularity, Swift maintained that the Dissenters were more wicked, if such were possible, than Roman Catholics, and that they were responsible for 'the Murder of a most pious King'. See also his sermon, *Upon the Martyrdom of King Charles* (1726), in Davis, *Prose Works*, ix, 219-31, and his pamphlet, *Queries relating to the Sacramental Test* (1733), in Davis, *Prose Works*, xii, 253-60. A portrait of King Charles I 'by Vandike' hung in Swift's deanery, a present from Rev James Stopford in 1726, which Swift bequeathed to Stopford in his will. See Woolley, *Correspondence*, ii, 621.

[31] Many years later, and probably at the suggestion of Alexander Pope, Swift softened his view of Vanbrugh, and actually complimented the architect's achievements. See 'Preface' to Swift's and Pope's *Miscellanies* (1727). For an account of this seeming conversion, see Morris Brownell, *Alexander Pope and the Arts of Georgian England* (Oxford 1978) 312-15.

[32] The relevant lines read as follows: 'In regard to two Persons only, we wish our Raillery, though ever so tender, or Resentment, though ever so just, had not been indulged. We speak of Sir John Vanbrugh, who was a man of wit, and of Honour; and of Mr. Addison, whose Name deserves all Respect from every Lover of Learning.' See *Miscellanies in Prose and Verse*, 3 vols (1727) i, 9.

[33] In the end, only twelve of these planned churches were built. For a detailed account of the plan and its results, see Summerson, *Georgian London*, 84-97.

[34] Davis, *Prose Works*, iii, 159.

[35] *ibid*. Swift wrote several attacks in the *Examiner* on Marlborough and his alleged greed; see no. 16, 19-24, and most notoriously, no. 27, 80-5, where he nicknames him 'Marcus Crassus'.

[36] This is one of the rare instances of Swift's use of the term 'Gothic' in an architectural sense. He generally used this term in a political sense, to distinguish an Anglo-Saxon tradition of parliamentary liberty from 'foreign' models of political tyranny. See, for example, his use of this term in *The Drapier's Letters*, in *Prose Works*, x, 86-7, or in his 'A Letter to Mr Pope', in *Prose Works*, ix, 32.

[37] See Brownell, *Alexander Pope*, 309f., 316, which includes a detailed account of why Blenheim is most likely the target of Pope's satire in *An Epistle to Richard Boyle, Earl of Burlington* (1731).

[38] Williams, *Journal*, i, 37-8.

[39] In November of the following year, he tells Stella that he had chosen not to accompany the Chief Secretary to Hampton Court because he could not get free lodgings there, and because

'the town is small, chargeable and inconvenient'. See Williams, *Journal*, ii, 400.

[40] Williams, *Journal*, i, 319, n.2.

[41] *ibid.*, 349-50.

[42] *ibid.*, 329.

[43] Williams, *Journal*, ii, 553.

[44] See Williams, *Journal*, i, 104, 122-3, 263.

[45] Williams, *Journal*,ii, 594. For illustrations of this famous mansion, see Summerson, *Architecture in Britain*, 74-6.

[46] Swift changed his lodgings nine times in his three year stay, residing at Chelsea from April 1711 to July 1712. See Williams, *Journal*, i, 142, n.16 for full details of these changes.

[47] Williams, *Journal*, ii, 648.

[48] See McParland, *Public Architecture*, 66-8, for an account and illustration of Tarbary's work. I have tried, without success, to discover why Swift should associate the name 'Tisdal' with Tarbary's work and Kilmainham, thinking first that he had in mind William Tisdall (1699-1735), an Irish clergyman whom Swift had known well in the early years of the century. David Woolley suggested, shrewdly, that Tisdall may once have been a chaplain at Kilmainham, and hence the association in Swift's memory between the chapel and the chaplain. The original minutes of Kilmainham Hospital (preserved from its opening, and held in the National Archives, Bishop Street in Dublin) do not, unfortunately, mention Tisdall as chaplain. My thanks to Gregory O'Connor of the National Archives, to Raymond Refaussé of the Representative Church Body Library, and to David Woolley, who helped me in these searches.

[49] See Brownell, *Alexander Pope*, 71-145.

[50] See Harold Williams (ed.), *The Correspondence of Jonathan Swift*, 5 vols (Oxford 1963-72), iii, 127, n.2. For additional and revised information, see Woolley, *Correspondence*, ii, 636.

[51] See Woolley, *Correspondence*, ii, 648, n.2. For Pope's accounts of these visits, see George Sherburn (ed.), *The Correspondence of Alexander Pope*, 5 vols (Oxford 1956) ii, 371-3, 387-8.

[52] For an account of this visit and gift, see Hermann Real and Heinz Vienken, 'A New Book from Swift's Library', *Bulletin of the John Rylands University*, 62, 2 (1980), 262-4. According to the authors, this copy of Fréart never appeared in any listing, or the sale catalogue, of Swift's personal library, and was eventually stolen from him. They also confirm that Swift, in turn, presented the book as a gift to the Irish portrait painter Francis Bindon, with a suitable adaptation of Burlington's original inscription. The present location of the book is not known. Fréart's *Parallèle* was a highly specialised volume on those authors, such as Palladio, who had retrieved and perfected the five Orders of ancient design – Doric, Ionian, Corinthian, Tuscan and Composite – rich with detailed and precise engravings. My thanks to Hermann Real of the Ehrenpreis Center for Swift Studies, Münster, Germany, for advice and information on several matters relating to Swift's library and architecture.

[53] See Williams, *Correspondence*, iii, 155, 244, 247.

[54] For a full account of this exchange, and the importance of this book to eighteenth-century scholarship, see Harold Williams, *Dean Swift's Library* (Cambridge 1932) 47-8.

[55] For bibliographical details, see Williams, *Dean Swift's Library*, sale catalogue, nos 556, 567, 579. See also Williams' commentary on these volumes, 46-7. Writing to Bolingbroke and Pope in April 1729, Swift remarked, 'I value the compilements of Graevius and Gronovius ... more than all my books besides.' Volume xii of the *Thesaurus Antiquitatum Graecarum* is dedicated to architecture, as is volume iii of the *Thesaurus Antiquitatum Romanorum*. Pope took an

active scholarly interest in the work of Graevius on Roman antiquities, and wrote a Latin treatise on the subject. See Brownell, *Alexander Pope*, 284-5.

[56] See Williams, *Correspondence*, iii, 189.

[57] See Woolley, *Correspondence*, ii, 93, n.4.

[58] Pat Rogers, *Grub Street: Studies in a Subculture* (London 1972) 237.

[59] *ibid.*, 6.

[60] See Rogers' detailed and persuasive reading of these poems, *ibid.*, 248-53.

[61] Ian Campbell Ross, 'The Scriblerians and Swift in Ireland' in Richard R. Rodino and Hermann J. Real (eds), *Reading Swift: Papers from the Second Münster Symposium on Jonathan Swift* (Munich 1993) 81-9.

[62] Woolley, *Correspondence*, i, 485.

[63] *ibid.*, 490.

[64] *ibid.*, 494.

[65] The granite spire was finally erected in 1749 by Dean Corbett after a design by George Semple. See J.H. Bernard and J.E.L. Oulton, *The Cathedral Church of St Patrick* (Dublin and Cork 1940), 27. This little classic, documenting the history of St Patrick's, includes many interesting and valuable illustrations of the cathedral down through the ages.

[66] *ibid.*, 13. Peter Galloway points out that St Patrick's was in 'a semi-ruinous condition from the 17th to the 19th centuries'. See his study, *The Cathedrals of Ireland* (Belfast 1992), 87.

[67] McParland, *Public Architecture*, 43-9.

[68] *ibid.*, 45-6.

[69] Patric Judge, 'State of Architecture in Ireland, in 1716', *Irish Arts Review*, iii, 4 (Dublin 1986) 62-3.

[70] Davis, *Prose Works*, x, 62. On King's views on *The Drapier's Letters*, see Ehrenpreis, *Swift*, iii, 264-7.

[71] Judge, 'State of Architecture', 63.

[72] On these divisions, see Oliver W. Ferguson, *Jonathan Swift and Ireland* (Urbana 1962) 17-19. Swift was a life-long opponent of toleration for Dissenters, especially in the pamphlets of his later years. See *ibid.*, 182-3.

[73] See McParland, *Public Architecture*, 45, and Rolf Loeber, 'Early Classicism in Ireland: Architecture before the Georgian Era', *Architectural History*, 22 (1979), 49-63, 59-60.

[74] McParland, *Public Architecture*, 9.

[75] *ibid.*

[76] See Ehrenpreis, *Swift*, iii, 287-8.

[77] See Davis, *Prose Works*, x, 77-94.

[78] On Swift's cultural xenophobia, especially with regard to Italian cultural influence, see Joseph McMinn, 'Was Swift a Philistine? The Evidence of Music', *Swift Studies*, 17 (2002) 59-74.

[79] See Toby Barnard, 'Improving clergymen, 1660-1760', in Alan Ford, James McGuire and Kenneth Milne (eds), *As by Law Established: The Church of Ireland since the Reformation* (Dublin 1995), 146.

[80] Craig, *Dublin*, 95.

[81] For a biographical sketch of Pearce, and a listing of his works, see Maurice Craig, 'Sir Edward Lovett Pearce', *Quarterly Bulletin of the Irish Georgian Society*, xvii, no. 1 (1974), 10-14.

[82] McParland, *Public Architecture*, 180-4.

[83] *ibid.*, 195.

[84] Craig, *Dublin*, 99.

[85] See Ehrenpreis, *Swift*, iii, 827-31.

[86] For the complete text, and history of the poem's publication, see Rogers, *Poems*, 550-6, 891-2.

[87] *ibid.*, 550.

[88] *ibid.*, 551-2.

[89] *ibid.*, 555: lines 173-80 and 894.

[90] See James Woolley (ed.), *The Intelligencer* (Oxford 1992) 275. Woolley points out that Sheridan's occasional remarks about architecture are informed by anti-Italian prejudice rather than specialised knowledge. See *ibid.*, 191.

[91] Irvin Ehrenpreis and James L. Clifford, 'Swiftiana in Rylands English MS 659 and related documents', *Bulletin of the John Rylands Library*, 37, 1955, 375-8. This copy of *Valerius Maximus* was in Swift's library at the time of his death. See Williams, *Dean Swift's Library*, sale catalogue, no. 624. At the time of writing this article, Ehrenpreis pointed out that Swift's copy was in the National Library of Ireland. At some point after that, however, it disappeared and has never been traced. My thanks to Andrew Carpenter, once again, for his knowledgeable advice on this matter.

[92] See Woolley, *Intelligencer*, 275. For full bibliographical details of the Ovid and Cicero editions, see *The Rothschild Library,* nos 2,308 and 2,315 (Cambridge 1954). For details of the Lactantius edition, see Sotheby's book sale catalogue, 23 June, lot 101. My thanks to Gail Ford of Sotheby's for supplying me with a copy of the details of this sale. These four gifts from Pearce are listed in Williams, *Dean Swift's Library*, sale catalogue, nos 620, 623, 624, 625.

[93] McParland, *Public Architecture*, 180-1.

[94] Campbell Ross, 'The Scriblerians', 88-9.

[95] Davis, *Prose Works*, xi, 176. While Swift held mixed and critical views about architecture, he was a resolute and enthusiastic gardener, very often showing greater interest in landscape than buildings. See Carole Fabricant, *Swift's landscape* (London 1982), and my 'Pastoral properties: Swift and gardens', *British Journal for Eighteenth-Century Studies*, 22, 1, 1999, 15-34.

[96] 'Horace, Lib.2, Sat.6', in Rogers, *Poems*, 167.

[97] This kind of moral and domestic fundamentalism, an extreme version of the classical code, was coincidentally the basis of one of the most important texts of neo-classical architectural theory in the eighteenth century, Laugier's *Essai sur L'Architecture* (1755), which proposed the 'cabane rustique' as the moral source of all architecture and the proper measure of contemporary architectural decadence.

[98] Mark R. Blackwell, 'The two Jonathans: Swift, Smedley and the Outhouse Ethic', in Aileen Douglas, Patrick Kelly and Ian Campbell Ross (eds), *Locating Swift* (Dublin 1998) 129-49.

———

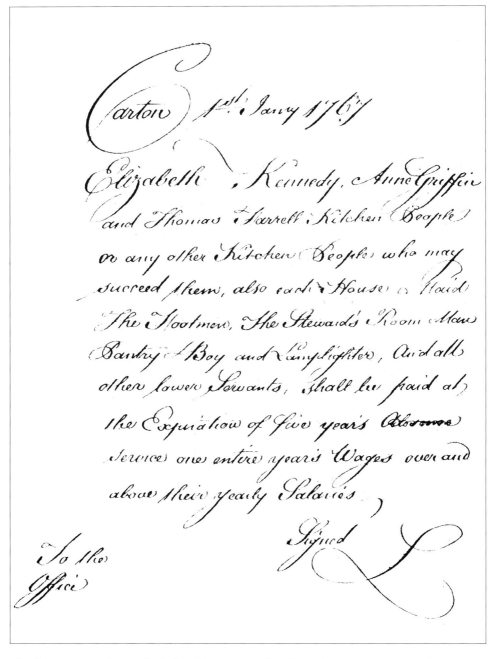

Carton 1st Jany 1767

Elizabeth Kennedy, Anne Griffin and Thomas Farrell Kitchen People or any other Kitchen People who may succeed them, also each House Maid The Footmen, The Steward's Room Man Pantry Boy and Lamplighter, And all other lower Servants, Shall be paid at the Expiration of five years Services one entire year's Wages over and above their yearly Salaries

Signed

To the Office

1 – Like many employers, the Duke of Leinster was forced to take measures to retain the services of his domestic staff. Here he offers an incentive of one year's wages to those of his 'lower' servants who complete five years' service in his household (fol. 78).

Vails and travails:
how Lord Kildare kept his
household in order

PATRICIA McCARTHY

'NOT TO ALLOW OF CURSING AND SWEARING ABOUT THE HOUSE &c. OR any riotous Behaviour but everything done in the most quiet and regular Manner. To see that every Person do their own Business in the proper Manner and times, and if not, to inform Lord or Lady Kildare of it.'

— 'Rules to be observed by the Marquis of Kildare's Steward at Carton'

So little has been written about servants in eighteenth-century Ireland that it is most gratifying to come across a document that gives an insight into the running of a large household in this period. The Marquis of Kildare (later Duke of Leinster) (1722-1773) had what is generally referred to as an 'army' of servants at Carton, county Kildare. He kept a small number of staff in Kildare House (later Leinster House) in Dublin, and a number who moved between the two. The document in question is a fairly sizeable manuscript, 113 pages in length including an index, and is among papers in the archives of Alnwick Castle, seat of the Dukes of Northumberland.[1] It is described as 'Rules for the government of the Marquis of Kildare's (Duke of Leinster's) household 1763-1773', and has a note attached which reads 'For his Grace the Duke of Northumberland with the Archbishop of Cashel's Compliments. 24 January 1795, Stephen's Green, Dublin'. It contains memos, timetables, instructions and orders, varying between 'Rules to be observed by the Marquis of Kildare's Steward at Carton' to 'How Ladders &c are to be painted that they may be known who they belong to'. Most entries are dated and are signed 'K' (Kildare), and from November 1766, 'L' (Leinster). It is probably safe to assume that these directives were given to the steward who dealt with them and retained the documents. How this document came into the possession of Charles Agar, the Archbishop of Cashel, and why he sent it to the 2nd Duke of Northumberland is not clear, but it may have been nothing more than a wish to compare ducal establishments on both sides of the Irish Sea. It is known that both men knew each other quite well, and Agar was second chaplain to the Duke's father when, as Earl of Northumberland, he came to Ireland as Lord Lieutenant in 1763.[2]

Bearing in mind that the document relates to the sole ducal household in Ireland, in many ways it reflects the responsibilities and the problems that presented themselves to all who employed servants in Ireland about this time. This article will look at how employers in less noble households met similar challenges to those that faced the household at Carton. Despite the detail in this document, such as the meticulously listed duties of the steward and the butler, little is dealt with, apart from diet, that gives an insight into basic aspects of the lives of the many servants who worked there.

FOOD AND DRINK

The document is paternalistic in tone; in common with many employers at the time Kildare refers to his servants as 'family', treating them like children who need a firm hand and to be disciplined when they misbehave. He takes an interest in the diet of his servants, ensuring that they eat well and on time. Among the rules for 'the feeding of the Family' in the absence of Lord and Lady Kildare, little distinction is made between the food in the steward's hall and in the servants' hall, apart from the times of meals. The upper servants (i.e. steward, housekeeper, butler, clerk of the kitchen, personal maids and valets) dined in the steward's hall at 4pm on 'Mutton and Broth, Mutton Chops, Harrico or Hashed, Roast or boiled Pork with Pease Pudding and Garden things or, Stakes, Roast, or boiled Veal with Garden things when Veal is killed at Carton'. Once a week they had mutton or beef pie, and each Sunday, roast beef and plum pudding. Leftover meat from this meal was to be eaten for supper and breakfast, 'adding some Potatoes or any kind of Garden Stuff, Cheese or Eggs'. In the servants' hall they fared almost as well, dining at 1pm on 'boiled Beef, Cabbage and Roots, every Sunday to have a Piece of Beef Roasted and Plumb Pudding, or any other kind of Pudding'. On Thursdays they had boiled mutton or pork with vegetables. The amount of meat consumed by the lower servants alone per annum must have been sizable, taking into account that their meat allowance was one-and-a-half pounds per person per week. For supper they had bread, butter and cheese. Salt fish was eaten once a week, probably Friday in deference to Catholic servants, with potatoes and cheese. If any of the meat was not 'well and cleanly dressed and good of the Kind, this should be reported' (fol. 18-21).

A pint of ale was given to each person who supped in the servants' hall. In addition, in 1758 the cook was allowed one quart of ale at 11am and another at 2pm, and laundrymaids, labouring like the cook in a hot atmosphere, were allowed one quart on two mornings per week. If there was a wet-nurse in the house (with nineteen children there generally was one) she was allowed one pint of ale at 9pm (fol. 22-3). As time went by, modifications appeared in the 'Rules'. By 1772 the cook was allowed one quart of ale or strong beer between 1pm and 2pm 'if he desires', and two or three quarts of small beer were to be provided for kitchen staff (fol. 91). Interestingly, small beer, which must have been very light, was virtually available to anyone: 'no Person of the Family to be refused ... as much as they shall drink' between breakfast and 6pm (fol. 25). Any malt liquor that remained after the Duke and Duchess dined was allowed to be taken to the second table (steward's room) (fol. 89).

While the family was in residence at Kildare House there was a constant flow of food from Carton. A mule or horse departed from there at 10am each Monday, Wednesday and Friday, carrying 'Rowls, Butter, Eggs, Fowl, Game &c and Sallading', returning the following day (fol. 29). On Tuesday and Saturday mornings a cart and two horses brought meat, garden produce, bread, and anything else that was required from Carton (fol. 27). In October 1769 the Duke was obviously planning a dinner in Dublin, as he instructed the farmer to send two 'good fat' sheep, a dozen or one-and-a-half dozen chickens, a goose or two, a couple of turkeys, and a pair or two of ducks, 'each to be extremely good in their Kinds' (fol. 86). At the same time, worried that fruit might be damaged in the cart during transportation, a note was dispatched to the gardener that in future it should be sent either with 'Joe' (by mule or horseback), or by a man on foot (a footman) on Mondays, Wednesdays and Fridays (fol. 88).[3] Any letters going to Dublin from Carton were to be left in the farmyard before 10pm for collection next morning by the carter (fol. 46).

DISCIPLINE

While he took good care of his servants, ensuring that those who arrived home from town 'of a very Wet Evening in Winter' were allowed some ale or strong beer, he was also firm. He frequently dismissed staff, but in the case of Thomas Rice, re-employed him twice, the first time at the solicitation of the Duchess, on 3 April 1767. The Duke stipulated that Rice be employed by the planter only, and 'if ever he is seen about my House or any of my Offices at Carton (except on Pay Nights in the Office Yard) he will be immediately discharged ... and whoever employs him in any shape in or about said House & Offices shall be stopped 10s'. The following year in March he was re-employed, this time in the brew-house, having been forgiven once more by the Duke, but after a further transgression 'his Grace hath turned him away never more to be employed at Carton' (fol. 80). The steward was instructed to be 'over strict at first as it is much easier to relax than to recover an Authority over People' (fol. 14).

Such philosophising over the handling of servants was not for John Scott, 1st Earl of Clonmell (d.1798). In a tirade against country-house living he calls servants 'an absolute band of robbers' explaining that:

> the men thieve and plunder, and sometimes ingratiate themselves dangerously and scandalously into the favour and affections of their superiors in the house, the wife, the sister, or daughter; the women servants ... pilfer and pillage, and constantly debauch the master, the sons, and the relations, and frequently seduce the male children, sometimes even to disgraceful marriages, oftener, disorder them, and at times, by pimping and intrigue, sell the daughters to swindlers, fortune-hunters, and vagabonds.

Incidentally, he rated the guests that are invited to country houses as 'often more dangerous'.[4]

Employers had different ways of punishing their unruly servants. Bishop Edward Synge of Elphin, county Roscommon, had Billy Smith put into the iron coal box for three hours, and when he repeated the misdemeanour he was whipped.[5] This seems surprisingly harsh in view of the fact that Synge looked after his servants or 'family' very well, ensuring that they received medical attention when required, that they were well fed, particularly after journeying from Elphin to Dublin, and were dressed well. He disapproved of his daughter Alicia's maid, and 'rather suffer'd than approv'd of her continuing in any shape in my family...'[6] He told Alicia, 'You know me to be strict and Severe with regard to the Conduct of Servants. This is not the effect of temper, but prudence. Harshness, irksome to my self, I find necessary to keep them in order.'[7] Many employers imposed fines for misbehaviour that were sometimes disproportionate, like Thomas Otway of Castle Otway, county Tipperary, who fined Daniel Mullowney one shilling and a penny in November 1772 'for going into the stables without orders', when his daily pay was five pence.[8] At Doneraile Court, county Cork, in 1734, the coachman, who was earning £8 a year, was ordered to pay £1 7s 6d to replace a broken glass.[9] Jonathan Swift imposed a fine of one shilling out of board wages for every lie told, and if either of his two manservants got drunk, he was fined an English crown.[10] The Kildares fined outdoor staff such as carters 2/6d for taking too long coming from Kildare House to Carton, and shepherds were fined 6d for every sheep or lamb found wandering (fol. 44, 41). For the most part, verbal warnings from superiors, followed, if needed, by a report to Lord or Lady Kildare, seemed to be the usual sanction, though the kitchen boy was to be immediately fined 2/6d if any 'kitchen garbage or greens' were found in the ash hole rather than the dung hill (fol. 51). In an effort to curb any excess among his staff, the Duke ruled in July 1769 that he would not for the future 'permit any dancing to be in any part of my House without my leave, or the Dutchess [sic] of Leinster's, which Occasions Neglect, Idleness and Drinking and makes the Family Irregular' (fol. 85). A letter that appeared in *Hibernian Magazine* in November 1781 indicates what could happen if discipline was not imposed:

> On Thursday evening last, or rather Friday morning, a scene of 'High life below stairs' was exhibited in the house of a person of distinction near Stephen's Green. Mrs Margery the cook gave a grand route [sic] to several ladies and gentlemen of her acquaintance. But they were all routed about 4 in the morning by the unexpected appearance of the house steward, who had come from his master's country seat on particular business. The butler was instantly discharged, just after having amused the company with the finest exertions of theatric excellence in the soliloquy of Hamlet.

WAGES

Wages in Ireland were low, on average 30% lower than in England, according to Arthur Young in 1780. This accounted for the large number of servants and retainers to be seen in houses. Frequently servants were not paid at all, having board and lodging in lieu, and when they were paid, it was at the end of each year of service. The result of this was that the servant had to borrow on his or her wages, leaving little to collect at the end of the year.

Edward Gore, employed by Lord Doneraile on 17 April 1727 at £7 10s a year borrowed £3 17s 10d from his employer the following November, and £2 19s 4d on 12 April 1728 (five days before his first year was completed), but the small balance due to him was not paid by his employer until 25 August that year, over four months late.[11] In his will made in 1765, Sir Edward O'Brien of Dromoland, county Clare, instructed his son to pay his debts 'in particular my poor servants wages to some of whom I stand indebted for many years'.[12] The Duke of Leinster's system was kinder to his servants. According to the 'Rules', in 1772 his footmen (if not the rest of his staff) were paid on a quarterly basis, receiving £8 a year (fol. 97). Charles Pocklington Domville had been paying his footman the same amount in 1768 at Templeogue House, county Dublin, and at Mount Coote, county Limerick, the footman was receiving ten guineas in 1776.[13] The Kildares, however, were generous when it came to securing the services of a head gardener, offering £30 per annum, plus board wages of seven shillings per week. The housekeeper did quite well – £25 for the first year, and £30 'if we approve of her afterwards' – as well as having her own maid who was to be on the same footing as an upper housemaid, according to Lady Kildare.[14]

In the first half of the eighteenth century it was considered fashionable to have a male cook – French, if possible. They were paid significantly more than their female counterparts. In 1744 at Monivea, county Galway, William Burke was paid £8 a year, plus the grazing of a mare. After he was discharged the same year, Mary Lavoy accepted the job at £6 for the first year and £7 thereafter, with no mention of grazing for her mare, if she had one.[15] This discrepancy in pay, together with the frequent comings and goings of staff, is underlined at Doneraile Court between the years 1787 and 1800 with reference to the cook. During that period seven cooks passed through its doors, two women and five men. The women were paid £20 and £22 15s respectively in 1787 and 1791, while the mens' lowest wage was £34 2s 6d in 1788, rising to £40 in 1790, and forty guineas by 1800.[16] At the other end of the scale, kitchenmaids, parlourmaids and dairymaids earned, on average, in the 1740s £2 10s a year, rising to £6 to £7 by the beginning of the nineteenth century.[17] Looking at servants' wages books throughout the eighteenth century, one is struck by the number of staff either being discharged or leaving their employment, often to get married, and who had to be replaced. In an effort to stem the tide of departures from his employment, in January 1767 the Duke of Leinster offered the following incentive to his servants:

> Elizabeth Kennedy, Anne Griffin and Thomas Farrell Kitchen People or any other Kitchen People who may succeed them, also each House Maid, The Footmen, The Steward's Room Man, Pantry Boy and Lamplighter, And all other lower Servants, shall be paid at the Expiration of five years' service one entire year's Wages over and above their yearly Salaries (fol. 78) (Plate 1).

The scheme was extended and modified from January 1772: each household upper manservant out of livery who remained for five years was entitled to a flat rate of ten guineas; to each livery servant of household or stables, seven guineas; and to each household lower woman servant, five guineas (fol. 100).

Among the Ballyglunin Papers is an agreement drawn up between Walter Blake of Ballyglunin and his servant Peter Hillery, dated 3 February 1774.[18] Hillery seems to have been his farmer. He received £10 a year, plus a '1/4 acre muck yearly at Ballyglunin, greasing of 6 collops yearly' on any of Blake's land 'most convenient to him'; he can keep one cow to fatten, and also received two stone of 'cast fleece wooll'.[19] Blake also gave him annually sixty labourers for such work as his servant saw fit. In return Hillery would live with him always and look for 'no more wages whilst I keep him and it is my present intention always to keep him'. Hillery's wife, Cathy Mannin, in a separate agreement, received a house, garden, and 'the greasing of two collops', plus £4 a year in return for her services as cook and housekeeper in town and country.[20]

In addition to wages and board wages, already mentioned, were weekly cash payments to servants in lieu of meals. They were given when employers were away from home or when servants travelled with the family. While their employers were at Kildare House, servants on board wages at Carton were allowed such garden produce as they desired (fol. 88). Married servants were not allowed to live in the house, but were given board wages for living outside the estate. The steward was instructed that they were not to eat or drink in the house 'except now and then, they and their Wives may be asked to Dinner on Sunday to live in Harmony with them so far as to carry on their mutual Business to Lord Kildare's advantage' (fol. 15). Servants managed to find many ways of saving portions of their board wages, one of which was to get themselves invited to eat in the servants' halls of houses where they had friends. It also gave them more free time and more independence than most employers desired.[21]

Working in large houses such as Carton or Castletown where great numbers of servants were employed had advantages. On paper (as in the 'Rules') it would appear that there was a strong demarcation between the duties of each category of servant, unlike that in a smaller house where staff would be expected to do whatever job needed to be done. That stated, frequently outdoor staff, such as postilions, were expected to wait at table as required, even in the most noble houses. The Duke, among his rules for footmen, ordered that they 'and Stable Men, if they should be ordered to attend', must be in wait at the kitchen door ten minutes before the bell for the Duke's dinner was rung, ready to bring in the dinner (fol. 79). The social life of the house brought visiting maids, valets and coachmen, animating the servants' hall with gossip and new faces. For servants, 'a berth within a comfortable house was to be preferred before many more precarious situations', as put by Toby Barnard, quoting Samuel Madden, who criticises the many who 'squeeze into houses for an easy and indolent life where they may feed and lie well'.[22]

Before discussing a number of ways by which servants could increase their earnings, it seems apposite at this point to take a look at what was probably much less important to them, but an aspect of their lives that is of interest to us: where did the servants sleep? In larger Irish households, generally, was the accommodation allocated to servants' sleeping quarters on architectural plans sufficient for the numbers of servants employed?

ACCOMMODATION

Research shows that Barnard's 'berth' and Madden's 'squeeze' appear to be apt descriptions of the sleeping accommodation for servants in many houses, both large and small, in the eighteenth century. The Irish nobility and gentry were well known for the numbers of servants they kept. This excess 'are in the lower sort', said Arthur Young in 1772, 'owing not only to the general laziness but also to the number of attendants everyone of a higher class will have'.[23] The numbers pandered to the employers' desire for status. 'We keep many of them in our houses, as we do our plate on our sideboards', wrote Samuel Madden in 1738, 'more for show than use, and rather to let people see that we have them than that we have any occasion for them.'[24] Lady Caroline Dawson in 1778 remarked on the 'servants without end' at Carton,[25] and, at a dinner in Kilkenny Castle about a decade later, James Dowling Herbert noted 'a servant nearly behind every man'.[26] Taking advantage of the 'open door' hospitality, visitors were frequently coming and going. Invited guests arrived with their servants, like Mrs Delany and her husband, the Dean of Down. When travelling between Delville, their Dublin home, and the Dean's residence in Down, they travelled in the chaise, the cook and housemaid travelled in the coach and four, and another maid in a car for baggage. Including three men to drive the carriages, this meant that their entourage totalled eight people, plus horses, all requiring food and a night's accommodation.[27]

With large numbers of staff and a fairly constant stream of visitors accompanied by servants and horses, one wonders about the servants' sleeping arrangements, and how much thought was invested in the provision of such accommodation for them. On paper, as in architectural drawings, it looks neat and ordered. But whether or not it reflects the numbers of staff in the house is not easy to ascertain. The constant comings and goings of servants makes it difficult to calculate how many were living in a house at any particular time in the eighteenth century. Furthermore, the total numbers of servants mentioned per house do not differentiate between domestic and outdoor staff,[28] the latter, usually in the majority, being accommodated elsewhere. Annotated plans of houses give an indication of where they slept – usually the garret or the basement – but do not tell us whether they slept two or three to a bed, if any slept on the floor, or if, indeed, they actually slept in a bedroom. Nor is it possible in most cases to work out where visiting servants slept. Isaac Ware in 1756 advised that if garrets proved too small, 'a bed for one man, or two maid-servants is contrived to let down in the kitchen'.[29] Accommodation for servants was fairly rough, according to Mahaffy, and some may have slept on straw or on rugs on the floor, particularly in town houses.[30]

Lady Sarah Bunbury gave some thought to the matter when she advised her sister, the Duchess of Leinster, on the layout of the servants' quarters at Frescati, Blackrock, county Dublin, in 1775. However, one cannot help getting the impression that the thought was directed more towards filling any gaps in the house with servants' quarters, rather than to a consideration of their comfort. She recommended that the servants' hall should be located under the dining room, where the smell of food and the 'riot that goes on at supper wouldn't disturb you there, as it would under your sitting room'. Two rooms could be made into one for 'the men lie there', and another room, which would seem to be a small space, could be used as a 'lock-up' plate room for the butler, 'or that space can be given to the footmen for another bedchamber'. She also suggests that the maids could be 'sent' to 'that long strip up at the top of the house over your bed', presumably an awkward space in the garret.[31]

Pole Cosby, on the other hand, provided new rooms for maidservants and six rooms for manservants at Stradbally, county Leix, after his father's death, when his mother and sister came to live with him in 1729. Together with the furniture from her house, his mother brought a coach and six horses, coachman, postilion, footman and one maid, while his sister brought her maid and a manservant. Cosby was forced to provide more accommodation, building not just for the servants but for his extended family.[32]

Significantly, among the linen listed in an inventory of goods sent from Howth Castle to the Dublin residence of Lord Howth at St Mary's Abbey, is a footman's bed, indicating that this was something that was foldable and portable.[33] Field beds with foldable frames are frequently mentioned in inventories.[34] Christina Hardyment found sufficient references in a 1710 inventory of Dyrham Park, Gloucestershire, to pallet beds in workrooms and in employers' bedrooms to confirm that personal servants slept all over the place, in order to be on call quickly if they were needed.[35] Stable boys frequently slept in the stable, and personal maids sometimes slept in the same bed with their mistress, particularly when travelling.[36]

Often mentioned in architectural plans, diaries and novels are barrack rooms, a name that is probably a throwback to fortified dwellings of the sixteenth and seventeenth centuries when soldiers doubled as servants. References to these (similar to dormitories) apply usually to surplus single male guests, but not exclusively, as is clear from Richard Johnston's plans for Castle Coole, county Fermanagh, of 1789, where it applies equally to young lady guests.[37] But the term is used also for male servants. Instead of a number of rooms each accommodating two or three servants, it made more sense and was less expensive to provide a barrack room.[38]

In an interesting plan for servants' quarters by James Playfair of 1792 for Townley Hall, county Louth, four blocks of offices and accommodation range around a court.[39] On the second floor he organised his accommodation for servants in a most orderly fashion. One range of rooms is for women servants, another is for upper servants, a third for footmen, and the fourth for 'strangers' servants'. Accommodation for the steward, butler, housekeeper, and for 'strangers' upper servants' was located in the four projecting corners of the square. Within the footmens' range is a 'hospital' or sickroom. A 'powdering room', where servants could powder their wigs (or hair), adjoined the servants' hall.

In the kitchen and laundry block in Richard Castle's plans for Kildare House of about 1745, a bedroom for the laundrymaids is located off the wash-house on the ground floor. There too is the clerk of the kitchen's bedroom. On the first floor are the housekeeper's and cook's bedrooms, with adjoining closets, and here the architect has illustrated four beds in the maidservants' lodging room.[40] One pair of beds is larger than the other pair. Might these be double beds? Similarly, listed in a mid-nineteenth-century inventory of the Provost's House at Trinity College Dublin are two 'painted wood press bedsteads with double pallyasses on each' in the maidservants' room in the basement.[41] Valets and ladies' maids slept either in designated servants' bedrooms or frequently in dressing rooms attached to their masters' and mistresses' bedrooms, a practice that all but disappeared in the course of the eighteenth century. Lord and Lady Kildare's bedrooms and dressing rooms were the only sleeping accommodation on the first floor in Kildare House. Their personal servants may have slept in their apartment or in the two rooms in the attic directly over their employers' dressing rooms, both of which had staircases adjoining.[42] In the attic were five bedrooms with closets, as well as the nursery suite, but most of the limited accommodation must have been reserved for the Kildare's numerous children. Apart from a servants' lodging room in the basement of the main block, there were two manservants' lodging rooms on the upper floor of the stable and coach-house block, and also a small gate-lodge at the entrance to the house on Kildare Street. As can be seen, not much space at Kildare House was devoted to bedrooms. Visitors to the house would probably have their own residences in Dublin or would stay in hotels. As in London, visitors expected to be well entertained, but not invited to stay.

It would appear, therefore, that there was a degree of complacency in the provision of sleeping accommodation for servants on the part of the employer, and perhaps on the part of the servant too. In most cases it must have been an improvement on what they experienced in their own family homes. While most servants seem to have slept in rooms – single, shared, or barracks, depending on their status – a study of inventories has shown that press beds and portable beds, even a straw palliass upon the floor, were fairly common. Kitchen maids or boys frequently slept in the kitchen where, on the one hand, it would be warm, but they were prey to unwanted advances from other staff or from employers. An inventory of furniture at Leinster House has not been found, but according to the Knight of Glin, one dated 1805 for

Carton has recently been discovered, and it is hoped that when this becomes available it will shed some light on, among other things, the servants' sleeping quarters.[43]

VAILS

Returning to the subject of servants' earnings, there were a number of ways in which they could supplement their wages. The expectation of visitors to be well entertained by their host was justified in at least one respect: the cost to the guest incurred by the distribution of vails to servants. This was a problem not just for the 'family' at Carton, but for employers throughout the country, and in Scotland and England. The system of vails for servants – 'tipping', as we would call it – appears to have been well established by the eighteenth century. It is not clear how it came into being, but it obviously had the tacit agreement of employers for as long as it suited them. Defined by the *Oxford English Dictionary* as 'a gratuity given by a visitor on his departure to servants of the house',[44] it became a problem in the first half of the century when there was a feeling among employers that it had got out of hand. The customary scene in the hall, as their guest waited for his carriage or horse to be brought to the door, embarrassed many.[45]

Perhaps servants were taking to heart the advice offered to them in Jonathan Swift's ironic *Directions to Servants* (begun 1731). Swift suggested such methods, in the event of a gentleman who often dines with their master and gives no vails, 'to shew him some Marks of your Displeasure & quicken his Memory', and he concludes, 'By these, and the like Expedients, you may probably be a better Man by Half a Crown before he leaves the house.'[46] He further urged those servants who expected vails

> always to stand Rank and File when a Stranger is taking his Leave so that he must of Necessity pass between you; and he must have more Confidence or less Money than usual, if any of you let him escape; and according as he behaves himself, remember to treat him the next Time he comes.[47]

Hosts pretended not to notice guests fumbling in their pockets to find shillings and half-crowns to distribute to servants who had lined themselves up expectantly. Whether the motive for allowing it was to enable the aristocracy to display their wealth or to salve their conscience at paying such low wages is not clear.[48] The giving of vails was not confined to great houses; it was also expected in more modest establishments, though the amounts given were less.[49]

For potential guests it led to a situation where in many cases it became prohibitively expensive to accept invitations either to dine or stay overnight. Richard

Griffith from Bennetsbridge, county Kilkenny, complained in about 1760 in a letter to his wife that:

> an heavy and unprofitable Tax still subsists upon the Hospitality of this Neighbourhood ... In short while this Perquisite continues, a Country Gentleman may be considered but as a generous Kind of Inn-holder, who keeps open House, at his own Expence, for the sole Emolument of his Servants ... this Extravagance is not confined, at present, solely to the Country ... for a Dinner in Dublin, and all the Towns in Ireland, is become ... an expensive Ordinary. Nay, if you have any Sort of Business to transact, even in a Morning, with a Person who keeps his Port, you may levee him fifty Times, without being admitted by his Swiss Porter. So ... I shall consider a great Man as a Monster, who may not be seen, 'till you have fee'd his Keepers.[50]

Griffith was by no means alone in believing that he was being 'punished' by the porter or butler for the paucity of his vails, or perhaps his refusal to 'pay his way'. An unfortunate guest in England in 1754 found his punishment truly humiliating. 'I am a marked man,' he wrote,

> If I ask for beer I am presented with a piece of bread. If I am bold enough to call for wine, after a delay which would take its relish away were it good, I receive a mixture of the whole sideboard in a greasy glass. If I hold up my plate nobody sees me; so that I am forced to eat mutton with fish sauce, and pickles with my apple pie.[51]

For the servants it was a well-established way of increasing their income (often by 50% or more), and something to which they believed they were entitled. In 1750 John Macdonald accepted a position as a postilion in Scotland for £2 a year, clothes, and one-third of the vails, but it should be noted that it was the coachman who offered him the job and mentioned the vails.[52] Such an arrangement would have been most likely understood, but not spelt out, by the employer in Ireland.

However, the custom of vail-giving was the subject of much argument in the printed media in England. The writer Daniel Defoe abhorred the idea, and newspapers ran numerous articles and letters giving both sides of the argument.[53] In the *London Chronicle* a correspondent wrote in 1762 that 'Masters in England seldom pay their servants but in lieu of wages suffer them to prey upon their guests.'[54]

A crusade against the giving of vails began in Scotland in 1760 where seventeen counties issued appeals to abolish them. By 1764 the movement had spread to London, resulting in riots there by footmen – the servants who stood to lose the most.[55] It was probably at about the same time that employers from a number of counties in Ireland agreed among themselves to abolish vails to servants.[56] It seems likely that among these gentlemen was the Marquis of Kildare. Like a number of other employers, he decided to increase staff wages in an effort to compensate them for loss of earnings. In March 1765 he issued the following directive from Carton to members of his household:

> In Consideration of Vails &c, which I will not permit for the future to be received in any of my Houses upon any Account whatsoever from Company lying there or otherwise I shall give in lieu thereof viz.

To the House Keeper	}	
Maitre D'Hotel	}	£5 a year to each
Cook	}	
Confectioner	}	
Steward at Carton	}	
Present Butler and	}	£3 a year to each
Valet de Chambre	}	
Groom of the Chambers	}	
Gentn of Horse	£2 a year	

> To Commence the 1st day of April next and I depend upon them that they will not receive Money upon that Account from any Body, -

> I shall make no Allowance to either Livery Servants or Under Servants, and any of those who chuse to be discharged may

> All Stoppages for the future to be made out of the Wages of the respective Persons where any thing is lost (fol. 56-57).

It is interesting to note that these were all 'upper servants', and the housekeeper is the only female servant (the cook was often male). Perhaps these were the only servants in attendance at Carton or Kildare House as guests departed. However, seven years later, in 1772, the now Duke of Leinster directed that £4 per annum be paid to footmen in lieu of vails 'at the end of a year's service' (fol. 97).

Servants could also add to their income when the family was not at home by showing visitors around the house. With or without letters of introduction, visitors were quite likely to arrive unexpectedly at any large house in the country, and it was the custom for a member of the domestic staff – usually the housekeeper, butler or footman – to show them around the house. The rector of Navan, the Rev Daniel Augustus Beaufort (1739-1821), was a regular country house 'tourist' in the 1780s and the early nineteenth century, but while he left a valuable account of his visits, he did not disclose his contributions to servants' pockets. In the 1850s Sir Charles Domville of Santry House had special cards printed admitting parties of four or less to view his house on Tuesdays and Fridays between 2pm and 5pm.[57] Visitors generally were permitted to drive or walk about the gardens and grounds, but the Duke of Leinster was forced to erect a notice at Carton with instructions that none were to be admitted into the kitchen garden. It was addressed to anyone 'who comes to see the Improvements at Carton'. (fol. 83).

LIVERY

Vails, however, were not the sole perquisite of the servant at this period. Apart from cast-off clothes from the employer's family – the mainstay of the female servant's wardrobe – many male servants, for example, butlers, footmen, coachmen and postilions, had uniforms or livery made for them or were given an allowance for it. The Duke of Leinster ordered that his footmen, from 1 January 1767, were allowed twenty shillings a year for 'a Pair of black Worsted Shag Breeches, for a fine Felt Hat with a Silver Chain Loop and Button, and a Horse Hair Cockade'. He warned that 'Those who do not chuse to accept of it, to let me know that I may discharge them.' Between 1 April and 1 October they were instructed to wear 'clean Leather Breeches', with the warning that he will stop one shilling for each time he finds them disobeying this order (fol. 69). In 1772 the allowance had increased to thirty shillings a year, this time for leather breeches, shoes, stockings and boots (fol. 97). The Bellew family of Galway, in the 1770s, paid £5 a year, with a suit of clothes, for a butler in charge of plate and furniture 'if he behaves careful and honest'.[58]

There is little evidence of landlords like Robert French of Monivea in Galway issuing written warnings to staff about their dress, but undoubtedly there was a dress code in operation. French paid £24 9s 2d for servants' clothes in the year 1746-47, and £28 15s 5d in 1748-49.[59] Bishop Edward Synge of Elphin's servants were 'so shabby they will not be fit to appear in town', and he ordered, in September 1747, frocks and waistcoats for five liveried servants between his palace at Elphin and his Dublin home at Kevin Street.[60] In 1754 Lord Powerscourt paid a tailor for making livery 'two light colour coats and two scarlet waistcoats, two fustian frocks and four flanell waistcoats lapeld and lined all throw'.[61] At Strokestown House, county Roscommon, in 1844, Major Mahon purchased lengths of fabrics – Super Oxford cloth, drab twilled Silesia, black Silesia, padding, canvas, velvet facing, long cloth, linen, moleskin and calico – for manservants' suits, including livery. It seems likely that a tailor, probably an itinerant tailor, was commissioned to come to the house and make the servants' clothing. Both the kitchen and pantry boys were provided with moleskin suits, while Danny the kitchen man was given a suit of Barragon 'the time he came to live here'. Suits of clothes were also given to the men as Christmas presents.[62]

The wearing of livery proclaimed the wealth of the family. Pole Cosby of Stradbally was able to boast that having taken a house in 1739 on Dublin's Arran Quay at £55 for six months, he had five servants in complete livery, 'besides my own man'.[63] On the occasion of a visit by the Lord Lieutenant, the Duke of Richmond, to Charleville Forest, county Offaly, in October 1809, the Countess of Charleville wrote to her son, 'Magnificent full dress liveries have been made for the servants & a uniform of Blue and Scarlet for the upper men; in short it ought to go off handsome for money has not been spared.'[64] And at Baronscourt, county Tyrone, in 1844, Lord and Lady Abercorn impressed their guests with 'a house steward who lived with George IV, a most distinguished major-domo excellently got up, a first-rate cook, and remarkable lords-in-waiting dressed in crimson and silver. No livery could look richer.'[65] The fastidious Lord Abercorn, however, insisted that his rooms be fumigated after his liveried servants had removed themselves, and that the chambermaids should wear white kid gloves when making up his bed.[66]

BEQUESTS

Long-standing servants who had given five or more years' service were often left bequests in their employers' wills. These varied between employer's clothes or linen to sums of money. The dowager Viscountess Powerscourt, who died in 1785, was generous to the female servants who were in her service at the time of her death. Those who had been with her one year were given one year's wages, and those with her less than a year, a half-year's wages. But to every manservant she left just one month's wages.[67] However, female servants were not so highly esteemed by Sir Edward O'Brien of Dromoland. He left one year's wages to male servants of five or more year's standing, 'having met [with] not one woman servant worth salt to her pottage since Mrs Barnwell left me'.[68] Lady Powerscourt also bequeathed to every servant the sum of £5, which 'will do them more good' than putting them all in mourning clothes, a custom of the time.[69]

CARD MONEY

'If your Lady loves Play, your Fortune is fixed for ever; Moderate Gaming will be a Perquisite of ten Shillings a Week; and in such a Family I would rather chuse to be Butler than a Chaplain ... It is all ready Money, and got without Labour.[70]

So said Swift on a rather lucrative perk for the butler, or sometimes the footman, whose job it was to supply cards and candles whenever the lady of the house invited her friends to play cards. The system allowed for greater numbers at these parties than perhaps the hostess's own means would allow, as Marshall has pointed out, and the guests were expected to leave on the table double and treble the amount of the cards' worth. The higher the stakes, the more new decks of cards were called for, and the more money the butler made. Added to that, he was free to sell off the old cards to coffee houses, or to poorer families who liked to play cards.[71] It might be more difficult to cheat on candles, as wax candles would be expected, and those made of tallow were rather odorous.

While servants were undoubtedly paid little, there were possibilities for some of them to supplement their earnings, both with and without their employers' knowledge. The 'servant problem' seemed to come to a head with the controversy over vails in the 1750s and 1760s, at which time the behaviour of servants in general came under close scrutiny. It may have contributed to the gradual separation and distancing of servants from the employer that began in the late eighteenth century. The Duke signed the last 'Rule' in August 1773, the year of his death. Unfortunately, it is not known how his heir dealt with these problems or whether he drew up a new book of rules.

While this document (the 'Rules') is comprehensive in many ways, one also gets the impression that at times there is a knee-jerk reaction to situations as they develop. The fact that many of them are dated at different times seems to reinforce this. Kildare's own decency and humanity are evident in many of these rules, and one is given the strong impression that he was probably disregarded over and over again by his staff. His wishes in this document were conveyed to the steward and to others in charge of staff. It meant that everybody was made aware of the parameters within which they should operate. How well it worked in practice is a moot point. Perhaps the action by Charles Agar in sending such a document to the Duke of Northumberland implied that the Leinster household was looked upon as a model for other establishments. Or is that reading too much into it?

———

ACKNOWLEDGEMENTS

My thanks to John Cornforth for pointing me in the direction of the document. I would like to thank Dr Toby Barnard for his valued comments and suggestions, and my supervisor Dr Edward McParland for his continued help and guidance. I am also grateful to the Knight of Glin, to the staff of the Irish Architectural Archive, to Clare Baxter, Collections Manager, The Northumberland Estates, and to the Duke of Northumberland and his Trustees for permission to reproduce a page from the manuscript..

ENDNOTES

The following abbreviations are used:
IAA   Irish Architectural Archive
NA   National Archives, Dublin
NLI   National Library of Ireland
PRONI   Public Record Office of Northern Ireland, Belfast

[1] Northumberland, Alnwick Castle Archives, MS 670, 'Rules for the government of the Marquis of Kildare's (Duke of Leinster's) household 1763-1773'. My thanks to the Knight of Glin for making available his photocopy of the document, and to the Duke of Northumberland and his Trustees for permission to reproduce a page from the manuscript. References to this document are provided in the main body of the text in brackets. Stella Tillyard has made use of similar material in *Aristocrats* (London 1994).

[2] A.P.W. Malcomson, *Archbishop Charles Agar: Churchmanship and Politics in Ireland 1760-1810* (Dublin 2002) 138-9.

[3] Sometimes referred to as 'running' footmen, a part of whose duties was to run errands, often of great distances, taking shortcuts across the countryside. Part of their employer's equipage, he would run before the carriage to prepare an inn or lodging for the arrival of his master.

[4] John Scott, 1st Earl of Clonmell, 'Life in the Irish Country House', *Quarterly Bulletin of the Irish Georgian Society*, vii, Apr-Dec 1964, 68-70.

[5] Marie-Louise Legg (ed.), *The Synge Letters 1746-1752* (Dublin 1996) 22-3.

[6] *ibid.*, 271.

[7] *ibid.*, 383.

[8] M. Hewson, 'Eighteenth century directions to servants in Co. Tipperary', in E. Rynne (ed.), *North Munster Studies* (Limerick 1967) 332-4.

[9] NLI, Doneraile Papers, MS 34,112/10.

[10] Jonathan Swift, *Directions to Servants* (Berkshire, special ed. 1925) 35.

[11] NLI, Doneraile Papers, MS 34,112/10.

[12] J. Ainsworth (ed.), *The Inchiquin Manuscripts* (Dublin 1961) 525.

[13] NLI, Domville Papers, MS 11,844, Book of Servants; S.C. O'Mahony, 'Gleanings from the Coote Household Accounts 1776-85', *North Munster Antiquarian Journal*, xxiv (1982) 59.

[14] B. Fitzgerald, *Correspondence of Emily, Duchess of Leinster (1731-1814)*, i (Dublin 1949) 42, 100, 108.

[15] NLI, French of Monivea Papers, MS 4919.

[16] NLI, Doneraile Papers, MS 34,114/2.

[17] NLI, French of Monivea Papers, MSS 4919, 4928; NLI, Domville Papers, MS 11,844; S.C. O'Mahony, 'Gleanings', 59.

[18] NA, Ballyglunin Papers, M 6931, parcel 2, documents 96a and 96b.

[19] *Oxford English Dictionary*, iii (Oxford 1989), defines the Anglo-Irish version of 'collop' as 'a full-grown beast of the horse or cow kind. Six sheep are also called a colpa, as their grass is estimated as the same as that of full-grown cow or horse.' I understand the phrase 'greasing of 6 collops' to mean the grazing of six sheep, as Blake also allows his farmer to keep one cow.

[20] NA, Ballyglunin Papers, M 6931, Parcel 2, documents 96a and 96b.

[21] J.J. Hecht, *The domestic servant class in eighteenth-century England* (London 1956) 155.

[22] T. Barnard, *A New Anatomy of Ireland: The Irish Protestants, 1649-1770* (Yale 2003) 302.

[23] Arthur Young, *A Tour in Ireland in the years 1776, 1777, and 1778*, 2 vols, (Dublin 1780).

[24] S. Madden, *Reflections and Resolutions Proper for the Gentlemen of Ireland* (Dublin 1738), cited in C. Maxwell, *Dublin under the Georges* (Dublin 1997) 104.

[25] G. Clark (ed.), *Gleanings from an old portfolio*, i (Edinburgh 1895) 81.

[26] J.D. Herbert, *Irish Varieties for the last fifty years* (London 1836) 159. No date is given, but it must be between 1786 and 1795.

[27] A. Day (ed.), *Letters from Georgian Ireland* (Belfast 1991) 203.

[28] Barnard, *A New Anatomy of Ireland*, 295.

[29] Isaac Ware, *A Complete Body of Architecture* (London 1756) book iii, section ii, ch. i, 346-7.

[30] J.P. Mahaffy, 'The furnishing of Georgian houses in Dublin in the earlier part of the century', *The Georgian Society Records*, iv (Dublin 1912) 10.

[31] Fitzgerald, *Correspondence of Emily, Duchess of Leinster*, ii, 150.

[32] 'Autobiography of Pole Cosby of Stradbally, Queen's County, 1703-1737', *Kildare Archaeological Society Journal*, v, 1906-8, 184.

[33] J.P. Mahaffy, 'The furnishing of Georgian houses…', 8.

[34] These could be used by people when travelling, or as extra bedding for servants or visitors.

[35] C. Hardyment, *Behind the scenes: domestic arrangements in historic houses* (London 1997) 43.

[36] J. Macdonald, *Memoirs of an eighteenth-century footman* (London 1985) 87; E. Dillon, *Wild Geese* (New York 1980) 49.

[37] Lord Belmore's collection of Castle Coole drawings; photocopies in the IAA.

[38] J.H. Gebbie (ed.), *An introduction to the Abercorn Letters (as relating to Ireland 1736-1816)*, 5 November 1808 (Omagh 1972) 388.

[39] IAA, Townley Hall Collection, ref. 85/156.

[40] IAA, Guinness Collection, 96/68.1/1/21 and 96/68.1/1/22.

[41] My thanks to Dr Edward McParland for making available this document.

[42] Collection Patrick Guinness. D.J. Griffin and C. Pegum, *Leinster House* (Dublin 2000) 46.

[43] In conversation with the Knight of Glin, June 2003.

[44] *Oxford English Dictionary*, xix (Oxford 1989, 2nd ed.).

[45] D. Marshall, 'The domestic servants of the eighteenth century', *Economica*, April 1929, 26.

[46] Jonathan Swift, *Directions to Servants* (Dublin 1745) 13.

[47] Swift, 'Rules that concern all Servants in general', *Directions to Servants*, 14.

[48] B. Hill, *Servants: English domestics in the eighteenth century* (Oxford 1996) 77.

[49] Marshall, 'The domestic servants', 24.

[50] R. and E. Griffith, *A series of genuine letters between Henry and Frances*, iv (London 1770, 3rd ed.) letter dxii, 142-3.

[51] Quoted in Marshall, 'The domestic servants', 27.

[52] Macdonald, *Memoirs*, 20.

[53] Hill, *Servants*, 76-92.

[54] *London Chronicle*, 11 (1762) 164; quoted in Hill, *Servants*, 77.

[55] Marshall, 'The domestic servants', 35-7.

[56] Footnote to letter dxii (footnote 50 above): 'An Agreement entered into among the Gentlemen of several Counties in Ireland, not to give Vails to Servants'.

[57] NLI, Domville Papers, MS 9391.

[58] K.J. Harvey, *The Bellews of Mount Bellew* (Dublin 1998) 73.

[59] NLI, French of Monivea Papers, MS 4918.

[60] Legg (ed.), *The Synge Letters*, 83-4.

[61] NLI, Powerscourt Papers, MS 8367/1.

[62] NLI, Pakenham-Mahon Papers, MS 10,136.

[63] 'Autobiography of Pole Cosby of Stradbally', 435.

[64] R.W. Bond, *The Marlay Letters 1778-1820* (London 1937) 127-8.

[65] J.Y. Burges, *Chronicles of Parkanaur 1818-1883*, PRONI, Burges Papers, T.1282/1.

[66] W.H. Dixon (ed.), *Lady Morgan's memoirs: autobiography, diaries and correspondence*, i (London 1862) 391.

[67] NLI, unsorted Powerscourt Papers, box 10, legal advice and wills.

[68] Ainsworth (ed.), *The Inchiquin Manuscripts*, 525.

[69] NLI, unsorted Powerscourt Papers, box 10, legal advice and wills. When a member of the royal family died, prominent families, particularly those connected with the church or the parliament, put their servants into mourning. Three months full mourning meant dressing in matt black, followed by second mourning when the effect could be lightened somewhat; Legg, *The Synge Letters*, 294; L. Taylor, *Mourning Dress: a costume or social history* (London 1983) 104.

[70] Swift, 'Directions to the Butler', *Directions to Servants*, 14.

[71] *ibid.*, 14; Marshall, 'The domestic servants', 28.

———

1 – Hugh Howard, PORTRAIT OF ST GEORGE ASHE
(courtesy Board of Trinity College Dublin)

From Imperial Schatzkammer to the Giant's Causeway: collecting in eighteenth-century Ireland

TOBY BARNARD

I N 1690 S T G EORGE A SHE (P LATE 1), A RECENT GRADUATE OF T RINITY C OLLEGE Dublin, soon to be its provost and later a negligent Church of Ireland bishop, was in Vienna. Ashe acted as secretary to the English ambassador, Lord Paget of Beaudesert. More to the point, Ashe, a man of learning and curiosity, used the opportunity to scan the contents of the Imperial Library and the Schatzkammer, the imperial treasury of rarities and curiosities. In a letter to an acquaintance back in Ireland, he described the layout and contents of the Schatzkammer, with its thirteen cabinets holding precious and bizarre objects.[1] A few years later, Samuel Molyneux devoured the sights and sensations of London before crossing to continental Europe. Molyneux inspected a large variety of ancient and modern buildings. In addition, he was admitted into private collections of paintings, engravings, antiquities and curiosities. He singled out for particular praise those of lords Halifax and Pembroke; the latter had recently returned from a spell in Dublin as Lord Lieutenant. He also visited the museum of Dr Woodward. Over the last collection – the first systematic assemblage of geological items, later deposited with Cambridge University – Molyneux enthused that it 'contains the most elucidating materials that I have seen to a history of nature's hidden processes within the formation of minerals'.[2]

The reactions of Ashe and Molyneux introduce several themes deserving further pursuit. The most obvious is the fact of travel outside Ireland, and how it introduced travellers to fashions which they might then ship back home. One vogue was the assembling of cabinets of curiosities, treasuries, or – in Woodward's example – 'elucidating materials' that revealed 'nature's hidden processes'. Woodward, indeed, issued a manual to guide novices in harvesting and codifying geological specimens, and subsequently published a detailed catalogue of his collection, again as a model for others.[3] Secondly, the origins and functions of collections can throw light on wider intellectual and cultural currents.[4] Both Ashe and Molyneux were involved in co-operative efforts of investigation and improvement. For a time these endeavours were systematised by the Dublin Philosophical Society. Ashe had been present at its foundation in 1684, along with Samuel Molyneux's father, William. Samuel resuscitated the society for a year or two in Queen Anne's reign. Groups as much as individuals made collections. Sometimes, indeed, institutional collections stood a better chance of preservation and survival than those of private collectors, which were at risk of being dispersed after their owners' deaths.

A third point, evident from the approach of Ashe and Molyneux, is how making collections might advance the public good. They were not mere whimsies or self-indulgences, but intended to assemble materials through which the secrets of creation could be probed and better understood. Eventually, more precise knowledge would aid profitable exploitation. To take merely one example: geological specimens could be analysed in order to detect ores which could then justify investment in mining.[5] More precise information about the terrain of Ireland was not only a prelude to profiteering, but would confirm the omnipotence and omniscience of the deity which had created it. In this spirit, the study of the natural world – the book of nature, as it was often called – was deemed a form of worship, and particularly recommended to the clergy. One of their number, Richard Barton, active during the 1740s in the investigations of the Physico-Historical Society – a successor of the Dublin Philosophical Society – and obedient to the injunction, stated that 'the handiwork of God was a suitable subject for his ministers'.[6]

Apparently random assemblages of fossils, precious and semi-precious stones, petrifications and other mysterious objects do not immediately conform to the objects most usually connected with collecting: books and paintings. Of the collections formed in later-seventeenth and eighteenth-century Ireland, by far the most numerous and seemingly the earliest in date were indeed those of books and manuscripts.[7] Such collections are considered here only in so far as they relate to the principal themes. There were a few voracious bibliophiles whose addiction had to be fed by snapping up whatever rarities came on the market. They resembled collectors of other kinds of objects in employing agents who searched for rarities outside Ireland. Passionate book-collectors insisted that their libraries had practical purposes. In common with assemblages of antiquities and curios, if properly ordered and catalogued the volumes could spread useful knowledge more widely. Yet, alongside the purposefulness with which different collections were made, items frequently entered them by haphazard and serendipitous routes.

Paintings were the second object of desire. In collecting them, the inhabitants of Ireland lagged behind those of England, which in their turn trailed behind the connoisseurs of western Europe. In the seventeenth century, only the Ormondes at Kilkenny (Ireland's one ducal family) could properly be regarded as having a collection, housed in a gallery and shown to favoured guests.[8] By the start of the eighteenth century, one or two institutions – notably Trinity College, but then the Royal Hospital at Kilmainham, and even some of the chartered trading companies of the capital – were gathering collections of paintings. For the most part, and in distinction from the Ormondes' gallery, the canvases were portraits of worthies closely associated with the particular place. So, provosts, fellows and distinguished alumni hung in Trinity; governors of the hospital at Kilmainham; and masters and wardens in the guilds' halls. Most of these images were either presented by the subjects themselves or by sycophants.

Visitors and commentators continued to stress the backwardness of Ireland in the business of collecting pictures. A few prominent aristocrats were regularly credited with owning the only worthwhile galleries. This was perhaps to take an unduly restrictive view of what constituted a collection, and to endorse a familiar but sadly distorting notion that cultural innovation in eighteenth-century Ireland was monopolised by peers. This continues: only in republics, like France, America and Ireland, do those with titles receive so much deference. Some proud of their collections endowed them with the same ethical and moral worth that were invested in libraries, cabinets of fossils, and albums of pressed plants. These purposes are most loudly proclaimed in contemporary descriptions of two of the most notable: George Berkeley's, displayed in his episcopal palace in the hamlet of Cloyne, and Samuel Madden's, housed at his Fermanagh seat of Manor Waterhouse. Berkeley, an ardent crusader for improvement, annexed music, statuary, architecture and political economy to the cause. So too did Madden, a founder of the Dublin Society in 1731, then its reviver early in the 1740s. His pictures belonged to an ensemble in which landscape gardening, architecture, and practical improvements in manufactures all featured.[9] Berkeley and Madden seemed to subscribe to contemporary theories which arranged painting according to a hierarchy of genres and attributed to the highest – history painting – a capacity for moral enlightenment along the lines advocated by Lord Shaftesbury.[10] The same thinking led Madden to include painting and statuary among the activities which would be rewarded with premiums under the auspices of the revamped Dublin Society of the 1740s.

The reasonably well-known collections of Madden and Berkeley were not the only ones in Ireland before 1750. The right to import and auction paintings in Dublin had first been granted in 1681.[11] It may not have been exploited immediately, yet, in the 1690s, the younger John Evelyn, temporarily in Dublin, decided to sell part of his collection there. Canvases other than the family portraits were auctioned.[12] The availability of imported art, much of it engraved on paper, together

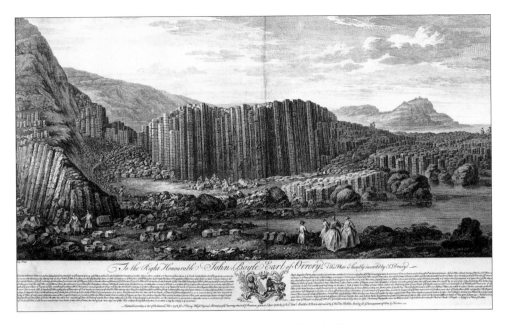

2 – Susannah Drury, VIEW OF THE GIANT'S CAUSEWAY
(courtesy Bodleian Library, Oxford)

with the opportunities to make collections, albeit modest in price and pretension, may have been seriously underestimated.[13] These supplies of 'improving' imagery, and the concern to improve the techniques through which it was produced, united in a project more directly linked with the cabinets of curiosities and proto-museums. It is reasonably well known that an early recipient of a bounty from the Dublin Society was a young lady, Susannah Drury, who painted the Giant's Causeway in county Antrim. Miss Drury, 'a young gentlewoman', 'a modest and well-behaved young person', spent several months at the bleak and remote spot, sketching the phenomenon. Plates were then engraved from her sketches (Plate 2).[14] This was not the first time that the Causeway had been drawn and engraved. In 1693, Edwin Sandys, the leading Dublin engraver of the day, an 'excellent artist', journeyed to county Antrim with the local Church of Ireland bishop to depict what others, encouraged by the Dublin Philosophical Society, had tried to describe in words. Sandys was paid £13 for these images.[15]

The origins and significance of the Causeway had long excited speculation. Pieces or 'pillars' from it were in demand among assiduous collectors. In 1697 William Molyneux, while defending in print Ireland's legislative sovereignty, sent a segment to the prime collector of the time, Dr (later Sir) Hans Sloane in London. 'Such a rude trifle' was thought worthy of Sloane's notice, not least because he had himself originated in Ulster.[16] Within a decade, Molyneux's son Samuel looked forward enthusiastically to inspecting the natural wonder. He was supplied with samples, as also of petrified matter from Lough Neagh, by a Mr Neve from Magherafelt.[17] Others continued the interest. In 1741 a new Dean of Clogher, John Copping, awaited samples of the basalt columns from Boyd of Ballycastle, another improver besotted with the doctrines of the Dublin Society and Physico-Historical Society.[18] Indeed, the Causeway was so renowned that the Bishop of Derry, Thomas Rundle, felt that pieces would make an appropriate present to the poet Alexander Pope, and soon adorned the latter's grotto at Twickenham.[19]

The trade in bits of the Giant's Causeway catered to the interest in the rare and wonderful. Some were sent to the curious in Dublin, not simply to enrich their collections, but in the hope that scientific analysis would penetrate the mysteries of its formation. But it is equally noteworthy that many of the pieces were shipped from Ireland. This reminded that the pre-eminent collectors were outside the island. Sloane and Dr Richard Mead were at this juncture the nonpareils. In consequence, Sloane received – usually unsolicited – a miscellany of oddities and artefacts: petrified moss sent by another improver, Dobbs; coins unearthed at Howth; motley shells; stones dug from a bog in the King's County.[20] This notion that the better destination for artefacts uncovered in Ireland was England inspired other gifts, such as the head of a giant elk presented by Bishop Wetenhall of Dromore to the Royal Society in London.[21] In the same mode, Ralph Thoresby in Yorkshire, the leading collector of coins, interested himself in a rarity found in Ireland by Thomas Putland, a functionary of the Irish treasury.[22] In time, the Putlands – quintessential Dublin rentiers – would become significant collectors, but as yet they had not acquired the habit and so did not keep the finds for themselves.

Sloane, as has been stressed, knew and was revered by virtuosi in Ireland. Acquaintances corresponded with him long after he had settled in London; tourists from Ireland saw and wondered at his collections. Two known to have done so were St George Ashe and Samuel Molyneux. The first was by then a hardened traveller, Molyneux a mere novice, although he had already ventured into the remoter regions of Ireland.[23] There was a tendency to deprecate what Ireland had to offer, and, in contrast, to enthuse, maybe excessively, over what was on view elsewhere. However, more than a courtly deference made Ashe praise Sloane's assemblage – reckoned the largest and most remarkable at the time – or the Schatzkammer in Vienna, thought by some a wonder of the modern world. As tourism gathered pace, travellers from Ireland headed for the standard spectacles, thereby experiencing what was common to the prosperous throughout much of Europe.[24] The curious viewed collections of paintings and statuary: the Arundel marbles or the contents of Northumberland House, Hampton Court and Wilton House in Wiltshire. Further

3 – Sir Joshua Reynolds,
GENERAL JOHN GUISE
(courtesy Christ Church, Oxford)

opposite
4 – French, c.1720-40,
GENERAL GUISE AND THE
CONNOISSEURS
(courtesy Christ Church, Oxford)

afield they were dazzled by the offerings of the Netherlands and Italy. These visits familiarised the untutored with what were accounted masterpieces, and inculcated a taste for collecting. Many accounts concentrate on the few who, especially from the 1740s, descended on Italy, commissioned works there, and patronised the local dealers and antiquaries. However, only a small proportion of those who travelled for pleasure beyond Ireland could afford to return with canvases by Claude, Batoni and Richard Wilson, or the fancies and fakes purveyed by Roman traders. The Netherlands were a much readier source of wares.

Handiest and least expensive as mementoes of these trips were engravings. Indeed, an enterprising group with strong Irish connections in the 1720s intended to cash in on this market by pioneering and popularising a new form of coloured engraving of favourite paintings. Collecting engravings has not received the attention it deserves, partly because the details of what arrived in late seventeenth and early eighteenth-century Ireland are frustratingly difficult to retrieve. Odd glimpses – a visitor to Rome from Ireland in 1688 or another in Paris of the 1730s – reveal the passions of the Irish.[25]

The provincial awestruck in front of acknowledged masterworks was a

favourite trope; it readily accommodated the reactions of the bemused and ignorant Irish. This was not how they always behaved. Tourists from Ireland, like their counterparts from other countries, couched their responses to what they were told to see in words that they were told to use. The quickening pace of travel hastened the printing of guidebooks and cribs so that the untutored could bluff their way around the palaces and galleries of Europe. Even so, a series of travellers from Ireland, both in England and in continental Europe, judged independently. They struggled to express the feelings evoked by works as various as the Raphael cartoons, then at Hampton Court, or a now-vanished altarpiece after Raphael drawings of St Paul striking Elymas the sorcerer in the cathedral at Chester.[26]

At this stage, one example must suffice. In early Georgian London, the equivalent for paintings to Sloane's miscellaneous collections was the collection of General John Guise (Plate 3). The general claimed a vestigial Irish link, via an ancestor's friendship with Archbishop Narcissus Marsh. Be that as it may, he welcomed visitors from Ireland – if vouched for – into his London house where the pictures were hung. One such unidentified guest, introduced to Guise by the heir of Lord Cavan, was not intimidated. In particular, he was sceptical about two alleged

Michelangelos: he thought that they looked little more than primed canvases. The sightseer moralised, 'this shows what sort of people connoisseurs are, and that all their curiosities are to be valued only by the great warmth and ardency of their own fancies and imaginations' (Plate 4).[27]

The critical note by this Irish observer, presently anonymous, sounds two warnings. Numerous itinerants crossed from Ireland into Britain, and then some ventured further. Not all arrived as cultural innocents or visual illiterates, although most acknowledged how seeing more enhanced their appreciation. Those who returned to Ireland, even if they were not laden with artistic booty, often retained an interest in the arts and collecting which they continued to express. Moreover, Ireland offered richer pickings for the hunters after the curious than is sometimes allowed. One reason was warfare. English and Scottish conquerors of Ireland habitually belittled the culture of the defeated. Notwithstanding this disparagement, Ireland was not altogether barren of novelties which might detain the interested. Again, most obvious among the treasures uprooted and transferred to newcomers were manuscripts and books, particularly those previously owned by now suppressed monasteries or by Catholic owners driven into exile. The Book of Kells was a striking example. Bestowed on Trinity College by its warrior vice-chancellor, Henry Jones, during the Cromwellian interregnum, it soon attracted the scholarly interest of those investigators of other aspects of Ireland through the Dublin Philosophical Society in the 1680s. Many other ancient documents and treasured books circulated in the unsettled conditions of the warfare in sixteenth and seventeenth-century Ireland. Prizes were to be had, but moved along lines which can seldom be recreated in their entirety. Typical are the Irish manuscripts of Henry Bathurst, an English lawyer who became a judge in Munster and proprietor of Old Park overlooking the harbour of Kinsale. In 1675 he bequeathed his doubtfully gotten gains to a brother, the head of an Oxford college, but the Bathurst collection is not now to be found there.[28]

Intermittent bursts of collective endeavour to forward the study of Ireland's topography and past encouraged collections. The successive groups, Hartlib's friends in the 1650s, the Philosophical Society, then the Dublin Society from 1731 and the Physico-Historical Society in the 1740s, valued samples on which they could experiment and speculate. As a result they encouraged their collection. Also, provincials, hearing of these Dublin cognoscenti, sent in curiosities. Samuel Molyneux, picking up where his father and uncle had left off, established contact with John Keogh in Roscommon. Keogh duly despatched to Molyneux a giant's tooth and a massive dog's skeleton from a second correspondent, James Reynolds, in county Leitrim.[29] Similarly, in 1708, another of Molyneux's correspondents, this time Walter Atkins, a vigorous cleric from county Cork, obliged with reports and examples of what had been unearthed in excavations on Lord Midleton's estate.[30] These materials were more than curiosities; they might help determine the veracity of more general theories about the earliest settlements in Ireland, the origins of Christianity and building there, or on pre- and post-lapsarian worlds.

A network of informants across the country was the ideal to which the learned collectives in Dublin aspired. In the main what was wanted from the provincial members were reports, but sometimes objects were also despatched. The problem was that once these materials arrived they had somehow to be stored. This was possible so long as the offerings remained few, but too many antlers, skeletons and columns from the Giant's Causeway would soon burst the closets of the fellows of Trinity, who, for the most part, made up the activists in these incipient societies.

The university promised secure and durable locations for collections. Oxford, with the Ashmolean Museum and the Bodleian Library, offered an obvious model. Soon enough Dublin University had its own impressive collection of books, to which were added a physic garden, with its useful plants, and a chemical laboratory, which may also have boasted collections for experimentation. During the 1690s, 'an handsome new skeleton of a man' was displayed in a chamber abutting on the old library. The skeleton had been presented by the physician Charles Gwithers. In a second chamber were kept 'a great many manuscripts, medals and other curiosities'. By 1729 the college possessed 'a little museum' as part of an ensemble, with an anatomy theatre, laboratory and herbarium, given striking architectural form.[31] These resources resembled those found in the Low Countries and Italy.[32] In 1732 the English visitor Loveday noted that the new library, not yet in use, included a room reserved for 'the museum of curiosities'. For the moment the curiosities were housed next to the chemical laboratory. One type of object was 'rare herbs pasted on paper in glass picture cases'. The anatomy school also contained striking exhibits, notably a skeleton of a man astride the skeleton of a horse, suspended from the ceiling.[33] Other treasures were added: two classical statues sent by an alumnus who had become a merchant in Hamburg; a gallery of portraits; and in the 1740s a series of commissioned busts of college notables (Plate 5).[34]

The collections associated with the Dublin Philosophical Society lacked the security of those in the college. The Society's meetings ceased after 1708, when, presumably, its possessions were dispersed among the surviving officers. Conspicuous among them was Samuel Molyneux, but his move to England did not increase the chances of survival. When, in 1730, his library was auctioned, it included 'all his mathematical, optical and mechanical instruments' useful to his (and perhaps even his father's) earlier experiments.[35] The Dublin Society seems not to have been so keen to assemble or receive donations. It is true that it was given, unsolicited, samples of volcanic rock from county Kerry. But this may have been an isolated donation. The Society preferred to stage exhibitions of modern inventions. In 1734, for

5 – The Long Room, Trinity College Dublin, showing busts of college notables
(photo David Davison; courtesy Board of Trinity College Dublin)

example, it organised a display of innovative farming implements in rooms adjacent to the House of Lords.[36] These were advertisements of its practical concerns, not museums. In contrast, the Physico-Historical Society, the group which in the 1740s sprang up alongside the Dublin Society, complementing and sometimes competing with it, did acquire a collection. In 1744, the well-meaning master of the free-school in Cavan, the Reverend James Moore, donated a horn 'of extraordinary shape'.[37] Next, the Society employed Isaac Butler as a botanist to collect rare plants, in rather the same way as earlier in England the Royal Society had used Thomas Willisel.[38] Others enlarged the collections: Charles Smith, the Dungarvan apothecary and author of histories, both natural and civil, of Cork, Waterford, Kerry and Limerick, unearthed fossils, stones and shells. Another enthusiast, the Lurgan curate Richard Barton sent down more materials from the neighbourhood of Lough Neagh.[39] The Physico-Historical Society cared enough about these goods to ask a member, James Simon, to prepare a repository for them.[40] In 1748, at least, the fossils were to be catalogued; probably the plants as well.[41]

The Physico-Historical Society undoubtedly retained the utilitarian objectives of its precursors. Hopes persisted that, through the minute study of clays and rocks, manufacturing techniques could be advanced. After the Physico-Historical Society petered out early in the 1750s, some of its preoccupations were continued by a smaller group, the Medico-Politico-Physico-Classico-Ethico-Puffical Society. Its members studied minerals, and proposed a museum to house fossils.[42] The Society sponsored botanical investigations that may have resulted in a *hortus sicus* being collected.[43] In 1766 one of its members, Samuel Caldwell, returning from Aix-la-Chapelle, entertained his colleagues with various 'substances'. The effects are not recorded in the society minutes; nor whether the substances were then to be stored somewhere.[44] These ephemeral groups, lacking permanent quarters, found it impossible to preserve their miscellaneous collections. Either they were dispersed to the individual members' custody or passed to successor bodies. The most important of these, which acquired a stable home, was the Royal Irish Academy.[45]

These groups, although wedded to utility, were fascinated by the odd. The curiosity of some members embraced relics of the Irish past. The Physico-Historical Society, in its publications, reiterated the credo of the earlier groups: namely that Ireland, with its untapped potential, was ripe for improvements, and that 'the English in Ireland' were solely responsible for what so far had been achieved.[46] Precious artefacts supported these contentions. Throughout the seventeenth century, ancient objects fashioned from precious metals were valued as bullion rather than as antiquities.[47] Hopes of profit led promising sites to be ransacked. The prospect of converting the objects easily into cash left scant space for an aesthetic or historical appreciation. But once collectors were known to pay a good price for rarities, then discoveries were more likely to be touted for sale to the cognoscenti. In 1747 the luminaries of the Physico-Historical society inspected an ancient gold plate belonging to Lord Newport, the Lord Chancellor. Newport, whether in his official or a private capacity, seems to have gathered a collection of such valuables; maybe the Lord Chancellor was given first refusal on treasure trove. During the 1750s the Medico-Politico society concerned itself with a gold plate, coins and medals, reputedly Roman, found in the north of Ireland. It is not clear whether these objects were sent to the Society in Dublin for opinions and safety.[48] In a similar way, Sloane had been apprised of the discovery of a copper trumpet in county Kildare in 1726.[49] Appreciation of the quality of the craftsmanship was slowly competing against avarice at the intrinsic worth of the metal. Moreover, curiosity about the past suggested by this material evidence could be detached from polemic over which ethnic or confessional group pioneered or monopolised such skills in an earlier Ireland.

A better appreciation of the shared past told, perhaps, of more relaxed conditions, in which the recently installed Protestant proprietors felt more confident that the new order would endure and thrive. Accordingly, survivals from an older Ireland were prized. The circumstances which brought rarities to light changed. In the seventeenth century, war delivered precious goods as well as land to fresh owners. Many more articles were probably destroyed. By the eighteenth century the characteristic exertions of improvers, set on foot by groups like the Dublin Philosophical Society or Dublin Society, were more likely to reveal the hidden as fields were ploughed, bogs drained and woodlands felled. In 1738 the Bishop of Cork informed Lord Egmont, an absentee owner of large estates in the diocese, of the recently discovered skeleton of a man alleged to have given suck to a child. The bishop thought it 'a most extraordinary natural curiosity ... I cannot forbear letting your lordship partake with me in the amusement.'[50] Paradoxically, improvement stirred an enthusiasm for relics of 'primitive' times. Yet, it would be dangerous to predate or exaggerate the extent of these antiquarian tastes. The topographical artist Jonas Blaymires was disappointed by the luke-warmness with which his engravings of medieval buildings were greeted.[51] Similarly, collectors deemed few productions of Ireland deserving of a place in their drawers or on their shelves. In 1726 the Reverend Nicholas Knight hoped 'to give the world a distinct view of the ancient and present state of Ireland in four parts'. To further this project he appealed for 'rarities of art and nature to be communicated'. Nothing seems to have come of Knight's design.[52] Moreover, the choicest discoveries tended to be earmarked for the discerning elsewhere, notably Sloane.

Collectors in Ireland generally looked overseas for their wants: books, paintings, prints, coins, medals, and even plants. Evidence abounds of these foreign quests: the plant-hunting expeditions in Jamaica on behalf of the Rawdons of Moira

county Down, which then spread a taste for exotic plantations among their neighbours and kindred. Here the only difficulty, as Brilliana Rawdon complained in
1703, was that the exotics were too dear for most in the region. Perforce, they made
do with curiosities more easily and cheaply obtained, including the arbutus or straw-
berry tree, in high repute and cultivated in the south-west.[53]

Coins and medals, important alike in establishing the chronology of obscure
societies and tracking forgotten trades, were prized by the virtuosi pushing back the
frontiers of knowledge. Ashe, while in Vienna, promised to bring back for one of
his Dublin friends, John Madden, also an avid collector of manuscripts, sufficient
ancient and modern medals to satiate him.[54] A member of a prominent Ulster
Presbyterian family, Samuel Haliday, in Switzerland, looked out for medals which
would please the exacting Sloane.[55] A fillip to these collecting passions among
Dubliners was offered by the cultivated Viceroy, Pembroke, and his exquisite aide-
de-camp, Sir Andrew Fountaine. The latter, an acknowledged connoisseur, published a treatise on Saxon coinage, and stimulated a more discriminating attitude
among Irish collectors, with whom he stayed in touch.[56]

Those who owned Fountaine's treatise on Anglo-Saxon and Danish coins
included the notable book collector and fellow and benefactor of Trinity, Claudius
Gilbert. Dr Gilbert also coveted and bought rare coins.[57] This genre of collecting
reached its apogee when Lord Charlemont commissioned a coin cabinet from
Chambers (Plate 6).[58] Before that, in 1720, Trinity College had caused a cabinet to
be made, thereby suggesting that the private interest of fellows such as Claudius
Gilbert, Robert Howard and John Ellwood spilled over into institutional collecting.[59]
The Squire of Barbavilla in Westmeath, William Smythe, in conjunction with a
well-travelled brother, ordered from Dublin a finely made cabinet which was probably intended for the display of coins and other curios (Plate 7).[60]

The forming of collections was eased by the brisk traffic in appropriate artefacts and the appearance of specialist dealers. Travel gave more people from Ireland
opportunities to see and purchase. Use of the chances is shown by the Howards,
sons of the foremost physician in Dublin at the turn of the seventeenth and eighteenth centuries. One, Hugh Howard, studied painting and employed his slender talents with the brush in London. The necessity to live on what he thereby earned was
ended by a fortunate marriage. Meanwhile, he developed a lucrative sideline as inter-
mediary for collectors. Hugh Howard's best markets were in England, but he did not
ignore his native Ireland. He returned to paint some luminaries of Trinity College,
so enlarging the modest gallery at the university (Plate 1). He also supplied customers in and around Dublin with works of art. A brother on the spot, Robert
Howard, successively Bishop of Killala and Elphin, assisted. Bishop Howard was a
willing customer for what Hugh Howard purveyed – decorative and furnishing pic-

*6 – Lord Charlemont's medal
and coin cabinet, designed
by Sir William Chambers
(1723-1796)*
(courtesy Courtauld Institute of Art
Gallery)

*7 – Cabinet at Barbavilla,
county Westmeath*
(courtesy Mrs Valerie Bunn)

tures, often with rather speculative attributions to distinguished masters like Guido Reni, Luca Giordano, Andrea del Sarto, Pellegrini, or Gaspar Poussin.[61]

This traffic was not entirely in one direction. The Howards, mingling easily in the upper echelons of Irish Protestant society, spotted desirable items already in Ireland. One in particular haunted Hugh Howard. It was a 'Caricatura' belonging to General Frederick Hamilton. At first, Hugh Howard wheedled to borrow it in order that he might copy it. Soon, it seems, he wanted to buy it outright in the hope then of selling it well.[62] The Howards exemplify the shadowy side of picture-dealing in early eighteenth-century Ireland. Their optimistic attributions, touched-up canvases, and complete forgeries matched the gullibility and cupidity of many would-be buyers.

More germane to the theme of collecting is the route by which the Caricatura had come to Ireland. Its owner Frederick Hamilton was one of a group, important alike in the cultural and socio-economic life of Protestant Ireland. Hamilton, originally from county Londonderry, rose high in society thanks to a successful career as a soldier. In retirement, surrounded by improvements and possessions, he was esteemed as much for his taste as his valour.[63] In this he was not unique among high-ranking officers. Continental warfare under William III in the 1690s, and then the War of Spanish Succession, gave ample opportunities for Protestants from Ireland – as from England and Scotland – to prosper and travel. Almost certainly, Hamilton's picture had been picked up while he was in the Low Countries, possibly though the good offices of the quartermaster of his regiment.

The latter functionary, William Leathes, also hailed from the north of Ireland. His forte was supplying fellow officers of the Royal Irish Regiment. Staying on as George I's emissary in Brussels, Leathes continued to cater to the varied wants of his comrades even after they had left the ranks. He knew his way around the art markets of the Low Countries as thoroughly as he knew the textile trades and the East India imports of the same region. Leathes' acumen rendered him invaluable to those back in Ireland, such as General Hamilton or Lord Kildare, who sought the wares of the United Provinces and Austrian Netherlands. Leathes himself made a collection, mainly of paintings, but it has only a tangential link with Ireland, since he retired to an estate in Suffolk. The remnant of the collection is in Christ Church mansion in Ipswich. Yet he acted as a conduit to bring goods from continental Europe to the grand and not so grand in Ireland. He helped a sister acquire engravings which enlivened her Dublin house. This was at almost the same moment that the viceregal couple, the Ormondes, lightened the look of the Castle by hanging its drawing room with engravings.[64]

Whether such decor should be dignified as a collection is a testing question. Two points emerge from this cursory assemblage of scattered information. At least some of components of collections were present in late seventeenth and early eighteenth-century Ireland, and in greater quantities than has often been supposed. Books, paintings and prints are the easiest to spot. However, there are odder items. By the 1730s a suit of armour was to be found in the Hall of the Painter-Stainers' Company of Dublin. It was presented by Colonel Joshua Paul, a Carlow squire of austere Protestant mien. It had previously belonged to a Pooley – perhaps the painter. Another member of the company was requested to make a face and hands for it, and equip it with a pair of boots and sword.[65] It is impossible to know if it was a painter's prop to assist in the portrayal of military heroes or the nucleus of a collection. The second point must be that what seemed aimless – the amassing of lumps of stone, petrified wood, dried flowers and bleached bones – was undertaken in the name of improvement as much as of amusement. Sentiment, serendipity, convention, even one-upmanship could dictate what entered collections. But delight and enlightenment were never far away. Unfortunately, the collections which have left the clearest traces and the collectors whose motives are sometimes recorded tend to be the ones who exercised power and asserted standing through the activity. Improvement through the rapt contemplation of a heap of stones may seem – and may be – the sublimation of psychological derangement.[66] But seventeenth and eighteenth-century enthusiasts in Ireland as elsewhere knew that collecting was a sociable, not a purely solitary pleasure that could yield public benefits as well as private gratification.

———

ENDNOTES

The following abbreviations are used:

BL	British Library, London	PRONI	Public Record Office of
Bodleian	Bodleian Library, Oxford		Northern Ireland, Belfast
CRO	County Record Office	RDS	Royal Dublin Society
NA	National Archives, Dublin	RIA	Royal Irish Academy
NLI	National Library of Ireland	TCD	Trinity College Dublin

[1] TCD, St George MSS, photocopy 175a, St G. Ashe to A. St George and S. Lightburn, 9/19 December 1690; same to unknown, 18/28 December 1690; R. Distelberger, 'The Habsburg collections in Vienna during the seventeenth century', in O. Impey and O. McGregor (eds), *The Origins of Museums: the cabinet of curiosities in sixteenth and seventeenth-century Europe* (Oxford 1985, reprinted Thirsk 2001) 51-61.

[2] Southampton Civic Archives, Molyneux MSS, S. Molyneux, tour, D/M, 1/3, f.94. For the collection: J.M. Levine, *Dr Woodward's Shield: History, Science and Satire in Augustan England* (Berkeley, London and Los Angeles 1977) 93-113; H. Torrens, 'Early collecting in the field of

geology', in Impey and McGregor (eds), *The Origins of Museums*, 289-90.

[3] J. Woodward, *Brief instructions for making observations in all parts of the world* (London 1696); J. Woodward, *Fossils of all kinds digested into a method* (London 1728).

[4] Examples of the approach include: Impey and McGregor (eds), *The Origins of Museums*; M. Swann, *Curiosities and Texts: the culture of collecting in early modern England* (Philadelphia 2001).

[5] BL, Evelyn MSS, formerly at Christ Church, Oxford, C. Monck to J. Evelyn, 29 October 1694, 16 March 1695[6]; mining company materials, *ibid.*, box viii.

[6] R. Barton, *Lectures in Natural Philosophy* (Dublin 1751) 111-12. A good guide to the Society's work is E. Magennis, '"A land of milk and honey": the Physico-Historical Society, improvement and the surveys of mid-eighteenth-century Ireland', *Proceedings of the Royal Irish Academy*, 102C, 2002, 199-217.

[7] T. Barnard, 'Libraries and collectors, 1700-1800', in R. Gillespie and A. Hadfield (eds), *Oxford History of the Book in Ireland*, volume 2, forthcoming; E.A. Boran, 'Libraries and collectors, 1600-1700', *ibid.*

[8] J. Fenlon, *The Ormonde Picture Collection* (Dublin 2001); J. Fenlon, 'Her grace's closet: paintings in the duchess of Ormond's closet at Kilkenny Castle', in *Bulletin of the Irish Georgian Society*, xxxvi (Dublin 1994); J. Loveday, *Diary of a tour in 1732 through parts of England, Wales, Ireland and Scotland* (Edinburgh 1890) 30-1; Markham, *John Loveday of Caversham, 1711-1789* (Salisbury 1984), 499.

[9] NA, M 2533, W. Henry, 'Hints towards a natural and typographical [sic] history of the Counties Sligo, Donegal, Fermanagh and Lough Erne', 464-5; A. Crookshank and D.A. Webb, *Paintings and Sculpture in Trinity College Dublin* (Dublin 1990) 94, 158-64.

[10] L. Lippincott, 'Expanding on portraiture: the market, the public and the hierarchy of genres in eighteenth-century Britain', in A. Bermingham and J. Brewer (eds), *The Consumption of Culture, 1600-1800: Image, Object, Text* (London 1995) 75-85.

[11] R. Loeber, *Biographical Dictionary of Irish Architects* (London 1981) 109, under Trotter, Robert.

[12] BL, Evelyn MSS, J. Evelyn to J. Evelyn, 26 March 1694, formerly at Christ Church, Oxford; Anne Crookshank and D. Fitzgerald, Knight of Glin, *Ireland's Painters, 1600-1940* (London and New Haven 2002) 52.

[13] B. Cowan, 'Arenas of connoisseurship: auctioning art in later Stuart England', in D. Ormrod and M. North (eds), *Art Markets in Europe, 1400-1800* (Aldershot 1998) 153-63; Crookshank and Glin, *Ireland's Painters*, 51-64.

[14] RDS, minutes, 26 October 1738; BL, Sloane MS 4057, f.68v, J. Copping to H. Sloane, 22 August 1741; A. Crookshank and D. Fitzgerald, Knight of Glin, *The Watercolours of Ireland* (London 1994) 28, 30.

[15] Bodleian, Lister MS 36, ff.57, 182, Sir R. Bulkeley to M. Lister, 22 July 1693, 13 April 1697; *Philosophical Transactions*, xx, 1698, 209-23; K.T. Hoppen, *The Common Scientist in the Seventeenth Century: A Study of the Dublin Philosophical Society*, 1683-1708 (London 1970) 105, 269, n.67; Pollard, *Dictionary of the Dublin Book Trade* (London 2000) 508-9.

[16] BL, Sloane MSS 4036, f.367; 4037, f.9, W. Molyneux to H. Sloane, 13 November 1697, 8 January 1697[8]; Crookshank and Glin, *The Watercolours of Ireland*, 34; Hoppen, *Common Scientist,* 182.

[17] BL, Sloane MS 4041, ff.190-90v, 235, S. Molyneux to H. Sloane, 5 August 1708; W. Dereham

to same, 26 October 1708.

[18] BL, Sloane MS 4057, ff.68-9, J. Copping to Sir H. Sloane, 22 August 1741; C. Dallat, 'Ballycastle's eighteenth-century industries', *The Glynns*, 3 (1975) 7-13.

[19] BL, Sloane MS 4057, ff.109, 117, 130, J. Copping to Sir H. Sloane, 15 February 1741[2]; A. Pope to same, 30 March 1742, 22 May 1742.

[20] BL, Sloane MSS 4052, ff.113, 189; 4054, f.200, T. Adams to H. Sloane, 15 May 1732, 19 September 1732, 14 March 1735[6].

[21] BL, Sloane MS 4042, f.48, Bp. E. Wetenhall to H. Sloane, 27 September 1709.

[22] BL, Sloane MS 4039, f.305, T. Putland to R. Thoresby, 27 November 1696, copied in R. Thoresby to H. Sloane, 7 June 1704. For Thoresby as a collector: P.C.D. Brears, 'Ralph Thoresby, a museum visitor in Stuart England', *Journal of the History of Collections*, i, 1989 213-24; *Musaeum Thoresbyanum* (London 1764).

[23] BL, Sloane MS 4043, f.129, St G. Ashe to H. Sloane, 9 March 1712[13].

[24] A. Maçzack, *Travel in Early Modern Europe* (Cambridge 1995).

[25] PRONI, D 695/226, p.29, S. Waring, tour notebook; NLI, PC 225, D. Molyneux to R. Howard, 20 June 1736; T. Clayton, *The English Print, 1688-1802* (New Haven and London 1997) 45; T. Barnard, *The Grand Figure: the material worlds of Ireland*, forthcoming, ch. 5.

[26] BL, Add. MS 27,951, f.69v, 'Itinerarium Londinense', 1761.

[27] BL, Add. MS 27,951, ff.64-4v, 'Itinerarium Londinense', 1761; cf. *ibid.*, Add. MS ff.93v-94, 'Itinerarium Bristoliense', 1772; J. Byam Shaw, *Paintings by Old Masters at Christ Church, Oxford* (London 1967) 9.

[28] Gloucestershire CRO, D 2525, Bathurst of Cirencester MSS, box 45, will of Henry Bathurst, 24 August 1675; T. Barnard, 'Learning, the learned and literacy in Ireland, 1650-1760', in T. Barnard, D. Ó Cróinín and K. Simms (eds), *'A Miracle of Learning': Studies in Irish manuscripts and learning. Essays in honour of William O'Sullivan* (Aldershot 1998) 207-32.

[29] Southampton Civic Archives, Molyneux MSS, DM 1/2, f.26, J. Keogh to S. Molyneux, 22 December 1707. For Keogh, see Hoppen, *Common Scientist*, 32-3, 155, 194.

[30] Southampton Civic Archives, Molyneux MSS, DM 1/2, ff.25-6, W. Atkins to S. Molyneux, 10 April 1708. On Atkins: T. Barnard, 'Protestants and the Irish language, c.1675-1725', *Journal of Ecclesiastical History*, 44, 1993, 243-72, reprinted in T. Barnard, *Irish Protestant Ascents and Descents* (Dublin 2003) 179-207; Hoppen, *Common Scientist*, 193.

[31] TCD, MUN/P/4/28/42; TCD, MUN/P/4/32/15, bursar's vouchers, *c.*1724, 26 January 1729[30]; E.A. Boran, 'The function of the library in the early seventeenth century', in V. Kinane and A. Walsh (eds), *Essays on the History of Trinity College Library* (Dublin 2000) 39-52; Southampton Civic Archives, Molyneux MSS, D/M 1/3, f.129, S. Molyneux to unknown, 28 February 1712[13]; E. MacLysaght, *Irish Life in the Seventeenth Century* (Shannon 1969, 3rd ed.) 378; E.C. Nelson, 'Botany, medicine and politics in eighteenth-century Dublin and the origin of Irish botanical gardens', *Moorea: the Journal of the Irish Plant Society*, 6, 1987, 34-6. For Gwithers, see Hoppen, *The Common Scientist*, 166, 180-1.

[32] E.J. McParland, *Public Architecture in Ireland, 1680-1760* (New Haven and London 2001) 147; M. Hunter, 'The cabinet institutionalized: the Royal society's "Repository" and its background', and W. Schupbach, 'Some cabinets of curiosities in European academic institutions', in Impey and McGregor (eds), *The Origins of Museums*, 217-30, 231-44.

[33] Loveday, *Diary of a tour in 1732*, 54-5.

[34] NLI, French of Monivea MSS, envelope 6, D. French to R. French, 14 April 1747; NLI, PC

227, Wicklow MSS, R. Howard to H. Howard, 18 September 1707; Bodleian, Smith MS 58, 257, T. Smith to N. Marsh, 4 November 1707; J.K. Bailie, 'Memoir on two large medallion busts which are preserved in the manuscript room of the library of Trinity College, Dublin', *Transactions, Royal Irish Academy*, 22, part 2, 1855, 85-107; J.H. Todd, note in *Proceedings of the Royal Irish Academy*, 2, 27, 1841, 49-52; Crookshank and Webb, *Paintings and Sculpture in Trinity College Dublin*, 132.

[35] *A catalogue of the library of the Honble. Samuel Molyneux, deceas'd* (London 1730); *A Catalogue of the Pitt Collection* (Southampton 1964).

[36] RDS, minutes, s.d. 29 March 1733, 12 December 1734.

[37] RIA, MS 24 E 28, Physico-Historical Society minutes, 15 May 1744.

[38] RIA, MS 24 E 28, Physico-Historical Society minutes, 28 May 1744, 1 October 1744, 1 and 10 June 1747, 6 July 1747, 9 February 1747[8], 19 December 1748.

[39] RIA, 24 E 28, Physico-Historical Society minutes, 1 April 1745, 5 August 1745, 7 December 1747, 7 March 1747[8].

[40] RIA, 24 E 28, Physico-Historical Society minutes, 7 April 1746.

[41] RIA, 24 E 28, Physico-Historical Society minutes, 14 March 1747[8].

[42] RIA, MS 24 K 31, minutes of the Medico-Politico Society, s.d. 22 July 1756, 6 January 1757.

[43] RIA, MS 24 K 31, minutes of the Medico-Politico Society, s.d. 7 December 1756, 7 April 1757, 5 May 1757.

[44] RIA, MS 24 E 5, papers of the Medico-Politico Society, 19 February 1766.

[45] R.B. McDowell, 'The main narrative', in T. O Raifeartaigh (ed.), *The Royal Irish Academy: A Bicentennial History, 1785-1985* (Dublin 1985), 19, 37-41.

[46] G. Boate, *Irelands naturall history* (London 1652), 114; W. Harris, *The antient and present state of the county of Down* (Dublin 1764) xii-xiv.

[47] D.M. Beaumont, *The Gentry of the King's and Queen's Counties: Protestant landed society, 1690-1760*, unpublished Ph.D. thesis, Trinity College Dublin, 2 vols (Dublin 2000), ii, 123-5.

[48] RIA, MS 24 E 28, Physico-Historical Society minutes, 18 May 1747; *ibid.*, MS 24 K 31, minutes of the Medico-Politico Society, s.d. 8 July 1756, 1 September 1757; 'Find of treasure trove, 1665', *Journal of Kildare Archaeological Society*, vii, 1912-14, 189.

[49] BL, Sloane MS 4048, f.209, 'A draught of a copper trumpet found ... Griffinrath, Co. Kildare, by Rev Sankey Winter ... 15 February 1725[6]'.

[50] *Philosophical Transactions*, no. 461, 810, 813.

[51] T. Barnard, 'Art, architecture, artefacts and ascendancy', *Bullán*, 1, 2, 1994, 26.

[52] Printed proposal, *Whereas the Revd. Nicholas Knight, D.D.* (Dublin 1726) 2 (copy in Marsh's Library, Dublin).

[53] BL, Evelyn MSS, C. Monck to J. Evelyn, 29 October 1694; *ibid.*, Sloane MS 4039, f.190, B. Rawdon to H. Sloane, 26 September 1703; E.C. Nelson, 'Sir Arthur Rawdon (1662-1695)', *Proceedings of the Belfast Natural History Society*, 2nd series, x (Belfast 1982).

[54] TCD, St George MSS, photocopy 175a, St G. Ashe to unknown, 18/28 December 1690; W. O'Sullivan, 'Dr John Madden', in Kinane and Walsh (eds), *Essays on the History of Trinity College Library*, 104-115.

[55] BL, Sloane MS 4046, f.132v, S. Haliday to H. Sloane, 13 February 1715[16]. For Sloane's collection: M. M. Archibald, 'Coins and medals', in A. MacGregor (ed.), *Sir Hans Sloane: collector, scientist, antiquary* (London 1994) 150-66.

[56] BL, Sloane MS 4041, ff.10-10v, T. Molyneux to H. Sloane, 7 August 1707; NLI, PC 227, R.

Howard to Hugh Howard, 15 July [1707], 18 September 1707; Southampton City Archives, Molyneux MSS, D/M, 1/3, pp.79-80, S. Molyneux to unknown, 20 December 1712; Hoppen, *The Common Scientist*, 192-3, 195; J. Ingamells, *A Dictionary of British and Irish Travellers in Italy, 1701-1800* (New Haven and London 1997) 376-7.

[57] A. Fountaine, *Numismata Anglo-Saxonica & Anglo-Danica breviter illustrata* (Oxford 1705), now in TCD, pressmark SS b 19; NLI, MS 8390/1, bills of Sir A. Fountaine to R. Mead, 1729; *ibid.*, MS 8390/2, 'Dr Gilbert's memorandum' on coins struck in England.

[58] C. O'Connor, 'The Charlemont House medal cabinet', *Irish Arts Review*, i, 2 (Dublin 1984), 23-7.

[59] TCD, MUN/P/24/18, bursar's vouchers, 20 April 1720. The price of £12 suggested it was large and elaborate.

[60] This piece is discussed in Barnard, *The Grand Figure*, ch. 4.

[61] NLI, PC 227, bill, 1 April 1729.

[62] NLI, PC 227, H. Howard to R. Howard, 2 January 1734[5], 20 November 1735, 4 December 1735.

[63] Barnard, *A New Anatomy*,196-7.

[64] Dublin City Libraries, Gilbert MS 81, abstract of records of St Luke's Guild, 18 October 1733, 21 February 1737[8].

[65] J. Brown, *Kings and Connoisseurs: collecting art in seventeenth-century Europe* (New Haven and London 1995); W. Muensterberger, *Collecting: An Unruly Passion* (Princeton 1994); S.N. Pearce, *On Collecting: an investigation into collecting in the European tradition* (London 1995); Swann, *Curiosities and Texts*.

———

Hugh Lane and mural painting: designs for the Gallery of Modern Art, Dublin

PHILIP McEVANSONEYA

THE CONTROVERSY SURROUNDING THE HOPES OF SIR HUGH LANE (1875-1915) to establish a gallery of modern art in Dublin in the first decade of the twentieth century is well known in outline, as are the problems surrounding the bequest of his collection of paintings.[1] These two areas have somewhat overshadowed Lane's activities as a patron, rather than collector, of art. Lane's relations with the contemporary art world in Britain and Ireland have not yet been discussed in full.[2] This article details one aspect of Lane's involvement with contemporary art, his promotion of mural painting and his abortive project for the mural decoration of the unbuilt gallery of modern art in Dublin designed by Edwin Lutyens. These activities must be seen in the context of the period from about 1880 to 1914 when a limited but important revival of interest in mural painting was taking place in the British Isles, Europe and the United States.[3]

After a short apprenticeship, Lane had set up as an independent art dealer in London by 1898.[4] Lane's early interests and dealing activities are becoming better known, but they seem to have been confined to Old Masters until Lane changed direction after 1901. That is not to say that he abandoned his interest in Old Masters, but rather that a new interest took on increasing, but parallel, importance. He began rapidly, and with the zeal of the convert, to inform himself about contemporary painting and art from the recent past. Although this activity was soon to focus on

1 – *William Walcott, DESIGN FOR A GALLERY OF MODERN ART IN ST STEPHEN'S GREEN WEST, BY SIR EDWIN LUTYENS (1912), watercolour, 25 x 58 cm (courtesy Dublin City Gallery, the Hugh Lane)*

2 – *William Walcott, DESIGN FOR THE GALLERY OF MODERN ART SPANNING THE LIFFEY, BY SIR EDWIN LUTYENS (c.1913), watercolour, 51 x 79 cm (courtesy Dublin City Gallery, the Hugh Lane)*

France, Lane quickly became a key figure in the promotion of recent and contemporary art on both sides of the Irish Sea.

Lane's Irish connections were not close, and it was only in adulthood that he developed an interest in Ireland which was encouraged by his aunt, Lady Gregory, an important figure in the Irish cultural scene. In 1902 Lane conceived the idea of setting up a permanent gallery of modern art in Dublin, feeling that such an institution was essential for the emergence of a distinctive Irish school of painting. This gallery may initially have been envisaged as a collection of Irish and British art, but by 1904 Lane had expanded his ideas to include European art too. Modern continental painting was barely known in Ireland then, so Lane organised a loan exhibition in Dublin in order to introduce it to an Irish audience in anticipation of the establishment of a permanent collection. For the exhibition of November 1904 loans were obtained from the Parisian dealer Paul Durand-Ruel and from the executors of James Staats Forbes, a voracious Scottish collector. Lane visited Durand-Ruel in Paris in September 1904, accompanied by the artist William Orpen, who advised Lane on his selections.[5]

Lane started to collect modern French works, acquiring between 1904 and 1912 a total of fifteen paintings from Durand-Ruel, and more from other sources. These included *Musique aux Tuileries* and *Eva Gonzalès* by Manet, *Les Parapluies* by Renoir, and others by such artists as Monet, Morisot and Pissarro. His intentions in this were to donate the paintings to the modern art gallery to supplement the 200 or so paintings, drawings, watercolours, prints and sculptures he had already given. By 1912 he had acquired the 39 modern works which were later caught up in the dispute over his bequest.[6] As Lane assembled the nucleus of the permanent collection, other exhibitions were held in Dublin in 1905 and Belfast in 1906. The Dublin gallery of modern art opened in temporary premises in 1908. Lane then offered to donate his collection of modern works, mostly French, if a permanent, purpose-built gallery on a prominent site were built 'within the next few years'. Ever ambitious, Lane engaged Lutyens in 1910 to design a gallery for Dublin. It is not known when Lane first met Lutyens, but in 1909-10 Lutyens redesigned the garden at Lane's London home, Lindsey House in Cheyne Walk, Chelsea. Lutyens produced designs for two sites – one on St Stephen's Green in 1912, for which permission was refused, and another for a gallery bridging the River Liffey in 1913 (Plates 1, 2).[7] Lutyens agreed with Lane that he would be remunerated for his design work on the Dublin gallery and its grounds with an Old Master painting. The presence of a work attributed to Poussin in the collection of Lutyens's son, with a provenance from Lane, suggests that this agreement was carried through.[8]

There were political objections to Lane's plans, which thrived in an atmosphere of suspicion of foreign influence, whether of the Anglo-Irish like Lane, or of continental works of art. In addition, Dublin Corporation could not make up its mind to spend the £22,000 required to top up the £23,000 to be raised from public subscription, of which £11,174 had been collected. Having set a final deadline which passed in September 1913 without the commitment he sought being given, Lane withdrew the offer and the paintings, and the project collapsed.[9]

Lane saw the purpose-built gallery not just as a shell to house the collection, but as part of a decorative ensemble. He was determined that the exterior should be a civic adornment, and, it seems, that the design and decoration of the interior should be complementary to the paintings displayed there. Lane claimed that 'a fine building ... is more necessary for Dublin than pictures. It is more than a hundred years since a good piece of architecture has been raised in Ireland'.[10] As regards the interior, Lane decided that the building should have mural paintings – probably in the entrance hall or on a staircase if, as is likely, continental models were being followed – to set the mood and context for the viewer's visit. On the basis of the known chronology of events, Lane must have come up with the idea to install mural paintings when the St Stephen's Green site was under consideration, and carried the idea over when the bridge site was proposed.

Mural painting was undergoing a revival not just in Britain, but across Europe and in American cities in the period between about 1880 and 1914. Lane would have known, or known of, such late nineteenth-century decorative schemes as those in the South Kensington Museum by Frederic Leighton, Edward Poynter and others, or that in the Scottish National Portrait Gallery by William Hole. A number of decorative schemes had been carried out in provincial French museums in the same period, including those by Puvis de Chavannes at Amiens and Rouen. The cities of Boston, Budapest, Oslo, Paris, Stockholm and Vienna all saw the completion of elaborate mural schemes in civic, gallery or museum buildings. These may not all have been known to Lane, who most likely was stimulated by examples from nearer home, such as the schemes in London at the Royal Exchange (begun 1892), Skinners' Hall (1902-9), and the renewed campaign at the Palace of Westminster (1906-27).

It was to the British and European context that Lane looked because there was no living or recent tradition of mural painting in Ireland in the early 1900s, very few projects having been completed after about 1820 owing to the almost total absence of patronage.[11] This may explain why Lane decided not to call on any Irish artists to tackle the projects he had in mind, even though there were one or two he might have contemplated using who had some experience in the field. George (AE) Russell, in addition to being a writer and art critic, was also an artist who had painted mural decorations such as those in the Dublin Theosophical Society Lodge in 1892-93, or those in the Irish Agricultural Organisation Society's headquarters, also in Dublin, in 1906 (now in the National Gallery of Ireland). Lane might also have considered James Ward, the headmaster of the Dublin Metropolitan School of Art since 1907. His main interest was in mural painting, which he introduced into the DMSA curriculum. Ward had assisted both Leighton and Poynter in their decorative works at South Kensington, and later designed a series of historical scenes which, between 1915 and 1919, were painted in spirit fresco in the rotunda of Dublin City Hall in collaboration with his pupils.[12] Lane may have found these artists inadequate in some way for the task in hand, but the process which Lane followed to find suitable artists for his Dublin scheme had the additional benefit of allowing him to increase the prominence of his role in the London art world, where, by 1909, he was already a patron of mural painting.

After his 'conversion', Lane began to develop his profile as a patron and supporter of modern and contemporary art on both sides of the Irish Sea. In London he came into contact with such painters as Augustus John and P.W. Steer, whose work he was soon supplying to the newly established gallery in Johannesburg, along with works by Monet, Sisley, Pissarro, Watts, Millais and Orpen. In 1912 Lane was active in a different area, being one of the first to contribute to the initial financial backing which permitted the Omega Workshops to get off the ground.[13] The first evidence of Lane's personal encouragement of mural painting comes from 1909. In that year he commissioned Augustus John to produce decorative works – on canvas rather than painted directly onto the wall – for the hall of Lindsey House, his London home which was also his showroom. John began work on these *in situ*, but after many delays and arguments with Lane he took the canvases away to his studio at the Chenil Galleries. John continued to work on them intermittently, and although two of the three large canvases were finished, none was ever installed.[14] Of the three, one was eventually obliterated and a replacement designed but not painted; one was partly repainted as *The Mumpers* (1911-13, Detroit Institute of Arts); and the third is *The Lyric Fantasy* (Plate 3). It has been suggested, albeit somewhat casually, that Lane even thought of John as a suitable artist to decorate public buildings in Dublin.[15] This is not credible in the light of Lane's declining enthusiasm for John and his unsuccessful project at Lindsey House.

Lane endeavoured further to enhance his status as an active figure in the contemporary art world when, in 1912, he became associated with a committee chaired by D.S. MacColl, the art critic and, since 1906, Keeper of the Tate Gallery, London, and a prominent supporter of Lane's plans for a gallery of modern art in Dublin.[16] MacColl's committee was formed at the end of 1911 with the complementary aims of promoting mural painting as an art, and of broadening the range of locations in which murals were painted to include schools, factories, hospitals and other public buildings. The committee decided to mount a three-part mural painting exhibition-cum-competition, which was held in the Crosby Hall in Chelsea in the summer of

3 – Augustus John, THE LYRIC FANTASY (begun 1913), oil on canvas, 234 x 470 cm
(courtesy Tate Enterprises © Tate London, 2003)

1912. A similarly orientated exhibition held in the autumn of 1911 at Patrick Geddes' Outlook Tower in Edinburgh may have been influential on MacColl and his colleagues.[17] The aims of these exhibitions can be traced back to the mid-nineteenth century, to the hopes of G.F. Watts, who, through practical example, sought to encourage mural painting among young artists, and to the original phase of mural painting in the Palace of Westminster from the 1840s to 1860s. The most noticeable consequence of this had been the expansion of interest in domestic decorative painting.[18]

On the committee chaired by MacColl, powerful gallery curators and administrators of art education in London joined forces with influential artists. The members included Henry Tonks, Principal of the Slade School of Art; Patrick Geddes (who in 1908 had been one of a small group responsible for saving Crosby Hall and its re-erection in Chelsea); Gerald Moira, Professor of Mural Painting at the Royal College of Art; and A.H. Christie, Art Inspector of the London County Council. The smaller executive committee included Charles Aitken, Director of the Tate Gallery; Gilbert Ramsey, Director of the Whitechapel Art Gallery; the painter John Singer Sargent; the architect and designer W.R. Lethaby, Professor of Design and Ornament at the Royal College of Art and former Principal of the Central School of Arts and Crafts in London; the architect Halsey Ricardo; and the patrons and collectors Sir Edmund and Lady Davis.[19] Interconnections between members of these groups were plentiful and need not be detailed here.

The location may have been coincidental, but Crosby Hall was near to Lane's home and to Chelsea Town Hall, which was then being decorated with murals by

Charles Sims, Mary Sargant Florence, both well known as muralists, George R. Woolway and Frank O. Salisbury. Salisbury had won a competition organised in 1911 by the Chelsea Arts Club for the purpose of finding an artist for that project, Steer, Sargent and the architect E.A. Rickards being the judges.[20]

The first section of the Crosby Hall exhibition was retrospective, being related to earlier projects; the second section gave an overview of recent projects and samples of work; the third was a competition with cash premiums and the possibility of commissions as prizes. Prizes and wall space were offered in a total of nine locations, including the Middlesex Hospital, sponsored by Sir Edmund Davis, two London County Council schools (hence the several LCC representatives on the two committees), and even in the canteen at the Crosse & Blackwell jam and pickle factory. Lane offered three £100 commissions for paintings to decorate his putative Dublin gallery.[21] Lane may have thought that there would be no point in offering such rewards in Dublin, but although entries were pseudonymous, at least one Irish artist participated (see below). Being seen as a sponsor and participant in the enterprise would also have been attractive to Lane, who certainly knew the value of publicity.

A total of 21 entries, all under different pseudonyms, were received for the Dublin element of the exhibition. It is not clear which subjects, if any, were stipulated, but most of the subjects submitted were taken from Irish myths and legends or history (see Appendix).[22] Lane's three prizes were won by Walter Bayes (1869-1956), Principal of the Royal College of Art, a member of the Camden Town and Fitzroy Street groups, and a member of the exhibition committee; Frederick Cayley Robinson (1862-1927), who was soon to become Professor of Figure Composition at Glasgow School of Art;[23] and a much less well-known artist, James Mark Willcox (1888-1932), the only artist with Irish connections who is known to have participated. With one possible exception (see below), none of their designs, nor any of those by other participants, is known to survive. Bayes' design was probably *Deirdre and Naoise*, submitted pseudonymously with a (presumably more finished) detail as by 'Every Cloud Has A Silver Lining'.[24] Robinson was the author of the design *The Coming of St Patrick to Ireland 430 AD* (Plate 4), also submitted with an enlarged detail as by 'Qualis ab Incepto'.[25] Willcox, as 'Corrib', sent a design and detail of *Deirdre Presenting Cuchullin, Born of the God Suel, to her husband Sualtana*.[26]

To the retrospective side of the exhibition Robinson sent under his own name a classical subject, *Aeneas and his Chieftains at the Shrine of Ceres, after the Fall of Troy*. This may have made his pseudonymous competition entry identifiable through stylistic comparison. Other competition entrants though had their eyes focused only on the competitive Irish section, Alfred Cooper sending *Cuchulan at Rosnaill*, and Colin Rae sending *The Meeting of Cuchulan and Emer* (Plates 5, 6).[27] So far as participants in the Dublin competition can be identified, they seem to have represented

4 – Preparatory study for Plate 7, c.1912, charcoal, watercolour, chalks and gouache on paperboard, 61 x 61 cm (courtesy William Morris Gallery, Walthamstow)

a wide variety of artists at vastly different stages in their careers. The presence of Bayes amongst the prize-winners indicates that someone of his stature was pre-pared, when an objective he agreed with was at stake, to participate in an ambitious and therefore potentially embarrassing event.

As it turned out, only one of Lane's prize-winners is known to have received a commission from him, Robinson working up his competition subject *The Coming of St Patrick to Ireland 430 AD* (Plate 4) into a large-scale painting in oil on canvas (Plate 7). The precise chronology of Robinson's works has not been established, but

5 – *Alfred Cooper,*
CUCHULAN AT
ROSNAILL, *design*
submitted to Crosby
Hall competition, 1912

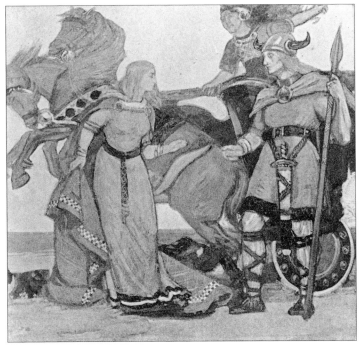

6 – *Colin Rae,* THE
MEETING OF CUCHULAN
AND EMER, *design*
submitted to Crosby
Hall competition, 1912

(both illustrations
reproduced from
THE STUDIO, *56 (August*
1912) 225; copy photo by
Brendan J. Dempsey)

7 – Frederick Cayley Robinson, THE COMING OF ST PATRICK TO IRELAND 430 AD (c.1912-13), oil on canvas, 201 x 191 cm (courtesy Dublin City Gallery, the Hugh Lane)

this large work produced for Lane (which is signed but not dated) must have been completed by September 1913 when Lane effectively cancelled the project to build the gallery in Dublin.[28] This version has not been published before; its origins deserve to be understood and its visual qualities to be discussed.[29] It corresponds closely to the type of work Robinson was producing in the 1910s under the combined influences of Walter Crane (a member of the Crosby Hall exhibition committee), Puvis de Chavannes, and the continental symbolism Robinson had absorbed during two sojourns in Paris from 1892 to 1894, and 1902 to 1906. A period in

8 – Preparatory study for Plate 7, c.1912, tempera on card, 23 x 22 cm
(courtesy Tullie House Museum and Arts Services, Carlisle)

Florence from 1898 to 1902 allowed Robinson to study early Italian artists and their techniques, including that of tempera painting. Like Mary Sargant Florence, who was also on the Crosby Hall committee and sent some examples of her work, but did not, so far as is known, enter any of the competitions there,[30] Robinson was later active in the Society of Mural Decorators and Painters in Tempera.

Robinson's style in about 1912 is characterised by his use of a frieze-like composition with strong verticals, the simplification of forms with clear, almost hard outlines, and Puvis-like, low, chalky tones.[31] Although his style was therefore well adapted to decorative purposes, not being visually strident but encouraging calm reverie, Robinson had not previously carried out any decorative projects.[32] There are two surviving preparatory works. A fairly sketchy work (Plate 8) must represent an early stage in the development of the subject, although the basic compositional schema was already established. A larger and much more highly finished work (Plate 4) is possibly the work shown at Crosby Hall in 1912.[33] Robinson's finished painting (which is in need of restoration) (Plate 7) is close to the latter version, although some changes have been made, notably in the number, position and gestures of the warrior figures. This is especially the case with the figure nearest the centre whose raised open hand registers as a peaceful gesture, in contrast to the prominent sword in the two preparatory works. This interesting late change turned an aggressive and defensive pose into a more welcoming one, perhaps being meant to indicate the future success of St Patrick's mission. The painting shows Irish warriors descending a cliff to investigate the imminent arrival of St Patrick, who stands silhouetted against the sail of a longboat. The use of receding planes, balancing foreground figures on one side and middleground or background figures on the other, replicates the composition of the design of the classical subject mentioned above which Robinson exhibited in 1912. The format and overall composition are comparable to those of a number of his other works, and the motif of interlocking figures arranged vertically was a favourite device.[34]

Although the Crosby Hall exhibition and competition were not seen as completely successful, they did afford an opportunity to focus attention on the prospects for mural painting. The main criticisms levelled at the exhibits were to do with the way in which some contributors had not realised the difference between a permanent mural and a large decorative exhibition picture. Similar criticisms had been made of the Chelsea Town Hall competition at the end of the previous year. Each design, it was stated, needed to be subordinate to its intended location. Divorced from that location, accurate appraisal of the effect of a work was difficult. Some entries were also thought to have failed for lack of human interest and excessive attention to decorative effect.[35]

The exhibition underlined what might be termed the democratisation of mural painting, taking it away from elite spaces such as parliament, guildhalls and town halls, and relocating it in publicly accessible places such as museums, hospitals and schools. This sort of action had been envisaged by Watts in the 1850s when he briefly considered the possibility of decorating the Great Hall at Euston Station with murals in accordance with the hopes of the architect Philip Hardwick, and similar ideas were later promoted by John Ruskin and then by Patrick Geddes.[36] The murals painted by Charles Mahoney at Morley College, London (1928, destroyed) and Brockley School, Kent (1934-36) are later examples which fit into this popularising pattern of murals in institutions associated with education and welfare.[37]

Only one commission, other than those for the Middlesex Hospital and for Dublin, is known to have resulted from the competition and to have been seen through to completion. The prize of a commission offered by Sutton Valence School in Kent was won by George Haghe Day, whose mural *The Mission of St Augustine* (Plate 9), based on his winning design, was painted later in 1912 in the school hall at a cost of £50. The mural was destroyed during modernisation work in 1956-57.[38] The £50 premium for a mural on the theme of the Nativity in the Lady Chapel in St Jude's-on-the-Hill, the newly built church designed by Lutyens in Hampstead Garden Suburb, was won by Mabel Esplin. What work she may have done there is not known. Lutyens is reported to have disapproved of the painted decoration with

9 – George Haghe Day, THE MISSION OF ST AUGUSTINE,
design submitted to Crosby Hall competition. c.1912
(reproduced from THE STUDIO, 56 (August 1912) 225; copy photo by Brendan J. Dempsey)

which the church was smothered by Walter Starmer, beginning in 1912.[39] Other pseudonymous competitors in the St Jude's section included Wooliscroft Rhead (no. 18) and Harry Mileham (no. 35).[40] The £25 prizes offered by the East End LCC schools in Cable Street and Commercial Street were won by Stanley H. North and Louise Jacobs respectively.[41] It has not been ascertained whether any mural paintings were carried out in either school or for the Cass Institute and the Cass Foundation School, which were amongst the organisations and institutions prepared to consider suitable designs.[42]

The Crosby Hall exhibition was but one manifestation of the growing interest which surrounded mural painting in the early twentieth century. It took place in the same year that the Society of Mural Decorators and Painters in Tempera was founded, and concurrently with reforms and innovations within teaching institutions, such as the Slade School's Rome Scholarship in Decorative Painting, first won by Colin Gill in 1913. The RA had inaugurated a competition 'for designs for the decoration of a portion of a public building' in 1881, but this encouragement of mural painting was not mirrored in other art schools until after 1900. During the period of the exhibition, both Walter Crane and Selwyn Image (who was also on the committee) made public speeches encouraging mural painting. Even Randall Davidson, the then Archbishop of Canterbury, joined the debate when he spoke in favour of decorative painting in public buildings at the Royal Academy banquet in 1912.[43]

The outbreak of the First World War did not result in mural painting being completely sidelined, as the murals included in the Arts and Crafts Society's exhibition held at the Royal Academy in 1916 prove.[44] The inter-war period saw a new flourishing of mural painting in private, institutional and commercial locations, which was celebrated in a photographic exhibition held at the Tate Gallery in 1939.[45]

The completion of some mural painting projects became the occasion for the expression of national feeling in the then constituent parts of Britain. Lane may not have been immune to such influences when the selection of the subjects for Dublin was made. Ward's murals in Dublin City Hall have Irish historical subjects; the programmes in the City Chambers of Glasgow and Edinburgh also have nationalistic themes, as does the contemporaneous scheme in the Glyndwr Institute, Machynlleth. Elsewhere, programmes were centred on regional activities, such as the scheme for the Tyne Improvement Commission.[46] It may be that for Lane the choice of St Patrick was not likely to be controversial, the saint being a pre-Reformation figure and the patron saint of Ireland, although it should be remembered that the competition took place when Irish Home Rule was again at the top of the political agenda. Lane's circle of friends associated with the Celtic Revival may well have encouraged him to consider Irish mythological subjects, but the identity of any other subjects, suggested or agreed, is not known.

If we accept the subject matter submitted to the Dublin section of the competition as indicative of what would have been included in the gallery mural scheme proper, it might be thought that Lane was trying to reconcile opposing views of what the modern school of Irish art should be. In 1903, at the time of Lane's first proposal to establish a modern art gallery, opinions were divided between those who saw the occasion as an opportunity for Ireland to integrate itself into a European stream of activity and those who thought that modern Irish art ought to refer to national art traditions. One proponent of the latter view, the Dublin entrepreneur and newspaper owner William Murphy, was explicit in promoting introspection:

> The stones of our Celtic legend and Celtic song, the dark but sometimes lightsome pages of the history of our country afford many subjects for the brushes of skilful painters ... We believe that what Ireland needs for the creation of a genuine school of native art is not the wholesale importation of works of alien painters, but the development of Irish artistic taste and skill on distinctly Celtic lines.[47]

Murphy's fear was that Lane would introduce paintings by the modern British school rather than by continental avant-garde artists (of whom in any case Lane in 1903 had only limited awareness). Lane's commission to Robinson seems to have sought a middle way by allying a traditional subject with an appropriate, understated, but fairly modern style. The opposition received from Murphy and others did not stop the establishment of the Municipal Gallery of Modern Art, but it did block Lane's plans for a purpose-built gallery designed by Lutyens and decorated by a group of able artists. Their opposition helped to keep the gallery in unsuitable accommodation until it moved to Charlemont House in 1933. However, it is possible that Murphy and his partisans inadvertently did the Municipal Gallery a very good turn: the bridge site would have made an attractive and vulnerable target at the time of the Easter Rising or in the Civil War.

Lane was ultimately unsuccessful in that his plans were never realised, although that failure was for reasons completely beyond his control. However, it cannot be denied that his plans indicate the prestige associated with mural decoration, the cachet of which Lane wanted to bring to Ireland.

———

APPENDIX

List of entries to the Dublin section of the Crosby Hall exhibition, 1912. (The identifications are based on information cited in notes 24 and 27 below.)

Competition II: Dublin (nos 23-25, 27-33, 139-48)

23	The Coming of St Patrick	Qualis ab Incepto	[F.C. Robinson]
24	Three Shouts of the sons of Tuirean	Paint Bender	[John M.B. Benson]
25	detail of above	Paintbender	
27	The Wooing of Emer, and enlarged detail	Emot	[William Wildman]
28	Irish Linen, and detail	Vieux Jeu	
29	Meeting of Cuchullin and Emer three designs and one full-size detail	Celt 1, 2, 3	[Alfred Cooper, H.B. Wright, Colin Rae]
30	Deirdre and Naoise, and detail	Every Cloud has a Silver Lining	[Walter Bayes]
31	One of the Four Seasons, and detail	Know Thyself	
32	Finn at the Well of Wisdom, and detail	King Arthur	
33	Deirdre presenting Cuchullin Born of the god Suel, to her Husband Sualtana, and detail	Corrib	[J.M. Willcox]
139	Meeting of Naoise and Deirdre, and detail	Ich Dien	
140	Finding of Oisin, and detail	Shamus	
141	Deirdre and Naoise Fate of the Sons of Usnach, and detail	Live and Learn	
142	Cuchullin, and detail	Belvedere	
143	The Coming of Tuatha de Danann, and detail	Celt	
144	Finn Macoul Making Lough Reagh, and two details	Base	
145	The Three Ages of Man, and detail	Childhood	
146	The Three Ages of Man, and detail	Old Age	
147	Meeting of Cathbad and Nessa, and detail	Franklin	
148	Design	Ern [sic]	

ACKNOWLEDGEMENTS

I am most grateful to Dr Clare Willsdon for her help in the preparation of this article, and for kindly bringing to my attention material in the Tate Gallery Archives and amongst the Geddes Papers at the University of Strathclyde, which material is cited by permission. My thanks also to Dr Nicola Gordon Bowe; Dr Edward McParland; Mike Thornton, Derby Local Studies Library; Norah C. Gillow, William Morris Gallery; Melanie Gardner, Tullie House, Carlisle (Carlisle City Art Gallery); Christina Kennedy and Liz Forster, Dublin City Gallery, the Hugh Lane; Colin Shaw, Sutton Valence School; and Stephen Freeth, Guildhall Library.

ENDNOTES

[1] Recently summarised by Barbara Dawson, 'Hugh Lane and the origins of the collection', in Elizabeth Mayes and Paula Murphy (eds), *Images and Insights* (Dublin 1993) 13-31, with details of the 1993 loan agreement between the National Gallery, London, and Dublin City Gallery, the Hugh Lane. For Lane's biography see Lady Gregory, *Hugh Lane's Life and Achievement, with Some Account of the Dublin Galleries* (London 1921), reprinted with a fore-word by James White as *Sir Hugh Lane, His Life and Legacy*; The Coole Edition of the Works of Lady Gregory, 10 (Gerrard's Cross 1973), and Robert O'Byrne, *Hugh Lane 1875-1915* (Dublin 2000). See also Jeanne Sheehy, *The Rediscovery of Ireland's Past, the Celtic Revival 1830-1930* (London 1980) 107-19, and Bruce Arnold, *Orpen, Mirror to an Age* (London 1981) 134-46 and *passim*.

[2] James White, 'Sir Hugh Lane as a Collector', *Apollo*, xcix, February 1974, 112-25, deals with Lane's donations of Old Masters to the National Gallery of Ireland. Lane's relations with con-temporary artists are touched on by Gregory, *Sir Hugh Lane*; Arnold, *Orpen*; John O'Grady, *The Life and Work of Sarah Purser* (Dublin 1996) 108-15 and *passim*, and most recently by O'Byrne, *Hugh Lane*.

[3] Clare A.P. Willsdon, *Mural Painting in Britain 1840-1940* (Oxford, 2000) is the definitive overview the topic has until now lacked.

[4] See Gregory, *Sir Hugh Lane*, and O'Byrne, *Hugh Lane*, for Lane's career.

[5] Arnold, *Orpen*, 143.

[6] Dawson, 'Hugh Lane', 27-9, 32. Lane's interest in Impressionism is contextualised by John House, 'Modern French Art for the Nation: Samuel Courtauld's Collection and Patronage in Context', *Impressionism for England, Samuel Courtauld as Patron and Collector*, exhibition catalogue, Courtauld Galleries (New Haven and London 1994) 9-33; Caroline Durand-Ruel Godfroy, 'Durand-Ruel's Influence on the Impressionist Collections of European Museums', and Christopher Lloyd, 'Britain and the Impressionists', both in Anne Dumas and Michael E. Shapiro (eds), *Impressionism, Paintings Collected by European Museums*, exhibition cata-logue, High Museum of Art, Atlanta (New York 1999) 29-38, 65-76.

[7] Jane Brown, *Lutyens and the Edwardians: an English Architect and his Clients* (London 1996) 145-58. Both were also involved in the founding of the Johannesburg Art Gallery, Lane as the chief supplier of paintings, and Lutyens as architect: Marybeth McTeague, 'The Johannesburg Art Gallery: Lutyens, Lane and Lady Phillips', *International Journal of Museum Management and Curatorship*, 3, 2, June 1984, 139-52. See also Michael Stevenson, 'History of the

Collection', in Hans Fransen (ed.), *Michaelis Collection: The Old Town House, Cape Town* (Zwolle 1997) 29-43.

[8]   Gregory, *Sir Hugh Lane*, 87; Mary Lutyens, *Edwin Lutyens by his Daughter* (London 1980; revised ed. 1991) 159, mentions 'some pictures' given to Lutyens by Lane in payment; Anthony Blunt, *The Paintings of Nicolas Poussin, a Critical Catalogue* (London 1966) 144, no. 210c, *Landscape with a Roman road*. See also O'Byrne, *Hugh Lane*, 120.

[9]   For a recent account of these events set in the context of Corporation politics, see Sheila Carden, 'Alderman Tom Kelly and the Municipal Gallery', *Dublin Historical Record*, liv. no. 2, 2001, 116-38.

[10]   Gregory, *Sir Hugh Lane*, 88.

[11]   Seán P. Popplewell, 'Domestic Decorative Painting in Ireland: 1720-1820', *Studies*, 68, spring-summer 1979, 46-65.

[12]   Nicola Gordon Bowe and Elizabeth Cumming, *The Arts and Crafts Movements in Dublin and Edinburgh 1885-1925* (Dublin 1998) 14-15, pl. 1; 185-8, nos 178-80; Philip McEvansoneya, 'History, Politics and Decorative Painting: James Ward's Murals in Dublin City Hall', *Irish Arts Review Yearbook 1999*, 15 (Dublin 1998) 142-7.

[13]   Judith Collins, *The Omega Workshops* (London 1983; reprinted 1984) 34.

[14]   Adrian Jenkins, *Augustus John: Studies for Compositions*, exhibition catalogue, National Museum of Wales (Cardiff 1978), nos 104-13; Lisa Tickner, *Modern Life and Modern Subjects, British Art in the Early Twentieth Century* (New Haven and London 2000) 70, 248-9, notes 72, 74.

[15]   William Rothenstein, *Men and Memories. Recollections of William Rothenstein 1900-1922* (London 1932) 144-5.

[16]   D.S. MacColl, 'A Modern Gallery in Dublin', *Saturday Review*, 98, 1 October 1904, 696-7, and 'Lessons from Dublin', *Saturday Review*, 105, 3 December 1908, 168-9.

[17]   Geddes' exhibition of 1911 is referred to in a circular for the Crosby Hall exhibition, as are Watts' earlier ambitions: *Exhibition of Designs for Mural Painting for the Decoration of Schools & other Institutions* (place and date of publication not given), the first of at least two editions, copy amongst the Geddes Papers, University of Strathclyde Archives, T-GED 5/3/22. The 1911 exhibition is also referred to in an unidentified newspaper clipping dated 30 November 1911: Geddes Papers, T-GED 5/4/24. 'Designs for Mural Painting – a Competitive Exhibition', *The Times*, 5 February 1912, 11.

[18]   See Helen Smith, *Decorative Painting in the Domestic Interior in England and Wales, c.1850-1890* (New York 1984).

[19]   *Exhibition of Designs for Mural Painting and for the Decoration of Schools and other Buildings* (place and date of publication not given [London 1912]) 3-4. Plans by the London County Council around 1912, and again in the early 1920s, for mural schemes in County Hall which was then being built eventually came to nothing: Hermione Hobhouse (ed.), *County Hall*, Survey of London Monograph, 17 (London 1991) 57, 65-7.

[20]   'Decoration of Chelsea Town Hall: Competition for Panel Designs', *The Times*, 5 May 1911, 11 (which erroneously referred to a 'Miss G. Woolway'); Tom Cross, *Artists and Bohemians. 100 years with the Chelsea Arts Club* (London 1992) 42. According to Salisbury's *Sarum Chase, New and Enlarged Edition of Portrait and Pageant* (London 1953) 29, the Chelsea Town Hall project was paid for by Lane. Whilst it was paid for by donations from prominent Chelsea individuals (Willsdon, *Mural Painting*, 187), no corroboration of Lane's involvement

DESIGNS FOR THE GALLERY OF MODERN ART, DUBLIN

has been found. Since Salisbury mistakenly says Lane died aboard the Titanic rather than the Lusitania, his claim may be unreliable. The Chelsea Town Hall project was briefly controversial owing to the inclusion in one panel of a likeness of Oscar Wilde.

[21] It is not absolutely clear whether the three sums of £100 offered by Lane were in fact prizes for the works themselves or the fees for commissions to be given to the three selected artists. The entry in *Exhibition of Designs*, 14, is ambiguous: Lane offers '£100 each for the execution of three panels from designs to be approved by him...' and the journalistic reports do not clarify this detail.

[22] *Exhibition of Designs*, Competition II, 6-7, nos 23-25, 27-33; 19, nos 139-48. It has not been possible to locate a full set of the circulars and supplements issued in promotion of the exhibition. *A Supplement to Final Circular for Competitors* exists specifying the details for 'Competition No I', the proposed murals at the Middlesex Hospital, which gives guidance on subject matter: Geddes Papers, University of Strathclyde Archives, T-GED 5/3/22. Perhaps the location in Dublin was sufficient guidance to participating artists.

[23] Robinson eventually carried out all the Middlesex Hospital murals too (on which see Alan Powers, 'Public Places and Private Faces – Narrative and Romanticism in English Mural Painting 1900-1935', in John Christian (ed.), *The Last Romantics, The Romantic Tradition in British Art, Burne-Jones to Stanley Spencer*, exhibition catalogue, Barbican Art Gallery (London 1989) 65, 68-9), although a £50 premium was awarded to Donald McClaren for his designs in this section of the competition: 'Designs for School Decoration', *The Times*, 19 June 1912, 15.

[24] Bayes' name is written next to this entry in a copy of *Exhibition of Designs*, 7, no. 30, in the Tate Gallery Archive, TG92/42/5, in which a partial list of prize-winners is also given. I can find no corroboration for O'Byrne, *Hugh Lane*, 171, who says, without giving a source, that Bayes' entry was *Irish linen* (no. 28, as by 'Vieux Jeu').

[25] Robinson is identified in *Exhibition of Designs*, 26, no. 23, copy in the Tate Gallery Archive, TG92/42/5.

[26] According to annotations on copies of *Exhibition of Designs*, 7, no. 33, in the Tate Gallery Archive, TG92/42/3 and /5. Willcox had Irish connections and may have been Irish. On the cover of the first cited copy of the catalogue appears the annotation: 'J.M. Willcox Lisnabruicka [?] Recess Co. Galway. Good. "Corrib". Sir H. Lane's Prize'. James Wilcox [sic] was a signatory in 1917 to a petition for the return of the Lane pictures (Gregory, *Sir Hugh Lane*, 309). James M. Willcox of Recess, county Galway sent a work to the Royal Hibernian Academy annual exhibition in 1918, no. 37, *A Connemara girl*, priced at £50. He was a member of the Society of Dublin Painters in 1920 (S.B. Kennedy, *Irish Art and Modernism 1880-1950* (Belfast 1991) 20, 368). As well as historical and genre subjects, he painted portraits, such as that of Nathaniel Hone the younger, *c*.1915-6, sold by James Adam of Dublin, 25 March 1998, lot 82, catalogued as by James M. Wilcox [sic].

[27] Robinson's *Aeneas* design (unlocated) is reproduced in *The Studio*, 56, August 1912, 226. A mural of this subject by Robinson was painted for Heanor Grammar School (now South East Derbyshire College), *c*.1919 (Willsdon, *Mural Painting*, 399). The works by Rae and Cooper were submitted with a third by H.B. Wright; see Appendix. This identification is made in 'Crosby Hall Exhibition of Mural Paintings and Decorations', *Building News*, cii, 7 June 1912, 797.

[28] Gregory, *Sir Hugh Lane*, 263, Appendix II: Gifts and Bequests to the Dublin Municipal

Gallery. The painting was accessioned at an unrecorded date in 1913 (gallery files). Robinson's participation in the Crosby Hall exhibition is misdated by Mary-Anne Stevens, 'Frederick Cayley Robinson', *Connoisseur*, 196, September 1977, 28, and in *Frederick Cayley Robinson ARA 1862-1927*, exhibition catalogue, Fine Art Society (London 1977) chronology (n.p.).

29 Kenneth McConkey, *A Free Spirit, Irish Art 1860-1960* (Woodbridge and London 1990) 46, reproduced the second preparatory work (Plate 4) rather than the finished work in Dublin (Plate 7).

30 *Exhibition of Designs*, 5, no. 1; 6, no. 14.

31 These qualities are also to be found in the four panels of modern subjects he painted in the entrance hall of the Middlesex Hospital in 1915-20: see *The Studio*, 65, August 1915, 181, 185; Powers, 'Public Places', 68-9, and Willsdon, *Mural Painting*, 290-92.

32 An annotation to a copy of *Exhibition of Designs*, 7, Tate Gallery Archive, TG92/42/5, notes 'Cayley Robinson colour scheme unfit'.

33 This version was reproduced in colour in *The Studio*, 62, August 1914, opposite 176. The signature it now bears is not apparent in that reproduction, and so must have been added after 1914.

34 This device can be seen in *Taking in Ballast*, *The Inland Sea* and *Souvenir of Claude Lorrain* (all untraced), reproduced in *The Studio*, 31, 1904, 241; *The Studio*, 83, 1922, 295, and Stevens, 'Frederick Cayley Robinson', 27.

35 'Chelsea Town Hall, Novel Scheme of Decoration', *The Times*, 9 December 1911, 6; 'Mural Decoration: Exhibition at Crosby Hall', *The Times*, 4 June 1912, 12; 'Studio-Talk', *The Studio*, 56, July 1912, 146, 149.

36 Willsdon, *Mural Painting*, 4, 311, 359, 364 (Euston); 50-1, 380-1 (Ruskin); 255-7, 282 and *passim* (Geddes).

37 Elizabeth Bulkeley *et al.*, *Charles Mahoney 1903-1968*, exhibition catalogue, Harris Museum and Art Gallery, Preston; Royal Museum and Art Gallery, Canterbury; and Fine Art Society, London (London 2000). Edward Bawden and Eric Ravilious also painted murals at Morley College.

38 'The Mural Painting Exhibition', *The Times*, 29 June 1912, 4, and information from Colin Shaw, the school archivist, to whom I am most grateful. Day's design was reproduced in *The Studio*, 56, August 1912, 225. Day was then the holder of the Royal College of Art travelling studentship in decorative painting: see *The Builder*, cii, 16 February 1912, 172. The mural may be seen *in situ* in a photograph in the school prospectus for 1917, 10.

39 'The Mural Painting Exhibition', *The Times*, 29 June 1912, 4. Christopher Hussey, *The Life of Sir Edwin Lutyens* (London 1950; reprint Woodbridge 1989) 192. It is not known whether Starmer had been a participant at Crosby Hall. A design by E.L.A. Appleby, Jessie Bayes and W.B. Savage for the St Jude's section of the Crosby Hall exhibition is reproduced in *The Studio*, 56, August 1912, 227.

40 These identifications are made in 'Crosby Hall Exhibition of Mural Paintings and Decorations', *Building News*, cii, 7 June 1912, 797.

41 'Designs for School Decoration', *The Times*, 19 June 1912, 15. North's prize-winning St George (no. 34 as 'Boreas') was reproduced in *The Builder*, cii, 16 August 1912, 211. Louise Jacobs as 'Lyon' sent 'Prince John Granting the Commune, 1191' and a detail (no. 84).

42 There are no records of any mural projects in the Cass Foundation's archives. Information from Stephen Freeth, Keeper of Manuscripts at Guildhall Library.

43 John Batten, preface and 'Resolution of the Society of Painters in Tempera', in John Batten

(ed.), *Papers of the Society of Mural Decorators & Painters in Tempera Second Volume 1907-1924* (London 1925) 62; 'Mr Walter Crane on the Revival of Mural Decoration', *Building News*, cii, 14 June 1912, 842; 'Professor Selwyn Image on the Future of Mural Decoration', *Building News*, cii, 21 June 1912, 876; 'Royal Academy Banquet, The Archbishop's Suggestion', *The Times*, 6 May 1912, 10.

[44] Alan Powers, 'Murals of the Arts and Crafts Movement at the 1916 Exhibition', *Craft History*, i, 1988, 23-30; P. Rose, '"It must be done now": the Arts and Crafts Exhibition at Burlington House, 1916', *Journal of the Decorative Arts Society*, 17, 1993, 3-12.

[45] *Mural Painting in Great Britain 1919-1939*, exhibition catalogue, Tate Gallery (London 1939).

[46] *Notes Historical and Descriptive on the Mural Decorations Painted by William Hole RSA in the ... Scottish National Portrait Gallery* (Edinburgh 1902); Gordon Bowe and Cumming, *Arts and Crafts Movements*, 15, 62, pl. xiii; Willsdon, *Mural Painting*, 184-5; 'Studio-Talk', *The Studio*, 61, March 1914, 144-5, John Oxberry, *Mural Decoration in the Frieze in the Boardroom of the Tyne Improvement Commission* (n.p. 1927), copy in Tate Gallery Archive, TG92/42/3.

[47] *Irish Daily Independent*, 16 January 1903. I owe this reference to Marta Herrero. Murphy was an early and enduring critic of Lane's plans: see O'Byrne, *Hugh Lane*, 176-7, 182-5, and Carden, 'Alderman Tom Kelly'.

1 – Float Station, Cavan branch (Street to Cavan)
(all photos by the authors)

The railway stations of
George Wilkinson

MICHAEL GOULD AND RONALD COX

C HRISTIAN BARMAN HAS SUGGESTED THAT 'THE AGE OF ... RAILWAY BUILDING IS not the only episode in the architectural history of the world that the historians have neglected, but it certainly is among the most important of them.'[1] The architect George Wilkinson (c 1814-1890) is best remembered for the design of the Irish workhouses. However, after he left the employ of the Poor Law Board in or around the end of 1854, and prior to taking up his duties as architect to the Board of Control for Lunatic Asylums in early 1860, he undertook private commissions, including work for a number of railway companies, but especially for the Midland Great Western Railway (MGWR). Until now this aspect of Wilkinson's work has been largely ignored. This article considers the buildings designed by Wilkinson for the railway companies, looking in turn at his mainline stations, the smaller intermediate stations, a number of extensions to existing stations, and finally some railway cottages.

DESIGN CONCEPTS

The railway stations designed by George Wilkinson are relatively uncomplicated in style. On the great majority he used a hipped roof, with a modest overhang at the wall. Windows, smaller on the upper floor, are rectangular, often four-pane, initially with a horizontal head, but later with a shallow-arched head. There was little in the way of architectural detailing, although he usually used dressed-stone quoins and window and door surrounds. The style has been described as 'Italianate', but some of his rural stations look more like country houses or rectories than industrial buildings.

Carrick-on-Shannon is representative of a Wilkinson country station (Plate 2). On one platform there is a station house, with a short veranda in front and a single-storey outshot (or projection) at one end. At some stations there was a separate goods shed, and at intervals along the line there were water tanks – usually raised on a tower – for the filling of the locomotive's tender. The other two elements of the station complex, the signal box and the cross-the-line footbridge, were normally of a standard pattern and were not designed by the architect to the railway company.

Station houses were a common feature of small country stations. The offices for tickets and parcels were built either within the overall structure of the house (the house normally being the larger part) or as an appendage.[2] Wilkinson favoured the incorporation of the offices within the overall structure. He liked to build in stone, and his workhouses were built in stone quarried as closely as practicable to the site. In the second half of his book on the practical geology of Ireland, he discusses all of the sources of stone used for workhouse construction, but also comments unfavourably on the quality of Irish brick.[3] It is therefore no surprise to find him using stone as the building material for his stations, including the goods shed and water-tank support.

It is possible that Wilkinson's rather plain designs may have reflected his lack of formal training.[4] On the other hand, two factors taken into account whenever he was employed to design the Irish workhouses were the low cost of his work and his ability to build to his estimate.[5] Such factors would have been equally important to the impecunious smaller Irish railway companies. The railway companies also had to decide whether to build in a majestic style, designed to impress the public of their power and strength, or in a semi-domestic style, designed to show that the railway was something more human and not an object of terror. Rural Ireland, not used in the 1850s to high technology, would seem not to have been a fitting place for intimidating majestic railway-station architecture.

The plain style of Wilkinson's country stations such as Carrick-on-Shannon may, however, be contrasted with those nearby at Moate and Killucan, attributed to John Skipton Mulvany (1813-1871).[6] Killucan has been demolished, but Moate, constructed in brick with stone dressings and now used as a house, is in a single-storey pavilion style. The gabled pavilions are finished with sash windows under a relieving arch, while the roof is carried forward between the pavilions to provide a shelter for waiting passengers. This style of station was quite popular in England at the time.

On the line between Mullingar and Athlone were two other stations – at Streamstown and Castletown Geoghegan. These presumably formed another pair, but again the former is demolished, while the latter is now a house. Castletown, constructed of dashed walls with stone dressings, has three forward-projecting gables, again with relieving arches like Moate, and it is likely that Mulvany also designed these.

MAINLINE STATIONS

George Wilkinson designed four large mainline stations, each to a different design, these being at Mullingar, Athlone, Harcourt Street in Dublin, and Sligo.

Mullingar (1856)

Mullingar, on the original MGWR main line from Dublin to Galway, was initially provided with 'an inconvenient accumulation of temporary arrangements'.[7] In 1856, with work then in progress on the extension to Sligo that branched from the main Galway line at Mullingar, the decision was taken to erect a more appropriate station there, and Wilkinson was given the commission. The new structure, which is still in use, has been described as 'the quirkiest nineteenth-century station in Ireland',[8] although Williams incorrectly dates it to about 1850 and attributes it to Mulvany. The building was bow-fronted into the internal apex of the V formed by the two diverging railway lines. The front windows were those of the refreshment room, and the various offices were arranged behind (Plate 4). The main entrance from the road had an appearance resembling an oriental temple, with a porch finished as an inverted V at roof level, with two supporting pillars and a downward curved crossbeam at eaves level. However, as the approach to it is flanked by the back wall (plain between pilasters) of the platform veranda on the left, and the blind arches (picked out in red stone) of the goods shed on the right, the effect is somewhat marred.

Wilkinson provided long verandas to the platforms, supported on solid walls at the rear, and on a row of cast-iron columns (one of which has the casting mark of I.S. Dawson & Sons Founders Dublin) set back from the front edge of the platform so as not to impede the opening of the doors of the carriages. The verandas had hipped roofs in slate and pierced wooden valances – an anti-drip feature. These were provided on both the up and down platforms on the line to Galway (currently not in use) and on the platform to Sligo. The veranda on the present Dublin platform, which is not in line with that opposite on the Sligo platform, is not shown on Byrne's survey of 1864,[9] and was added later; here the casting mark reads T Grendon & Cº Drogheda 1882. A nice touch is the way in which Wilkinson carried the end walls of the refreshment room half way across the verandas, allowing the exit doors to open directly under the protection of these verandas.

The bow-front of Wilkinson's refreshment room is shielded by a signal box, a feature he is unlikely to have asked for; whether this is a later addition or a carry-over from the older station is not clear. (Byrne's survey appears not to show it.) For some years there was a small single-stem metal water tower at the end of the platform, but this has been removed. (There is another at the Galway end of the unused platform.)

*2 – Carrick-on-Shannon
Station (the goods shed is out
of the picture to the right)*

*3 – The impressive entrance
to Harcourt Street Station,
Dublin*

opposite

*4 – Mullingar Station.
All three original verandas
can be seen (the signal box is
out of the picture the left)*

5 – Athlone East Station

Athlone (1858)

When the mainline of the MGWR was opened in 1851 from Mullingar to Athlone, it crossed to the west bank of the River Shannon to a large two-storey station designed by Mulvany, then architect to the company. The Great Southern and Western Railway (GSWR) built a branch line from near Portarlington on their main Dublin-Cork line. By 1854 the branch line had reached Tullamore. This was completed via Clara to Athlone, and Wilkinson was appointed to design a new station on the east bank of the river to serve the branch. The building, opened in 1860, has been described as an 'elegantly simple Italianate block with wide-hipped roof and over-sailing bracketed eaves ... flanked each side by single storey single-bay wings with shallow hipped roof', while the entrance was set behind 'a charming recessed loggia of three arches'.[10]

Following a rearrangement of rail services, Athlone West station was closed in 1985 and converted to offices, whilst Wilkinson's Athlone East station was given a new lease of life. One consequence has been the addition of 'Iarnród Éireann' in large letters above the loggia, although, as this is formed of single, open letters without a backing board, the sign is not as intrusive as it might have been (Plate 5). A single-storey circulation area, formed largely of glass, was also added, and this now masks the original platform elevation.

Harcourt Street, Dublin (1859)

The Dublin Wicklow and Wexford Railway (DWWR) opened to a temporary terminus at Harcourt Road in 1854, pending the construction of a bridge over the Grand Canal.[11] Wilkinson was appointed in 1858 to design a permanent terminal station. Although the new building was to be a 'less expensive and pretentious building' than the Dublin termini of the other railways,[12] many consider this to have been Wilkinson's best work, described recently as 'an exceptionally good piece of early railway architecture'.[13] In 1859 a writer in *The Dublin Builder* called the station 'the new pile of building' (although the term 'pile' was often used to mean one of irregular plan), but ended by saying 'it forms an important addition to the street architecture of this section of the city'.[14]

The frontage of Harcourt Street station extends for a length of 128ft 10in and reaches a height of 42ft. The entrance, 38ft by 25ft, on a plinth of steps and flanked by two colonnades of columns, led to two distinct flights of steps, 11ft wide, 'conducting first, second and third class passengers respectively to the platforms' (Plate 3).[15] Williams calls the design 'a successful adaptation of monumental Roman Baroque', whilst 'the harmony between its rubble calp (limestone), brown brick and dressed granite' has also been praised.[16]

Since the railway at Harcourt Street was at a higher level than the road (having had to cross over the Grand Canal), the building has a lower level of arched vaults under the platform. The line from Shanganagh Junction, near Bray, to Harcourt Street was closed in 1959. The vaulted area served originally as a bonded spirit store, but now serves as a wine store.

Sligo (1863)

Williams incorrectly dates the station at Sligo to about 1850, and attributes it to Mulvany.[17] However, the line from Mullingar, which opened in stages, was not opened throughout until 1862.[18] George Wilkinson was the architect for the stations and goods sheds, while the contractor for Sligo station and eight others along the line was Messrs Crowe Bros. Sligo station was still being built in 1863,[19] it being noted that it was fast approaching completion in July, and that 'it will be a handsome structure gas lit by Edmundson & Co. of Dublin'.[20] The station building at Sligo was 80ft by 30ft, being of 'plain rough hammered limestone with Portland cement cornices and dressings'. The building suffered severely during the Civil War, and the offices were rebuilt in 1928. The most spectacular architecture to survive is 'the massive windowless retaining wall, articulated by battered pilasters with a sense of the colossal'.[21] Wilkinson's original design also incorporated sheds, a carpenters' shop, smithy, and an 800ft long goods shed.

COUNTRY STATIONS

Small stations

Shepherd[22] has noted that, in December 1855, the Board of the MGWR received drawings from Wilkinson for Float and Crossdoney, the smaller stations on the Cavan branch. This branch commenced at Inny junction on the line to Sligo, where there was, apparently, also a station house, offices and water tower arranged into the V of land between the two lines of rail. Further plans for Float were received in April 1856, the platform being reduced to 200ft in length. The building, now a house, is typical of Wilkinson with its two-storey hipped-roof station house of three bays, and rectangular windows. There is one chimney stack, and small extensions to one side on the platform face, probably to provide access to the station house, and to the back, possibly covering the kitchen area. At the other side, on the platform face, are other entrances, presumably originally to privies, although one may have been to

6 – Clara Station
Note the horizontal window
heads, short veranda, and
outshot to the right

7 – Float Station, Cavan
branch (Street to Cavan)

opposite

8 – Longford Station
Note the extended veranda
and Z-shape floor plan

9 – Drumsna Station
Rear view showing door to
the stationhouse; note the
curved window heads

a lamp store. On this size of station there was no veranda, only a simple canopy over the central door into the waiting area (Plates 1, 7).

The design reappears on the main line at Ballysadare, now in ruinous condition, and at Newtownforbes, now used as a house (there are two chimneys and a long extension, perhaps added later). The canopy at Ballysadare was arched. This is seen again at Collooney station, a somewhat larger version of the design with four bays, although a detailed study of the stonework suggests that the original station house was extended at some later date.

In 1860 the DWWR decided to build a station on their line at Foxrock, county Dublin, this being considered a prime area for villa development.[23] A photograph taken just prior to its demolition in 1994 suggests that Wilkinson simply reused here his 'smaller station' design of the Cavan branch.[24]

Other country stations

Wilkinson also designed the larger station for Ballywillan on the Cavan branch. This is similar to his 'smaller station' arrangement, but it has four bays, round-headed windows (smaller to the top floor), and three chimneys. The station still exists as a house, although an unfortunate greenhouse-type porch has been added to the door on the street side. This door gave direct access to the station house. On the platform side, a centrally located door gave access to the waiting room, toilets, and the ticket and parcels offices, all on the ground floor to the left when facing the building.

Wilkinson used this style of station again on the Sligo line, initially with rectangular windows, but later with round-headed windows. The windows to the upper floor were also made somewhat taller. The stations had a slated veranda along the platform frontage, one end of which usually terminated in the single-storey outshot – a feature of many of Wilkinson's stations. The front of the veranda was supported on a row of square columns with a short base plinth. Those built were at Multyfarnham (now a house), Edgeworthstown (built on the edge of the town at the request of the local landowner, and now apparently a favourite of television film crews), Dromod (with an ugly door porch in concrete), Drumsna (now a house), Carrick-on-Shannon (high on the road side, so the door here is omitted), Boyle (handed, i.e. with the platform entrance to the right rather than the left), and Ballymote (no rear door). On the later stations, passenger access was via an opening in a screen wall provided as a stop to the other end of the veranda. The rear view of Drumsna, which is still very much in its original state, is shown (Plate 9).

It has not been recognised until now that Wilkinson must have also designed the other two stations on the Athlone branch from Tullamore. A new station was built there in 1865 (after Wilkinson went to work for the Asylum Board), and its design is quite different. Clara station, opened in 1859, is almost identical to Ballywillan except for the square-headed windows and a shorter veranda that extends only from the central door to the single-storey outshot (Plate 6). No details of the building at Prospect have been located, and this may, in fact, have been only a simple halt.

What is clearly the same design of station occurs again on the Portadown and Dungannon Railway (opened in 1858), and its extension, the Portadown, Dungannon and Omagh Junction Railway (opened in 1861). Here, the buildings are a handed version of the two-storey, four-bay arrangement, the door to the station house being moved one bay to the right. On the platform side there was the short veranda, as seen at Clara, but there was no outshot building and there were only two chimney stacks.

The arrangement of window heads was intermediate between that used at Edgeworthstown and that on the later stations on the Sligo line, with horizontal heads on the ground floor and curved heads on the upper floor. Stations in this lay-out (the line being closed, these are now used as houses) were built at Annaghmore[25] and Moy (later Trew and Moy) on the 1858 line, and at Donaghmore [26] and Beragh on the 1861 line. Another on the latter line, the station at Pomeroy (said to be the highest mainline station in Ireland) was of the smaller three-bay version, but it is the only one located which was gabled rather than hipped. These stations were described as being 'neat and commodious'.[27] Whilst the name of the engineer, George Willoughby Hemans, and that of the contractor, Messrs Gordon of London, was given, the name of the architect was not. Other stations on the line, such as Dungannon, built in 1861 after completion of the approach tunnel, and Vernor's Bridge (1862), as well as a couple of halts, appear to be by a different hand.[28]

The terminus at Cavan, built by the MGWR, but later used also by the Great Northern Railway and subsequently retained by that company until its services from Clones ceased in 1957, appears to be a direct derivative of Wilkinson's 'smaller sta-tion' layout. A central two-storey, three-bay section had extensions built out towards the platform at both ends (two-storey on the side next the town, one-storey by the signal box). The station veranda runs between these two extensions in a style very reminiscent of that used by Francis Thompson on the Chester to Holyhead Railway, a route that Wilkinson probably used when going from Dublin to his birth-place near Oxford.

The remaining station on the Sligo line, Longford, which served for some years as a temporary terminus, is a further modification of the Cavan design. The three-bay main section, with rectangular windows, smaller on the upper floor, had extensions at each end, one towards the road, the other towards the platform, giving

*12 – Ballinasloe Station
The original portion is
marked by the three tall
chimneys*

*13 – Stationmaster's house
near Bray Station*

opposite

*10 – Short goods shed at
Collooney
The station, with its curved
door canopy, may be seen to
the right*

*11 – The colonnaded car-
riage hall at Broadstone
Station,
the most obvious external
feature of Wilkinson's work*

a square Z-shape plan form. At Longford the veranda was carried from the face of this platform wing, along the three-bay section, round the corner, and along the face of the other wing (Plate 8). Passengers dropped by carriage at the entrance would thus have cover to the waiting room, although the front of the veranda would have stopped well short of the railway carriages. There is again a single-storey outshot. It was noted that the MGWR had decided to provide separate accommodation for third-class passengers at Longford, but this was presumably in the main structure. Thus the outshot probably held stores – for example, fuel for the fires and oil for the lamps. There may also have been a separate lamp room.

At certain stations a goods shed was also provided. They appear to have been typical of the genre (internal rail access to one side; road access externally on the other side, with cover formed by cantilevering out the roof), although Wilkinson inserted a semicircular opening in the upper part of the end gables, and a row of round windows on the railway side. What does seem surprising is the range of sizes seen. Cavan terminus had one with six round windows, as did the small wayside station at Ballysadare. Collooney, by contrast, had a short example with only three windows (Plate 10), although here there was also a loading dock which was longer that the station platform.

COSTS

The General Ledger Books of the MGWR for 1854 to 1866, held at the Irish Railway Record Society Archives, record payments made to Wilkinson and to the contractor for work on a number of stations. These are tabulated below:

stations	date	paid to contractor	paid to Wilkinson
Mullingar	14.4.57		£150
	23.9.59		£299 10s
	6.12.60		£17 10s
Mullingar to Longford	30.6.56		£473
	31.12.57		£74 15s
	23.9.59		£24 19s
Longford to Sligo	30.6.64		£1,217 6s
Sligo		£16,151	
Newtownforbes		£1,020	
Drumsna		£2,601	
Dromod		£2,785	

Carrick-on-Shannon		£3,349	
Boyle		£2,532	
Ballymote		£2,180	
Collooney		£1,476	
Ballysadare		£1,809	
Street to Cavan	31.12.57		£60
	23.9.59		£18 4s
Broadstone	10.61	£6,890	£345
Unspecified			c.£1,100

For the design of the extension and refurbishment at Broadstone Station in Dublin, Wilkinson appears to have received a fee of around 5% of the contract sum, although this is difficult to confirm due to some unspecified payments. At Mullingar, his fee at 5% would suggest a contract price of £9,080, whereas Crowe's tender was originally only for £7,240.[29] However, the final sum may well have been nearer to £9,000 allowing for extras. On the other hand, the figures recorded for the Longford to Sligo section indicate that Wilkinson received only a 3½% fee. It would appear, then, that the payments might not necessarily indicate a fixed fee. Similar GSWR General Ledger Books for 1859 to 1861 show that the company paid Wilkinson over £550, and that the payment was made via the company's resident engineer J.J. Bagnell.

EXTENSIONS

George Wilkinson designed significant extensions to three existing stations, these being Ballinasloe (on the main line from Athlone to Galway) and the Dublin terminus stations at Broadstone and at Westland Row.

Ballinasloe (1859)

Rothery[30] and Williams[31] state that Wilkinson designed the station at Ballinasloe, but both are incorrect. This was already a station when the main line opened in the early 1850s; at that time the architect to the MGWR was Mulvany. It was reported late in 1859 that Wilkinson had been briefed 'to extend the handsome railway station at Ballinasloe'.[32] A study of the building, which is still in use, allows the work of the two architects to be clearly delineated (Plate 12).

The central section, with gables visible in the extended roof, is built in snecked limestone, obtained locally, and is described as 'a successful foray in the

197

Tudor style',[33] but as this is not by Wilkinson, the use of the word 'foray' appears inappropriate. Although his workhouses are sometimes described at Tudoresque, or as Tudor-Gothic, none of Wilkinson's known work is in a style which could be properly described as 'Tudor'. Williams describes 'a picturesque massing of steep roofs hipped and gabled against a variety of chimney stacks', but notes that the roof tiles are modern replacements in asbestos cement. There is some attractive detailing around the windows and in the moulding under the eaves, as well as in the stone chimneys, which shows what was achievable in small station design.

This central section represents the original station by Mulvany. To either side may be seen the extensions added by Wilkinson, which are very much in the simplified style used by him on most of his stations. There is a further single-storey outshot to the south. The confusion over architectural attribution probably arose from the way in which the original door, with its inscribed 1851 date and opening onto the platform, has been incorporated into Wilkinson's extension to the north. Unless he relocated the whole door and surround, which seems unlikely as much of his design work seems to have been aimed at keeping costs down, this door must originally have been in the form of a porch. A porch in this position on a railway station would be quite unusual, unless it had served as a special entrance for some local dignitary.

Broadstone, Dublin (1861)

Wilkinson is generally credited with the construction in 1861 of the carriage shelter at Broadstone station. However, it is clear from contemporary descriptions of the work, undertaken by Crowe Bros, that a major reconstruction of the station interior was also undertaken.[34] At this time arrivals and departures took place from different platforms, and the purpose of the reconstruction was to reverse their function in order to eliminate the need for trains to make a potentially dangerous crossing movement at the station entrance. Passengers from Dublin now accessed the departure platform 'by a handsome colonnade, supported with metal pillars and through a spacious ticket-office. On the departure platform will now be found the waiting-rooms and, in an additional storey, the offices of the traffic manager, engineer, and auditor, also spare rooms ... to the number of nine, opening on a corridor 300 feet in length.' The carriage shelter, on the new arrival side, included 'a magnificent colonnade, 50 feet in width 300 feet in length'.[35]

Broadstone station is now used for non-railway purposes, and Wilkinson's 'magnificent colonnade' is crudely closed in (Plate 11). There is, however, in the Lawrence Collection (National Library of Ireland), a fine photograph of the station in its heyday.

Westland Row, Dublin (1862)

On 15 February 1861, *The Dublin Builder* announced that Wilkinson was to design a new front 'of an architectural character' to Westland Row terminus station, utilising the sites of three existing houses in order to face the new front on to Great Brunswick Street (now Pearse Street). In a later issue they had to print a retraction,[36] following questions asked by the railway's shareholders at a general meeting. The newspaper clearly felt somewhat aggrieved, as a notice appeared shortly after this meeting stating that 'Mr. O'Gorman, auctioneer and valuator, begs to inform ... that in consequence of the Dublin and Wicklow Railway Company requiring the premises occupied by him in Westland-Row, for the purposes of altering and extending the terminus, he has removed.'

Nothing more is heard until late in 1862, when the building of an extension was again announced.[37] A contract in the sum of £2,200 was awarded to T. Byrne for approach works to Westland Row, designed by 'Mr Wilkinson, Architect'.[38] No description of the work is given, but it is understood that the site of the various houses fronting Great Brunswick Street was used, not in the construction of a new front, but to provide better access to the station for the post office. The general plan of the extension was designed by William LeFanu, the engineer to the railway company. The English/Irish mails were sent from here by rail to Kingstown (now Dun Laoghaire), where a direct rail connection to Carlisle Pier had been completed by 1859.

RAILWAY COTTAGES

The bulk of Wilkinson's known design work relates to public buildings. However, it was announced in 1859 that he was to build a large house and two cottages (actually semi-detached) adjacent to Bray station for the use of Dublin and Wicklow Railway Company staff.[39] In the following year, it was announced that another two were to be built near Dalkey station.[40] Those at Dalkey are no longer extant, but the houses at Bray are still in use, although extended and no longer owned by the railway. The pair of cottages is very simple in style, with flat-pitch dormers over the first-floor windows. The detached house, apparently provided for the stationmaster, is somewhat grander, with gables to the L-shaped plan and round-headed windows, paired on the gable ends (Plate 13).

It may be noted here that the suggestion made by Garner[41] that Wilkinson designed Bray station itself is unlikely to be correct, as this station opened with the line in 1854.

CONCLUSION

George Wilkinson's railway commissions form a distinct segment of his professional work, although when he applied in 1878 for election to fellowship of the Royal Institute of British Architects, he did not mention on his application form either his workhouses, a very significant contribution to his professional output, or his work for the railway companies.

Many of the buildings he designed remain in use, in many cases still fulfilling their original design function. This is a good indication that, overall, Wilkinson's railway station designs were both sound and functional.

———

ENDNOTES

[1] Christian Barman, *An Introduction to Railway Architecture* (London 1950) 9.
[2] Marcus Binney and David Pearce (eds), *Railway Architecture* (London 1979) 88.
[3] George Wilkinson, *Practical Geology and Ancient Architecture of Ireland* (London 1845) *passim*.
[4] Andrew Saint, 'Three Oxford Architects', *Oxoniensia*, xxxv, 1970, 56.
[5] Michael H.Gould, *George Wilkinson and the Irish Workhouse*, thesis submitted for MPhil degree, The Queen's University of Belfast, 2002.
[6] Christine Casey and Alistair Rowan, *North Leinster: the counties of Longford, Louth, Meath and Westmeath* (London 1993) 74.
[7] Ernie Shepherd, *The Midland Great Western Railway of Ireland* (Leicester 1994) 21.
[8] Jeremy Williams, *A Companion Guide to Architecture in Ireland 1837-1921* (Dublin 1994) 372.
[9] Shepherd, *Midland Great Western Railway of Ireland*, 16.
[10] Casey and Rowan, *North Leinster*, 136.
[11] Fergus Mulligan, *One hundred years of Irish railways* (Belfast 1983) 30.
[12] *The Building News*, 26 February 1858, 214.
[13] Michael Morris Killanin and Michael Vincent Duignan, *Shell Guide to Ireland* (Dublin 1962) 226.
[14] *The Dublin Builder*, 1 March 1859, 32.
[15] *ibid.*
[16] Maurice Craig, *Dublin 1660-1860* (London 1992) 301.
[17] Williams, *Architecture in Ireland*, 339.
[18] *The Dublin Builder*, 15 December 1862, 325.
[19] *ibid.*, 1 February 1863, 17.
[20] *ibid.*, 15 July 1863, 125.
[21] Williams, *Architecture in Ireland*, 339.
[22] Shepherd, *Midland Great Western Railway of Ireland*, 19.
[23] *The Dublin Builder*, 1 November 1860, 363, 375.

[24] Peter Pearson, *Between the Mountains and the Sea* (Dublin 1998) 284.
[25] Ian McLarnon Sinclair, *Along UTA Lines* (Newtownards 2002) 47.
[26] *ibid.*, 56.
[27] *The Belfast Newsletter*, 3 September 1861.
[28] Sinclair, *Along UTA Lines*, 52, 47.
[29] Shepherd, *Midland Great Western Railway of Ireland*, 15.
[30] Seán Rothery, *Field Guide to Buildings of Ireland* (Dublin 1997) 204.
[31] Williams, *Architecture in Ireland*, 205.
[32] *The Dublin Builder*, 1 December 1859, 164.
[33] Williams, *Architecture in Ireland*, 205.
[34] *The Dublin Builder*, 1 April 1860, 239.
[35] *ibid.*, 1 April 1861, 469.
[36] *ibid.*, 1 May 1861, 498.
[37] *ibid.*, 15 December 1862, 320.
[38] *ibid.*, 15 January 1863, 10.
[39] *ibid.*, 1 November 1859, 147; *Freemans Magazine*, 13 November 1859.
[40] *The Dublin Builder*, 1 November 1860, 352.
[41] William Garner, *Bray – Architectural Heritage* (Dublin 1980) 29.

———

*1 – Rosalba Carriera, PORTRAIT OF GUSTAVUS HAMILTON, 2ND VISCOUNT BOYNE,
c.1730-31, pastel on paper, 56.5 x 42.9 cm*
(courtesy Metropolitan Museum of Modern Art, New York)

The Irish patrons of Rosalba Carriera (1675-1757)

SARAH RHIANNON DRUMM

THIS ARTICLE IS PRIMARILY CONCERNED WITH ESTABLISHING THE IDENTITY OF Rosalba's Irish patrons. Despite the fact that several of them commissioned more than one pastel from Rosalba, only eight Irish pastels survive that can be attributed to her with any certainty. Of the remaining works, the location of six has not been ascertained, and the identity of the sitters in two more has yet to be confirmed.

Rosalba was born in Chioggia, Venice, in October 1675, the daughter of Andrea Carriera, who worked in the mainland *podesteria* of the Republic of Venice, and Alba Foresti, an embroiderer. She had two sisters: Angela, who married the artist Giovanni Antonio Pellegrini (1675-1741), and Giovanna, who worked as an assistant in Rosalba's studio, and, like her, remained unmarried.

Although there are no records relating to her artistic training, Pier Caterino Zeno, along with the anonymous author of *Vita di Rosalba Carriera* (1755), both claimed that she was the pupil of the Venetian portrait painter Giuseppe Diamantini (1621-1705).[1] Pierre Jean Mariette in the *Abecedario* wrote that Rosalba originally painted snuffboxes under the guidance of Jean Steve, a French painter.[2] Blashfield and Dobson stated that Rosalba's paternal grandfather was an artist by the name of Antonio Pasqualini, but there is no documentation to support this.[3]

Rosalba received many honours during her lifetime. In 1705 she was admitted to the Academy of St Luke in Rome, for which her reception piece was *Girl Holding a Dove*. In 1720/21, she was elected to the Académie Royale in Paris, where her *morceau de reception* was *A Nymph*. While in Paris, she executed a pastel portrait of Louis XV as a child. In 1730 she visited Vienna to work for Emperor Charles VI. She received many other royal commissions, and a major collector of her work was the Prince Elector of Saxony, later Augustus III of Poland. By the time of his death he had collected 150 pastels by her.

Rosalba had begun her artistic career by painting miniatures in enamel, but later changed to the larger format of pastel, which was less taxing for her eyes. In the early 1740s her eyesight began to fail, but she continued to work intermittently until she went completely blind in 1746. It was a poignant end to a distinguished career. The influence of Rosalba was keenly felt outside Italy. The English artists Francis Cotes (1726-1770) and John Russell (1745-1806)[4] were both influenced by Rosalba's style, as was Maurice Quentin de la Tour (1704-1788) in France.[5] De la Tour, encouraged by Rosalba's success, made a copy of her *Nymph of Apollo's Retinue*, and from then on pastel became his chosen medium. By 1780 pastels had become so popular that there were more than 2,500 pastellists in the Académie Royale.[6] According to Anthony Pasquin in his book *History of the Professors of Painting, Sculpture and Architecture, who have practised in Ireland* (1796), the Irish artist Hugh Douglas Hamilton (1740-1808) owned several pastels by Carriera, and her influence can be seen in such portraits as *Emilia Olivia, 2nd Duchess of Leinster* (NGI; see Appendix). Pasquin also wrote, without foundation, that Rosalba had visited Ireland. Rosalba's reputation was held in such high regard in Ireland that often pastels were ascribed to her despite lack of evidence, as is the case with the pastels at Carton (see Appendix).

In Venice it became popular with those on the Grand Tour to visit her studio. Irish tourists followed this fashion and sat to her for their portraits or bought pastels by her as a souvenir of their trip. To this end, they often used agents like Joseph Smith (1674-1770) to assist them. Rosalba's godfather Carlo Gabrieli was Smith's lawyer,[7] and she received regular payments from Smith from 1725 to 1728 on behalf of patrons like the Hon Alan Brodrick. Smith eventually owned 38 works by her. Pietro Filippo Jamineau, a merchant in Venice from 1735 to 1745, also occasionally acted as an agent for Rosalba. Another agent was Owen McSwiney, also known as Swiney (1676-1745), son of Rev Miles McSwiney of Ballyteige, county Wexford. From 1721 until his death, McSwiney commissioned and handled paintings for sale in Venice and acted as an agent for such artists as Rosalba and Canaletto.

Rosalba was an incredibly prolific artist, and this is partly due to her chosen medium of pastel. Unlike oil, pastel requires no drying time and works could be completed more rapidly than with the use of other media. Rosalba's huge output raises a problem, however, as she executed many of the same subjects repeatedly – *The Seasons*, or *The Elements*, for example, or portraits of such celebrities as Faustina Bordoni, the distinguished contralto. In her diary for the year 1725, published by Sani,[8] Rosalba mentions four portraits of Faustina. Rosalba also had many followers who used a similar style, and her sister Giovanna sometimes copied her work, leading to difficulty with attributions.

In researching her Irish patrons, Rosalba's diary, kept from 1720 to 1728, and mainly spanning her visit to Paris from 1720 to 1721, provides a useful source of information. The later years have fewer entries, but, importantly, these record the names of her sitters. She also kept both letters she received and rough copies of those she sent. The first Irish man for whom we have any documentary proof of a link with Rosalba is Richard Tighe MP (1678-1736) of Rosanna, county Wicklow (cat. 9). A kinsman of Tighe was the Hon John Molesworth (1679-1726), who was a regular correspondent of Rosalba. Her portraits of Molesworth are known from the existence of copies by Godfrey Kneller and Anthony Lee (cats 7b, 7c). Richard Cantillon (c.1680-1734) had his name recorded in Rosalba's diary and appears to have sat for his portrait (see cat. 2). The portrait of another Irish sitter, the Hon Alan Brodrick (1702-1747), who was mentioned by her several times in 1725, is of interest as he used both McSwiney and Smith as agents in his dealings with her (cat. 1).

Various portraits by Rosalba have given rise to some speculation in relation to the identity of the sitter. Lady Mary Ferrers (1684-1740) sat to Rosalba in around 1729/30; however, the identity of the male pair to her portrait has yet to be confirmed. The portrait of Gustavus Hamilton, 2nd Viscount Boyne (1710-1746) (Metropolitan Museum of Art, New York), was formerly identified as Horace Walpole, and has already been the subject of much discussion (cat. 4) (Plate 1).

The works acquired by Joseph Leeson, later 1st Earl of Milltown (Milltown Collection, NGI) may have been acquired by someone else acting on his behalf, most likely Robert Wood, who in Rome had been responsible for the acquisition of seascapes by Vernet.[9] Although Benedetti states that Robert Wood 'had his portrait made by Rosalba',[10] there is no mention of this in either of Sani's texts.[11] However, it is recorded that in 1742 Wood purchased a number of works from Rosalba, including a *Diana* and a portrait of Flavia Arista, Princess Trivulzi.[12]

Rosalba's Irish patrons are a diverse group, many of them involved in politics but of differing ages and backgrounds. Some of them, discussed in detail in the following catalogue, do not fit the usual profile of a Grand Tourist. John Molesworth, 2nd Viscount Molesworth, worked in Italy, and Joseph Leeson, later 1st Earl of Milltown, was unusually old. If Cantillon's trip was a Grand Tour, then he, like Leeson, was older than the average tourist. Generally those who went on the Grand Tour were young men, probably between the age of 17 and 22, from a wealthy family, who were sent abroad to further their education. The Hon Alan Brodrick fits this profile and his letters reflect the nature of such a trip.[13]

Only two of Rosalba's Irish patrons, Molesworth and Mary, Countess Ferrers (cat. 3) are included by Russell in his list of British sitters for Rosalba.[14] Rosalba's Irish patrons are, however, a separate entity, and although the list is naturally shorter than that of her British sitters, they have considerable interest and importance from an Irish perspective.

CATALOGUE OF WORKS

1   *The Honourable Alan Brodrick (1720-1747)*
Pastel on paper, 53.3 x 40.6 cm
LOCATION: Midleton Collection at Malton, Yorkshire

Brodrick was the oldest surviving son of the 1st Viscount Midleton of Ballyanan, Cork, and Pepper Harrow, Surrey. His mother was Alice, daughter of Sir Peter Courthorpe of Little Island, county Cork. The 1st Viscount Midleton was a Whig politician who was Speaker for the Irish House of Commons, Lord Chancellor, and Attorney General for Ireland. He was an adversary of William 'Speaker' Conolly, and it was Brodrick's enforced resignation that elevated Conolly to the position of Speaker. His father was possibly the Alan Brodrick who kept the cyphers of the group of royalist nobles and gentlemen called 'The Sealed Knot'.[15] It was he who reported to Charles II on the state of politics and the intentions of the army in 1659 and early 1660, prior to the restoration of the monarchy, and was Surveyor General of Ireland from 1660. Brodrick was educated at Clare College, Cambridge, in 1718, and the Inner Temple in 1721. He succeeded his father as 2nd Viscount in 1728, and in 1729 married Lady Mary Capel, daughter of the 2nd Earl of Essex.

On the Grand Tour he sought to broaden his education, and in a letter of 8 November 1724 he wrote to his father:

> Have no reason to be discontented with ... my travels, since I have used my utmost endeavours to improve myself in whatever the place I was in, could inform me of. I have done what has been in my power towards perfecting myself in French, and have learnt as much Italian as the small share of conversation, which strangers can have with the people of the country would admit of.[16]

In 1724 Brodrick is recorded at Venice. He was in Padua on 15 September, in Bologna by 8 November, and in Rome by 1 March 1725. In the same year he visited Naples in March, Parma by 1 June, and was back in Venice during July and August.

During his second visit to Venice, Brodrick was mentioned in Rosalba's diary on several occasions. On 5 July 1725 she wrote: '*Incominciato il ritratto in piccolo di Faustina [Bordoni] per Mr. Brodrier*'.[17] Later, on 28 July, she wrote: '*Incominciato Sig. r Brodrick*'.[18] On 1 August she noted: '*Incominciato ... il Sig. Brodrick*',[19] and on 14 August: '*Avuto da Mr. Suini* [Owen McSwiney] *cinquantaquattro cecchini per li ritratti a Mr. Brodrick*'.[20] On 27 August she wrote: '*Avuto dal Sig. Smith cecchini 44 per li due ritratti piccioli del Sig. B.ro*'.[21] These last two references to Brodrick reveal that he was using two different agents for the purchase of Rosalba's pastels – McSwiney and Smith.

2 – Rosalba Carriera, WINTER, pastel on paper, 34 x 28 cm (detail)
(courtesy National Gallery of Ireland, Milltown Collection)

2   *Richard Cantillon (c.1680-1734)*
     LOCATION: unknown

Richard Cantillon was the second son of Thomas Cantillon of Ballyheigue, county Kerry. His mother was Brigid Cantillon of Kilgobbin, Limerick, a kinswoman of his father. Cantillon was Catholic, and his parents' marriage clashed with the Catholic Church's rules on consanguinity. A special dispensation was made for the couple to allow them to marry. In 1708 Cantillon became a French national, and in 1717 he took over the running of the financial house belonging to his relative, the Chevalier Richard Cantillon in Paris. In 1722 he married Mary Anne O'Mahony (1702-1751), the daughter of Count Daniel O'Mahony, a friend of the Chevalier Cantillon.

Cantillon died in mysterious circumstances in a fire in his house in Albemarle Street, London, on 14 May 1734. It was suggested that he was murdered by his own servants before the fire. However he had previously withdrawn £10,000 from his bank which threw a suspicious light upon the ensuing events. The mystery was further compounded by the discovery of a mysterious Chevalier de Louvigny roaming the jungles of Surinam with a large amount of documentation belonging to Cantillon, six months after the fire.[22] Cantillon's present fame however rests solely on a work published 21 years after his death, *Essai sur la Nature du Commerce en General*. This is considered along with Adam Smith's *Wealth of Nations*, written in 1776, to be an outstanding work on economic theory.[23]

Between 1724 and 1725 Cantillon was in Italy. He visited Venice in December 1724, before travelling to Naples and Florence, where he is recorded on 28 March 1725 with his wife. Listed in Rosalba's diary on 4 December 1724 is a 'Mr. Chantiglion',[24] and on 16 December she wrote: '*Avuto da M.r Cantillion cecchini novantacinque*'.[25] On 9 February 1728 Rosalba noted: '*Incominciato M. di Cantilion*',[26] which final mention of Cantillon would seem to imply that she had begun a portrait of him.

3a/3b *Mary, Countess of Ferrers (1684-1740) and Male Sitter*, c.1729-1730
       Pastel on paper
       LOCATION: private collection

Lady Ferrers' father Sir Richard Levinge of Mullalea, county Westmeath, was Speaker of the Irish House of Commons in Ireland in 1692, and Attorney General for Ireland in 1712. In 1703 Mary married Washington Shirley, 2nd Earl Ferrers (1677-1729), who attended Trinity College in Oxford between 1693 and 1697. They had one daughter, Selina, who married Theophilus Hastings, 9th Earl of Huntingdon.

Selina's portrait in pastels was executed by Samuel Cotes, brother of Francis, both of whom were influenced by Rosalba's style.

After the death of her husband, Lady Ferrers travelled to Paris and took a Mr Campbell as her lover, who was, at the time, acting as Charles Wyndham's travelling tutor. Campbell abandoned Wyndham on the grounds that he 'understood the language enough to travel without him which my Lady Ferrers did not'.[27] They travelled together to Rome, Venice (where they were recorded on 29 December 1729) and Naples. By 1730 Lady Ferrers and Campbell had been joined by her brother Sir Richard Levinge.

This pair of portraits by Rosalba has been traditionally identified as of Lord and Lady Ferrers, but since Lord Ferrers had died in 1729, the male portrait may have been of her brother, or perhaps even of Campbell. Another possibility is that it is a posthumous portrait of Lord Ferrers and that it was copied from a miniature.

4   *Gustavus Hamilton, 2nd Viscount Boyne (1710-46)* c.1730-1731 (Plate 1)

Pastel on paper; 56.5 x 42.9 cm

INSCRIPTION: on reverse: ...vus Viscount B ... drawn at Venice by Rosalba

PROVENANCE: The Rt Hon Nathaniel Clements (1705-1777), of the Ranger's Lodge, Phoenix Park, Dublin; to his son Robert Clements (1732-1804), and later, at Killadoon House, Celbridge, county Kildare (after the sale of the Ranger's Lodge); thence by descent to Charles Clements; sold on 24 January 2002 at Sotheby's New York to Sayn Wittgenstein Fine Arts acting for the Metropolitan Museum of Art, New York for $621,750.

EXHIBITED: John Paul Getty Museum, Los Angeles, 2000-01

LOCATION: Metropolitan Museum of Art, New York

In 1723 Gustavus Hamilton succeeded his grandfather as the 2nd Viscount Boyne, his father having died in 1715. Lord Boyne travelled to Italy with Edward Walpole, second son of Sir Robert and brother of Horace. They were in Venice on 20 January 1730 in time for Carnival, and remained, as recorded by Boyne, 'til ye Opera begins at Piacenza, rather than go to any other town in Italy'.[28] By 11 July 1730 Lord Boyne and Walpole were in Padua, and in December they were again in Venice. While Walpole returned to England in January 1731, Boyne remained in northern Italy, visiting Venice again in April 1731.

This particular pastel proves how difficult it can be to identify the sitter of a portrait by Rosalba, as different patrons were often posed in similar garments. Here we see Boyne wearing the black 'bautta' and mask of the Venetian masquerade costume, a white shirt and cravat, and a blue fur-trimmed coat. For a long time this portrait was considered incorrectly to be of Horace Walpole. The confusion over the

*3 – Rosalba Carriera,
SPRING, pastel on paper,
34 x 26.7 cm*

*4 – Rosalba Carriera,
SUMMER, pastel on paper,
35 x 28 cm*

*(courtesy National Gallery of
Ireland, Milltown Collection)*

210

*5 – Rosalba Carriera,
AUTUMN, pastel on paper,
34 x 28 cm*

*6 – Rosalba Carriera,
WINTER, pastel on paper, 34 x
28 cm*

*(courtesy National Gallery of
Ireland, Milltown Collection)*

identity of the sitter had been complicated by a second version of the pastel in the collection of Lord Walpole of Wolterton, which had been identified since at least 1820 as being of Horace Walpole (who, incidentally sat to Rosalba in 1741).[29] This misidentification was compounded in 1831 when the sitter's identity was provided as Horace Walpole in the engraving by J. Cochrane for Edmund Lodge's *Portraits of Illustrious Persons of Great Britain*.

It was first identified as Viscount Boyne when a third version of the pastel by Rosalba was sold by Lord Boyne from Burwarton House, Bridgenorth, Salop, in June 1956.[30] The latter pastel was catalogued at the time of the sale as Gustavus, Viscount Boyne, and was bought by Mr Ivor Worsfold, London. An inscription on the reverse reads: '...vus Viscount B ... drawn at Venice by Rosalba'.

The correct identification of Lord Boyne was convincingly proposed by C. Kingsley Adams.[31] He noted the physical similarity between the portrait by Rosalba and known depictions of Lord Boyne by Hogarth. He further pointed out that the portrait by Rosalba had been the property of the Clements family for many years, belonging first to the Rt Hon Nathaniel Clements MP (1705-1777). Clements had acted as Ranger of the King's Game in Ireland, and was also a banker and an amateur architect, and became Deputy Treasurer of Ireland and Paymaster General. He had been a close friend of the 2nd Viscount Boyne in his youth. The Clements and Hamilton families enjoyed close relations throughout the eighteenth century, and Clements acquired a large estate in county Donegal from Lord Boyne. It is therefore possible that since Boyne died early and unmarried, he left this work to his friend as a memento of their previous travels together, or, perhaps, his family presented it to Clements on the death of Lord Boyne.

5   Joseph Leeson (1711-1783), later 1st Earl of Milltown

Leeson was the son of a brewer, also Joseph Leeson, who, on his death in 1741, left his son £50,000 plus £6,000 per annum. Leeson Junior used this considerable sum of money to purchase land in Russellstown, county Wicklow, where he built Russborough House, designed by Richard Castle. He married three times: Cecilia Leigh in 1729 (d.1737), Anne Preston in 1739 (d.1766), and Elizabeth French in 1768. In 1743 he became MP for Rathcormack, county Cork. In 1756 he became 1st Baron Russborough, in 1760 1st Viscount Russborough, and in 1763 1st Earl of Milltown.

Leeson went twice to Italy: firstly from 1744 to 1745, which included Florence and Rome, and secondly in 1750 to 1751 to Rome. On Leeson's trip in 1745 he used as his secretary the archaeologist Robert Wood (*c*.1717-1771), son of

Alexander Wood. During his first visit he amassed £60,000 worth of goods, includ-ing statues and pictures which were seized by the French in transit to Ireland. There are no known records indicating what was included in this shipment.

Although Leeson is not recorded as having been in Venice, there are six paintings by Rosalba in the Milltown Collection, bequeathed to the National Gallery of Ireland in 1902. They are *Spring* (Plate 3), *Summer* (Plate 4), *Autumn* (Plate 5), *Winter* (Plates 2, 6), *Diana* (Plate 7), and *Venus* (Plate 8). The four seasons were a common subject for a series in painting. The theme recurred frequently throughout Rosalba's career, particularly during the 1720s, including 1725, the year that the first advertised performance of Vivaldi's *Four Seasons* took place.[32]

Benedetti suggests that as Dr John Clephane, an acquaintance of Leeson, pur-chased a set of Rosalba's seasons on behalf of James Dawkin; it is possible that he (Clephane) was involved in the purchase.[33] In a letter from Pietro Filippo Jamineau in Venice to Rosalba on 27 September 1742 ,Wood is mentioned in connection with a Diana and *Four Heads of Nymphs*, which could perhaps be the Four Seasons bought on behalf of Leeson. The original titles of the pastels in the Milltown Collec-tion are not known, only *Diana*, *Autumn* and *Winter* are certain; the rest were labelled according to the plants or flowers depicted. Benedetti proposes that Rosalba was assisted by either her sister Angela or her assistant Angioletta Sartori in the pas-tels in the Milltown Collection as her sight was failing at that time. However, her marvellous self-portrait for Joseph Smith, now in the Royal Collection, was not completed until 1744, thus suggesting that it was still possible for the Milltown pas-tels to have been her own work, with the possible exception of *Spring* (see below).

5a   *Spring*, sometimes called *Venus* (Plate 3)
       Pastel on paper, 34 x 26.7 cm
       LOCATION: Milltown Collection, National Gallery of Ireland

This bust-length pastel shows a female with her head turned to the right, holding a bouquet of flowers. The quality of the work in this pastel, which has smaller dimen-sions, is inferior to that of the rest of Rosalba's pastels in the Milltown collection.

5b   *Summer* (Plate 4)
       Pastel on paper, 35 x 28 cm
       LOCATION: Milltown Collection, National Gallery of Ireland

In this bust-length pastel the female figure is shown with head tilted slightly downwards and with flowers in her hair, indicating the season.

5c   *Autumn* (Plate 5)
        Pastel on paper, 34 x 28 cm
        LOCATION: Milltown Collection, National Gallery of Ireland

A bust-length pastel of a female figure is shown turning to the left. Vine leaves in her hair and a bunch of grapes in her hand indicate that this depicts autumn.

5d   *Winter* (Plates 2, 6)
        Pastel on paper, 34 x 28 cm
        LOCATION: Milltown Collection, National Gallery of Ireland

This is a bust-length pastel of a female, with her head turned to the right, wearing a blue velvet cloak trimmed with fur, and warming her hands on a small flame in the bottom right corner, appropriate for cold conditions.

Winter also appeared in Rosalba's work as *The Tirolese Girl*. In *Rosalba Carriera*, Sani refers to the National Gallery of Ireland's *Winter* with the title *Testa di Donna*, but she does mention the inclusion of the flame indicating that it is probably an allegory of winter.[34]

5e   *Diana* (Plate 7)
        Pastel on paper, 35 x 28 cm
        LOCATION: Milltown Collection, National Gallery of Ireland

A bust-length female figure is shown draped in blue, with matching tones in the background and ropes of pearls through her hair. The crescent moon on her forehead serves to identify her as Diana.

5f   *Venus*, sometimes called *A Female Head* (Plate 8)
        Pastel on paper, 35 x 28 cm
        LOCATION: Milltown Collection, National Gallery of Ireland

This bust-length female is shown turned slightly to the right, her head tilted downwards to the left, eyes downcast. She wears beads intertwined in her hair and Baroque pearl earrings.

7 – Rosalba Carriera, DIANA,
pastel on paper, 35 x 28 cm

8 – Rosalba Carriera, VENUS,
pastel on paper, 35 x 28 cm

(courtesy National Gallery of
Ireland, Milltown Collection)

6   *Charles Lennox, 2nd Duke of Richmond (1701-1750)* (Plate 9)

Pastel on paper, 56.5 x 44 cm
CONDITION: recently conserved
LOCATION: Castletown House, Celbridge, county Kildare

Charles Lennox, 1st Earl of March, whose wife Sarah Cadogan (1706-1751) was Irish, was the eldest son of the 1st Duke of Richmond, the illegitimate son of King Charles II and Louise de Kéroualle, a French courtesan. In 1719 he married the thirteen-year-old daughter of Lord Cadogan, Lady Sarah, in order to cancel a gambling debt between their parents. He left on his Grand Tour, immediately travelling to Parma, Rome, Naples, Milan, Padua, and Venice for the Carnival, and by May 1722 was in The Hague.

On 11 November 1726 Rosalba wrote: 'Incominciato la copia di Milord ecc. di Richemond'.[35] Although there is no record of the Duke of Richmond having visited Italy in 1726, it is most probably he. It may have been painted from a miniature. An earlier pastel of the Duke of Richmond mentioned in Rosalba's diary of 1720 would have to be of his father, the 1st Duke, whom the former succeeded in 1723.

Lennox was in partnership with Owen McSwiney over the allegorical tomb paintings commemorating British Whig heroes. According to Sani, McSwiney also acquired works for him by Rosalba, including *A Tirolese Girl*, and in 1728 he ordered *A German Girl* from her, which was not finished until July 1730.[36]

7   John Molesworth, 2nd Viscount Molesworth (1679-1726)

The Hon John Molesworth was the eldest son of the 1st Viscount Molesworth of Edlington, Yorkshire, and Breckdenstown, Swords, county Dublin, and Letitia, third daughter of Richard Coote, 1st Baron Coote.

In 1710 Molesworth was appointed Envoy Extraordinary to Genoa, but instead chose to be envoy to Florence from 1711 to 1714, a post for which he was not paid. While in Italy he made the acquaintance of the Florentine architect, Alessandro Galilei (1691-1736), whom he later induced to visit England and Ireland in 1714.[37] In 1720 Molesworth served as Envoy Extraordinary to the Casa Savoia in Turin.

Molesworth is Rosalba's second known Irish link. There are two known portraits of Molesworth, both purportedly copies of different pastels by Rosalba; the originals are missing. A letter of 1710 referred to the English envoy, whom Sani presumed was Molesworth:

Illustrious Sir, I humbly beseech you, that the portrait in question, which I think you have, will pass through the hands of the English envoy, so that he can keep it for the person for whom it is intended.[38]

However, as Molesworth was not appointed envoy until 1711, it seems likely that this may have been his predecessor.[39] In 1712 Molesworth wrote to Rosalba from Florence,[40] referring to a portrait. He apologised for his inability to render a service to Rosalba, and recorded his gratitude for her help. He also mentioned other letters from him, fearful that they had gone astray on the country roads, which indeed may have happened, as there are no other letters in existence between the two.

7a   *John, 2nd Viscount Molesworth*, c.1722

Pastel

PROVENANCE: presumably by family descent to Hender Delves Molesworth (great-great-great-great grandson of 1st Viscount); to his widow and bequeathed by her will to her nephew-in-law Allan Henry Neville Molesworth, but believed to have disappeared from her house in the 1990s.

LOCATION: unknown

7b   Copy of portrait by Rosalba of *John, 2nd Viscount Molesworth*, attributed to Anthony Lee (fl.1724-67) 1742

Oil on canvas; 74.9 x 62.6 cm

INSCRIPTION: on tablet: 'JOHN 2nd VISCOUNT MOLESWORTH/1679-1726.'; label on reverse written in black on stretcher-bearer: 'John 2nd Viscount.'; in black ink on the stretcher-bearer: 'Copy/Richard 3rd Viscount Molesworth/copied from crayon of Rosa Alba by Mr. Lee Painted [Painter?] in Dublin/in the Year 1744 – the original was done in crayons in Florence by Rosa Alba about 1742 [1722?]/The Property of Coote Molesworth 1745.' Inscription added by later hand 'Wrong! A.R.'

PROVENANCE: In 1745 Coote Molesworth, a brother of the sitter, probably that listed as 'Portrait of John 2nd Viscount Molesworth' in 8th Viscount's Will dated 15 September 1905; presumably to Molesworth Trustees upon death of 8th Viscount, 7 June 1906; probably that listed as 'Portrait of John 2nd Viscount' in care of Trustees in Pedigree of the Molesworth Family c.1937; listed as 'Copy Portrait of John 2nd Viscount Molesworth' in receipt signed by 11th Viscount 15 September 1961; listed as 'Portrait of John, 2nd Viscount Molesworth' by Christie's 1963, when valued at £20; listed as 'Portrait of John 2nd Viscount Molesworth' (as by follower of Kneller) by Sotheby's in 1999.

LOCATION: Molesworth Trust

In 1712 John's brother Richard visited him in Italy and it was possibly on this visit that they both had the portrait medals struck by Antonio Selvi (*c*.1679-1755) (British Museum), who spent most of his life in the service of the ducal court in

Tuscany. The medal shows John wearing a long wig with Prudence, Abundance, Peace and Commerce, with the Molesworth arms on the reverse.

The half-length portrait attributed to Lee shows John turned slightly to the right, his face turned and looking to the front, wearing a brown cloak with a long flowing wig and white cravat in a painted oval. The portrait has similarities to Selvi's medal, both using the high wig and drapery, and Rosalba may well have used it as a model for the portrait.

The inscription on the reverse may have been added by John's brother, Coote (named after his mother's family), who was briefly his secretary in 1722. The misidentification of the sitter as Richard, the 3rd Viscount, is curious, as all his other portraiture alludes to his military status. The initials 'A.R.' on the reverse can be identified as those of Athelstan Riley, a founder trustee of the 8th Viscount's Will Trust in 1906.[41]

7c   Copy of Rosalba's portrait of *John 2nd Viscount Molesworth*, by Sir Godfrey Kneller (1646-1723).

Oil on canvas; 123.8 x 99 cm

SIGNED: in monogram on lower left: GK

INSCRIPTION: on tablet: 'JOHN 2nd VISCOUNT MOLESWORTH/1679-1726/PAINTED BY LEE OF DUBLIN IN 1744/FROM AN ORIGINAL IN CRAYONS BY ROSALBI OF ROME/ Molesworth Heirloom.'

PROVENANCE: by descent to Mrs Marcus Gage of Streeve, county Londonderry, great-great-niece of the sitter; bequeathed to Molesworth Trustees sometime thereafter; listed as 'Portrait of John 2nd Viscount Molesworth' on receipt signed by 11th Viscount 15 September 1961; listed as 'Portrait of John 2nd Viscount Molesworth' (as by Lee after Carriera) by Christie's 1963, when valued at £300; listed as 'Portrait of John 2nd Viscount Molesworth' (as by Kneller) by Sotheby's 1999.

LITERATURE: Crookshank and Glin, *The Painters of Ireland c.1660-1920* (London 1978) 41.

LOCATION: Molesworth Trust

This three-quarter-length Baroque-style portrait shows Molesworth standing with his face turned to the right, showing him with his natural long hair, wearing a purple velvet coat unbuttoned at the chest, white shirt open at the neck with collar upturned. His right hand holds a walking cane, his left hand is drawing up a flowing brown cloak draped around the hilt of his sword. In the left background there is a rock arch, and on the right there is the interior of a dungeon chamber. Molesworth's stylised dress, known as a 'civic vest', was usually reserved for writers and men of learning.

Originally identified as by Anthony Lee, this painting was reattributed to

9 – Rosalba Carriera, CHARLES LENNOX, 2ND DUKE OF RICHMOND (1701-1750),
pastel on paper, 56.5 x 44 cm
(courtesy Castletown Foundation, Celbridge, county Kildare)

Godfrey Kneller in 1988 by Victor Fauville of Sotheby's. The location and date of the original by Rosalba is unknown, although since Kneller died in 1723, it would date to before then.

8   *Mary Middleton, Viscountess Molesworth (c.1697-1766), c.1700-1725*
        Pastel drawing.
        PROVENANCE: presumably by family descent to Hender Delves Molesworth (great-great-great-great grandson of 1st Viscount); to his widow and bequeathed by her will to her nephew-in-law Allan Henry Neville Molesworth, but believed to have disappeared from her house as recently as the 1990s.
        LOCATION: unknown

Molesworth's wife Mary also commissioned a portrait from Rosalba, most likely executed between 1720 and 1725, during her husband's residence in Italy. Her father Thomas Middleton (1694-1742) also sat to Rosalba c.1720 (Middleton family collection).

9   *Richard Tighe (1678-1736)*
        LOCATION: unknown

Tighe was the eldest son of William Tighe (d.1679) and Anne, the eldest daughter of Sir Christopher Lovett. He attended Trinity College from 1693 to 1696, receiving his BA in 1696. Tighe was small in stature and known for his love of fashion. He was nicknamed Little Dick Tighe and Beau Tighe. He married Barbara Bor, daughter and co-heir of Christian Bor of Drinagh, county Wexford.
        Tighe was recorded in Padua on 29 May 1700, and again on 17 March 1705.[41] He was acquainted with the British Resident of Venice, Christian Cole (fl.1697-1735), who first met Rosalba in 1701, and, while away from Venice, kept up a correspondence with her. Cole acquired high-quality pastel crayons for her while in Rome. From Rome on 9 May 1705 Cole wrote to Rosalba: '*La Prego de riverir della parte mi il signor Riccardo Tye.*'[42] On 16 May 1705 the artist replied from Venice:

> It is this Sig.r Taie, who in a few days will depart for there, and meanwhile I cordially recommend him ... still it upsets me to lose the company of Sig. Tighe but I do not despair of another opportunity during your stay there at the end of the summer.[44]

Tighe left soon afterwards, spending the summer in Florence. According to Rosalba's diary, he made a return visit to Venice in September. On 19 September

1705 Cole wrote from Rome to Rosalba, '*Saluto la sua madre, il Sig. Tighe etc*'.[45] There is no further mention of Tighe, and no location is known for his portrait, if it still exists.

———

APPENDIX

WORKS RELEVANT TO ROSALBA FORMERLY IN THE COLLECTION
OF THE DUKE OF LEINSTER

Notes on the pictures, plate and antiquities etc. at Carton, Kilkea Castle, 13 Dominick Street, Dublin and 6 Carlton House Terrace (London 1885)[46]

Duke's Study
i)   G. Caroline, Lady Holland, d.1774 (in crayons), Rosalba ... [1'7$\frac{1}{2}$" x 10"]

Duchess's Sitting Room
ii)   E. O. Duchess of Leinster (in crayons), Rosalba ... [2'5" x 1'9"]

Autumn Bedroom
iii)   7 female heads (in crayons), Rosalba Carriera of Venice ... [each 11$\frac{1}{2}$" x 10"]
iv)   2 female heads (in crayons) Rosalba Carriera ... [each 1'5$\frac{1}{2}$" x 1'2"]
v)   One of Rosalba herself drawing. She died 1757
vi)   St. George, Lord St. George, d. 1775 (in crayons), Rosalba ... [1'11" x 1'7"]

Catalogue of an important and valuable collection of works of art (removal from carton, Co. Kildare) which with the consent of His Grace The Duke of Leinster will be sold by auction by Messrs Bennett and Son, Limited M.I.A.A. at their Galleries 6 Upper Ormond Quay, Dublin on Wednesday December 2nd 1925 and two following days.[47]

Pastels
vii)   428:   Emilia Olivia Duchess of Leinster – small oval, Hugh Hamilton
viii)   431:   Lady Georgina Holland, Liotard
ix)   440:   Do. [portrait] of a lady wearing pearl necklet and flowers in her hair, Rosalba
x)   444:   4 classical heads, in finely carved and giltwood frames, Rosalba
xi)   445:   3 classical heads, in finely carved and giltwood frames, Rosalba
xii)   446:   Pomona; and The Art of Painting – a pair, Rosalba
xiii)   447:   Lord St. George, in carved and giltwood frame, Rosalba
xiv)   454:   Girl with a basket of fruit, Rosalba

Oil Paintings
xv)   532:   Oval [portrait] of Lady St. George, in carved and giltwood frame.

NOTES

Caroline, Lady Holland

Lady Caroline Lennox, the eldest daughter of the Duke and Duchess of Richmond, married Henry Fox (1705-1774), a Whig MP in 1744. She travelled abroad on several occasions. In the late 1720s she visited Louise de Kéroualle in Aubigny. In 1763 she was in Belgium and Paris, and in 1765 she was again in Paris. Caroline undertook her own Grand Tour in 1766, travelling to Lyon, Susa, Turin, Bologna, Florence, Rome and Naples, and was in France again in 1767 and 1769. She travelled mainly for the sake of her own and her family's health, believing like many at the time that the continental air was beneficial.

It seems likely that item (i) from the 1885 inventory, a portrait of 'G. Caroline, Lady Holland' by Rosalba and item (viii) from the 1925 sale catalogue, a portrait of 'Lady Georgina Holland' by Jean-Etienne Liotard, are the same piece. Although Lady Caroline Holland's Christian name was Georgina, she was known as Caroline. Since she is not recorded as being in Italy during Rosalba's lifetime, it is more likely that she sat to Liotard, who was in England painting portraits from 1753 to 1755 and from 1772 to 1774.

Emilia Olivia, 2nd Duchess of Leinster (1759-1798)

LITERATURE: W.G. Strickland, *Dictionary of Irish Artists* i (Dublin 1913), 441-2, lists two portraits by H.D. Hamilton of Emilia Olivia, Duchess of Leinster, in the collection of of the Duke of Leinster at Carton, as well as another at Castletown.

LOCATION: possibly the pastel in the National Gallery of Ireland (no. 6088) dateable to the 1790s.

In 1775 the Hon Emilia Olivia, daughter of Baron St George (*q.v.*) married William Fitzgerald, 2nd Duke of Leinster (1749-1804). Given the similarity of their names, she has previously been confused with William's mother, Emily (Emilia Mary) FitzGerald, 1st Duchess of Leinster.

Item (ii) in the 1885 inventory, 'E. O. Duchess of Leinster', and item (vii) in the 1925 sale catalogue, 'Emilia Olivia Duchess of Leinster', are likely to be the same picture. The former is listed as by Rosalba, and the latter as by Hugh Douglas Hamilton, but as the 2nd Duchess was born two years after Rosalba's death, the earlier attribution is obviously incorrect.

Baron St George MP (1715-1754)

Baron St George MP was the eldest son of John Usher of Headford, county Galway, taking the name of St George in 1734. In 1752 he married Elizabeth Dominick (*q.v.*), daughter of Christopher Dominick of Dublin. In 1774 they travelled to Italy with their daughter Emilia Olivia (1759-1798) (*q.v.*) for the sake of St George's health, but he died shortly after their arrival in Naples. Upon his death his collection of paintings was placed in the gallery of Leinster House until after the sale of 1815, when they were removed to Carton. A portrait of 'St. George, Lord St. George' (item (vi), 1885 inventory) and 'Lord St. George' (item (xiii), the 1925 sale catalogue) would appear to be the same work. Both are attributed to Rosalba. A much more likely candidate for the artist is Hugh Douglas Hamilton, who, according to W.G. Strickland, painted his portrait in oils and produced other pastels of his wife and daughter.

Elizabeth, Lady St George (née Dominick)

The attribution of the oval oil painting of 'Lady St. George' listed in the 1925 sale catalogue as item (xv), by Rosalba, would appear to be incorrect as Lady St George did not visit Venice until after Rosalba's death. Strickland records a portrait in crayons by Hamilton of this sitter, which would point to his authorship of this oil portrait, which was possibly a copy of the pastel.[48]

———

ACKNOWLEDGEMENTS

The author wishes to acknowledge the guidance and support of the following people: Dr Christine Casey, Department of History of Art, University College Dublin, and the Hon William Molesworth for his generous help with the portraits of John Molesworth; Sergio Benedetti for his help, especially with translations from Italian; her parents and sister Anna for their patience.

ENDNOTES

[1] Bernardina Sani, *Rosalba Carriera* (Turin 1988) 12. Zeno, in a letter of 1729 to Cav. Marmi, published in G. Campori (ed.), *Lettere Artistiche Inedite* (Modena 1886), asserts that Rosalba was the pupil of Diamantini.

[2] *ibid.*, 12. P. de Chennevière and A. de Montaiglon, *Abecedario de Pierre Jean Mariette et autres notes sur les arts et les artistes* (Paris 1851-1853).

[3] Evangeline Wilbour Blashfield, *Portraits and Background* (New York 1917) 398; Austin Dobson, *Rosalba's Journal and Other Papers* (London 1915) 5.

[4] Francis Russell, 'Drawings by Rosalba', *Burlington Magazine*, 139, 1997, 196.

[5] *The Art of Pastel*, exhibition catalogue, National Gallery of Ireland (Dublin 1996) 2.

[6] *ibid.*

[7] *The Glory of Venice: Art in the Eighteenth Century*, exhibition catalogue (London 1994) 445.

[8] Bernardina Sani, *Lettere, Diari, Frammenti* (Florence 1985) 90.

[9] Sergio Benedetti, *The Milltowns: A Family Reunion* (Dublin 1997) 82.

[10] *ibid.* Sani, *Rosalba Carriera*, is quoted as the source for this.

[11] Sani, *Rosalba Carriera*, 31. '*Il 27 Settembre (1742) è sollecitata a dipingere quattro teste di ninfe e una Diana per Robert Wood, gentiluomo inglese appassionato di archeologia orientale*'. ['On the 27 September 1742 she was asked to painting four heads of nymphs and one Diana for Robert Wood, an English gentleman with a passion for eastern archaeology']; Sani, *Lettere, Diari, Frammenti*, 684. Letter from Pietro Filippo Jamineau in Venice to Rosalba Carriera in Venice, 27 September 1742.

> Since I did not have the chance to meet you yesterday, I send mine (for not to give you the inconvenience of sending a person) I beg you let me know at what advanced stage you are in painting 4 heads of Nymphs and one Diana destined for Mr. Robert Wood, English Gentleman and when you foresee the possibility to deliver those same because

I am going to write to him next Saturday in the east where you will remember him making a journey of pleasure with his companion and they met in Constantinople, after that I will wait for your reply to know exactly about this matter.

I am your servant

Pietro Filippo Jamineau

From the House, Thursday 27 September 1742.

When they are ready; I will receive them, together with that of Princess Trivulzi and the other larger one for the same friend.

[12] Sani, *Rosalba Carriera*, 31.

[13] Jeremy Black, *The British Abroad: The Grand Tour in the Eighteenth Century* (Stroud 1992) 291.

[14] Russell, 'Drawings by Rosalba' 196-7.

[15] His letters are in the Surrey History Centre, www.surreycc.gov.uk/surreyhistoryservice

[16] Black, *The British Abroad*, 291.

[17] Sani, *Lettere, Diari, Frammenti*, 787. 'I began the small portrait of Faustina for Mr. Brodrier.' Sani provided the date for this incorrectly as 15 July.

[18] *ibid.*, 'I started Sig.r Brodrick.'

[19] *ibid.*, 'I began ... Sig. Brodrick.'

[20] *ibid.*, 788. 'I had from Mr. Suini 54 cecchini for the portraits of Mr. Brodrick.'

[21] *ibid.* 'I had from Mr. Smith 44 cecchini for the two small portraits of Sig. B.ro.'

[22] Antoine Murphy, *Richard Cantillon* (Oxford, 1986) 9.

[23] *ibid.*, 4.

[24] Sani, *Lettere, Diari, Frammenti*, 785.

[25] *ibid.* 'I had from M.r Cantillion 95 cecchini.'

[26] *ibid.*, 793. 'I started M. di Cantilion.'

[27] John Ingamells, *A Dictionary of British and Irish Travellers in Italy 1701-1800* (New Haven and London 1997) 353.

[28] C. Kingsley Adams, 'Portraiture Problems and Genealogy', *The Genealogists Magazine*, xiv, 11 September 1964, 115.

[29] Information from www.sothebys.com in connection with the sale of the portrait of Boyne on 24 January 2002.

[30] Sotheby's house sale: Burwarton House, Bridgenorth, Salop, 17 June 1956, lot 23.

[31] Kingsley Adams, 382-8.

[32] *The Art of Pastel*, 2.

[33] Benedetti, *The Milltowns*, 82.

[34] Sani, *Rosalba Carriera*, 308.

[35] Sani, *Lettere, Diari, Frammenti*, 790. 'I began the copy of Milord Richmond.'

[36] *ibid.*, 308.

[37] E. McParland, 'The Honourable John Molesworth', *A Dictionary of British and Irish Travellers in Italy 1701-1800* (New Haven and London 1997) 666.

[38] Sani, *Lettere, Diari, Frammenti*, 178: '*Ill. ma ch'è humilmente supplicata, essendo il detto ritratto, come mi figuro appresso di lei, farlo passare nelle mani del Sig.r Inviato d'Inghilterra, perche lo possa far tenere a chi l'ha commendato.*'

[39] In conversation with the Hon William Molesworth.

40 Sani, *Lettere, Diari, Frammenti*, 211-12. Extract from letter from the Hon John Molesworth in Florence to Rosalba Carriera in Venice, 6 August 1712.

> Mr. Drake is perfectly well acquainted with your commission, with much pleasure on my part in seeing the sign of memory, that you retain for me, that which I assure you will be agreeable to me.
>
> The time of my stay here is not less uncertain than the one of my departure, which I still do not have a fixed idea of; but, in the season that I arrive in, I hope to have the benefit of your greeting in Venice.
>
> I fear that my letters become lost on the country roads, then that has already occurred several times, that I ask you the fate of your Portrait which is in no way not in proportion to your merit, nor to another.
>
> I am very angry to not be able to return your help but you should be assured that I continue to do all that you depend on, according to the occasions that present themselves.

According to Sani this is the *Self-portrait* of Rosalba in the Uffizi previously dated to 1715, but dated by Sani to 1712.

41 The Hon William Molesworth, Inventory of the Portraiture of the Viscounts Molesworth and their Families, 2002 (unpublished work in progress, unpaginated, page numbers given in square brackets here) [4].

42 Ingamells, *A Dictionary of British and Irish Travellers in Italy*, 943.

43 Sani, *Lettere, Diari, Frammenti*, 90. 'Please convey my respects to signor Riccardo Tye.'

44 *ibid.*, 91. '*É questi il Sig.r Taie, che tra pochi giorni parte per costì, e fratanta cordialmente la riverisce...ancora mi da disgusto il perder l'occasione del Sig. Taie, ma non ne dispero qualche altra mentre lei si ferma costì sino al fin dell'estate.*'

45 *ibid.*, 94–5. 'Greetings to your mother, Sig. Tighe etc.'

46 Irish Architectural Archive.

47 Irish Architectural Archive. The 1925 sale catalogue also lists three engravings after Rosalba for sale, including the Seasons.

48 W.G. Strickland, *Dictionary of Irish Artists*, 2 vols (Dublin 1913) i, 443.

―――――

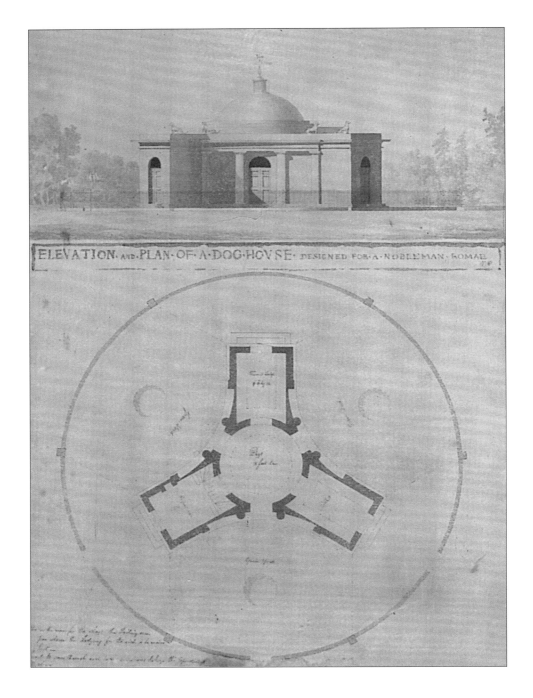

1– Soane's ELEVATION AND PLAN OF A DOG-HOUSE DESIGNED FOR A NOBLEMAN ROMAE 1779
The original drawing hangs in Sir John Soane's Museum, London.

An unpublished watercolour by James Malton from the collection of Desmond Guinness

DESMOND GUINNESS

T HE YOUNG JOHN SOANE AND HIS POTENTIAL PATRON FREDERICK HERVEY, Bishop of Derry, later 4th Earl of Bristol, together concocted an idea for a kennel or 'dog-house' (Plates 1, 5-7). It owes its inspiration to a visit by Hervey and Soane to the Villa of Lucullus, near Terracina, as they travelled south to Naples together in December 1778. Soane remembered the bishop saying, 'I should like to form some idea of a classical dog kennel, as I intend to build one at the Downhill for the hounds of my eldest son.'[1]

Soane produced a drawing (Sir John Soane's Museum, London) which 'provided for a circular fenced-in yard with three separate drinking basins linked to the separate functions of the three arms of the little building. One arm contained the kennel attendant's residence, the second a heated veterinary sick-bay, and the third kept the bitches from mingling with the male dogs, housed in the central rotunda.'[2] The kennel featured the baseless Greek Doric columns seen by Soane at Paestum, and the attic of the drum was borrowed from the Temple of Vesta at Tivoli, with Soane replacing the traditional bucrania with dogs' heads.[3] In the Age of Reason it made sense to ornament a kennel with hounds and huntsmen. As du Prey points out, 'The purpose of Soane's doghouse proclaims itself as loudly as if it barked.'[4]

Earlier in 1778, Soane had been awarded a three-year scholarship by the Royal Academy of Arts which enabled him to measure the buildings of ancient Rome. Also, as the son of a bricklayer, it was essential for him to look out for prospective patrons in England or Ireland so that his designs could materialise into buildings. The 'Edifying Bishop' seemed the ideal patron to cultivate. He was enormously rich, very extravagant, and was in the process of building two vast country houses in Ireland – Downhill (Plate 2) and Ballyscullion (Plate 3), both in county

2 – View of Downhill, county Londonderry, in its ruined state
(courtesy National Trust Photographic Library; photo Mike Williams)

3 – Engraving by J. Ford of Ballyscullion, county Londonderry
(reproduced from E.V. Sampson, STATISTICAL SURVEY OF COUNTY LONDONDERRY (Dublin 1802))

4 – Ickworth, Suffolk
(courtesy National Trust Photographic Library; photo Rupert Truman)

Londonderry; he later embarked on Ickworth in Suffolk (Plate 4).

Frederick Hervey was born in 1730 and named after Frederick, Prince of Wales, one of the sponsors at his christening. The year 2003 marks the bicentenary of his death, which occurred on 18 July 1803, when he was on the way from Albano to Rome, accompanied by a splendid cortege. The Earl-Bishop was taken ill, and the owner of the first cottage they found was approached for water for the dying man. Amazed by the splendour of the equipages, the farmer who provided the water made enquiries, and when he discovered the cortege belonged to a heretic prelate, he feared that if the Earl-Bishop expired under his roof, it might bring a curse on his family. Accordingly, the grand old man was bundled into a stable where he breathed his last.

The Earl-Bishop had a marked preference for domes, and had actually made an offer to purchase the Temple of Vesta at Tivoli so as to have it shipped, stone by

5 – Soane's elevation for a dog kennel, drawn by his pupil C.J. Richardson (1809-1872) c.1835
6 – Detail of the dome

7 – Detail of Soane's elevation for a dog kennel
(all illustrations courtesy Trustees of Sir John Soane's Museum)

8 – Mussenden Temple, Downhill, county Londonderry
(courtesy National Trust Photographic Library; photo Mike Williams)

stone, to Downhill. Instead, the circular Mussenden Temple, designed by the Cork architect Michael Shanahan, was built in 1783, perching on the cliff-top looking out to sea. The dome was to have been gilded. The frieze is ornamented by a Latin inscription carved into the stone, which translates:

> IT IS NOT UNPLEASANT WHEN SAFE ON DRY LAND TO WATCH THOSE FLOUNDERING ABOUT IN THE DEEP

...not a particularly Christian sentiment. It was fitted up as a library. However, it was

9 – Mausoleum at Downhill, modelled on the Roman monument of the Julii at Saint-Rémy, Provence (courtesy National Trust Photographic Library; photo Steven Wooster)

built too near the edge of the cliff which has eroded, but fortunately the American-based World Monuments Fund became aware of the problem and recently shored it up at a cost of £300,000.

The Earl-Bishop adored his young and beautiful kinswoman Mrs Frideswide Mussenden, who, in 1783, tragically died at the age of 22. He always put her beside him at table, but their relationship was platonic, although, of course, tongues wagged. The Mussenden Temple (Plate 8), which commemorates her, is Ulster's answer to the Casino at Marino near Dublin, designed by Sir William Chambers for the Earl-

Bishop's great enemy, Lord Charlemont, in 1758. Roman Catholics in the vicinity of Downhill were invited to celebrate Mass in the basement of the temple, a gesture of which Charlemont might not have approved. Both buildings were designed with hollow columns for the rainwater, avoiding unsightly gutters and downpipes.

Also at Downhill, Shanahan was responsible for the design of the mausoleum, erected to the memory of the bishop's brother, the Lord Lieutenant (Plate 9). It was begun in 1779, and was modelled on the Roman monument of the Julii at Saint-Rémy in Provence. The pedestal and lower Ionic stage originally supported eight Corinthian columns surmounted by a cupola, under which was placed a marble statue of the Lord Lieutenant, which had been carved in Dublin by Van Nost. Both cupola and statue were blown down in the Great Wind of January 1839, and the damage was never repaired.

Ballyscullion, the Earl-Bishop's other house in county Londonderry, had a vast dome over the central block, curved sweeps and wings. It was designed by the Cork architect Michael Shanahan, and the foundation stone was laid in 1787. Much of it was complete and habitable, but nothing now remains of this remarkable building except the portico which fronts St George's church in Belfast.

Ickworth was built on land which the Herveys had owned in Suffolk since the fifteenth century. It is a version of Ballyscullion, again with a large central dome, built by the Irish architect Francis Sandys in 1796, on the basis of a design by the Italian architect Mario Asprucci. It was completed long after the death of the Earl-Bishop but the interior became heavier with the passage of time and the family's advancement to a marquessate. The Earl-Bishop's three great houses were supposed to display to the general public the works of art amassed by him on his travels – some of it commissioned, some bought from dealers – so as to educate and enthral his visitors. This was, sadly, never to take place.

Having made friends with the bishop, Soane cut short his Italian stay. Work was in progress at Downhill, and if he declined the invitation to help complete the job, many a hungry architect would have taken his place. However, the bishop neglected to send for Soane when he reached Ulster, and he had to carry his luggage from country Antrim to county Londonderry. Downhill was upside down, leaking, unfinished – in chaos. Plans by Soane were agreed and soon abandoned; his note-book survives at Sir John Soane's Museum in London.[5] One commission was for a dining room. Soane came up with an oblong room that had an oval of columns and a floor plan, echoed in the ceiling, that was based on Michelangelo's pavement at the Capitoline Hill in Rome – very handsome designs that came to nothing and for which he received no payment. His dreadful experience in Ireland as a young man apparently haunted Soane for the rest of his days.

Evidently the Earl-Bishop kept the idea of a domed triangular dog kennel in mind. Thirty years ago, I purchased a watercolour from the Dublin antique dealer Gerry Kenyon, who had bought it from Monty Sainsbury of Bath (Plate 11). It is signed 'Ja.s Malton Arch..s et Del..t 1792' (Plate 12).[6] Malton's watercolour shows a domed building with three smaller domed offshoots, the triangular ground plan being held up by the artist himself. A second figure wearing a black hat, white cravat, black coat, black breeches, stockings and shoes (with silver buckles) is without doubt the Earl-Bishop, easily recognisable from his many portraits, such as that by Elizabeth Vigée le Brun (Plate 10).

The plan in the watercolour (Plate 13) shows each of the three offshoots from the central dome, measuring a slightly different length. It must have been a preliminary drawing for the bishop – shown pointing at the plan with his stick – to choose the length he preferred, or else a very lopsided building would have resulted.

The triangle is seldom found in architectural conceits. The earliest and best known of all is Longford Castle in Wiltshire, built by Sir Thomas Gorges in 1591. Sir Thomas Tresham, who spent years in the Tower of London for clinging to the Old Faith, built Triangular Lodge at Rushton, Northhamptonshire, in 1597, symbolising the Holy Trinity. Midford Castle near Bath (1775) was designed by John Carter for H. Disney Roebuck in the form of an ace of clubs, the winning card that paid for it. Severndroog Castle (1784) on Shooters Hill in Kent, is a triangular redbrick tower with turrets, built to commemorate Sir William James's victory over a pirate captain near Goa off the Indian coast. A folly castle called Gibraltar, on an island in the lake at Larchill, county Meath, is the only eighteenth-century example in Ireland of which the writer is aware.

––––––

ACKNOWLEDGEMENTS

Thanks are due to Naomi Gordon, World Monuments Fund; National Trust (Committee for Northern Ireland); Sir Charles Brett; Susan Palmer, Sir John Soane's Museum, London; Sarah Blackburn, National Trust Photo Library, London; Arthur Prager, Irish Georgian Society, New York, John Jolliffe; Charles Campbell, photographer, Leixlip; and Christopher Moore.

ENDNOTES

By far the most useful source for this article was Peter Rankin's, *Irish Building Ventures of the Earl-Bishop of Derry* (Ulster Architectural Heritage Society, Belfast 1972).

1. John Soane, *Memoirs of the Professional Life of an Architect* (privately printed 1835), 15.
2. Pierre du Prey, 'Je n'oublieray jamais, John Soane and Downhill', *Bulletin of the Irish Georgian Society*, xxi, July-December 1978, 19.
3. Margaret Richardson and Mary-Anne Stevens (eds), *John Soane Architect: Master of Space and Light*, exhibition catalogue, Royal Academy of Arts (London 1999), cat. 26.
4. du Prey, 'Je n'oublieray jamais', 20.
5. Pierre du Prey has analysed Soane's 'Downhill Notebook' brilliantly in John Soane, *The Making of an Architect* (Chicago and London 1982).
6. It was James Malton who produced the wonderful series of *25 Views of Dublin* (1791-1799), unsurpassed for their beauty and the accuracy of their architectural detail.

———

12 – James Malton, PROPOSAL FOR A TRIANGULAR BUILDING, 1792 detail of inscription (photo Charles Campbell)

13 – James Malton, PROPOSAL FOR A TRIANGULAR BUILDING, 1792 detail of figures shown with architectural plan (photo Charles Campbell)

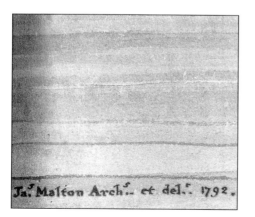

IRISH ARCHITECTURAL AND DECORATIVE STUDIES

THE JOURNAL OF THE IRISH GEORGIAN SOCIETY – VOLUMES I-VI, 1998-2003

vol. I (1998), 224pp, 128 illus
ISBN 0946846 162

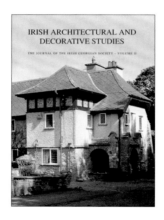

vol. II (1999), 208pp, 110 illus
ISBN 0946846 324

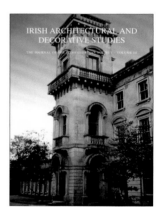

vol. III (2000), 192pp, 143 illus
ISBN 0946846 480

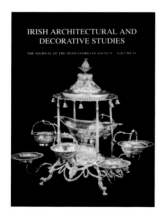

vol. IV (2001), 224pp, 109 illus
ISBN 0946846 723

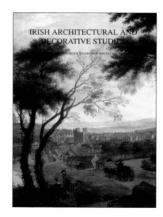

vol. V (2002), 208pp, 136 illus
ISBN 0946846 960

vol. VI (2003), 240pp, 120 illus
ISBN 0946846 979

Back-issues available from Irish Georgian Society and Gandon Editions at €20 each – contact information on page 4

Irish Georgian Society

CONSERVING IRELAND'S ARCHITECTURAL HERITAGE

THE IRISH GEORGIAN SOCIETY AIMS TO ENCOURAGE AN INTEREST IN AND TO promote the preservation of distinguished examples of architecture and the allied arts in Ireland. These aims are achieved by:

MEMBERSHIP – The Society has 3,000 members worldwide. Its headquarters are in Dublin, and there is a thriving and long-established London Chapter and two local Irish chapters in Birr and Limerick. The headquarters of the US membership, IGS Inc., is in New York, and there are local chapters in Boston, Chicago, Cleveland, Columbus, Washington, Minneapolis and Atlanta. The benefits of membership include: (i) a twice-yearly newsletter which includes the events programme; (ii) the annual journal; (iii) free entry to selected historic houses in Ireland.

FUNDRAISING – The Society runs an events programme which includes: (i) lectures, (ii) private theatre evenings, (iii) architectural walking tours, (iv) conferences and seminars, (v) day tours, including visits to houses not normally open to the public, and (vi) tours abroad.

EDUCATION – The Society's annual journal, *Irish Architectural and Decorative Studies,* contains articles of original research, and is the only Irish periodical devoted entirely to the architectural history of Ireland. In addition, valuable research in the field of conservation is funded by the Desmond Guinness Scholarship.

GRANTS – Donations to the Society and funds raised through the events programme enable the Society to make grants towards the restoration of historic properties.

PLANNING PARTICIPATION – The Society takes an active part in the planning process on a country-wide basis, and opposes planning applications which are not compatible with the principles of good conservation. It also provides general advice on other aspects of conservation.

The Society liaises with government departments in the area of conservation. The Government has accepted that the preservation and conservation of Ireland's historic buildings, precincts, properties and collections should be given high priority.

HISTORY

The Irish Georgian Society was founded in 1958 by the Hon Desmond Guinness and his late wife, Mariga, for the protection of buildings of architectural merit in Ireland. Many fine houses have been saved through their enthusiasm and commitment, and the dedication of members and supporters. The current President is Desmond FitzGerald, Knight of Glin.

The Society's main achievements include, among others, the saving of threatened great buildings such as: Castletown, county Kildare; Damer House, county Tipperary; Doneraile Court, county Cork; Roundwood, county Laois; Tailors Hall, Dublin, and 13 Henrietta Street, Dublin. Restoration work is being carried out at Ledwithstown, county Longford, and Mount Ievers Court, county Clare, and the Society is assisting with the urban restoration at 2 Pery Square, Limerick. The Society has provided grants for many other projects, including the restoration of correct windows in historic urban houses, such as 20 Lr Dominick Street, George Bernard Shaw's house in Synge Street, and 3-4 Fownes Street, Dublin.

These efforts are funded by our members' participation in the events programme, by the fundraising activities of our chapters, by donations, by sales from the Society's book and gift shop, and by generous royalties from Kindel & Co Inc., Scalamandre Inc., Chelsea House, and the Obelisk Collection.

MEMBERSHIP APPLICATION FORMS ARE AVAILABLE FROM:

IRISH GEORGIAN SOCIETY
74 Merrion Square, Dublin 2
tel: +353 (0)1-676 7053 / fax: +353 (0)1-662 0290 / e-mail: info@igs.ie

IRISH GEORGIAN SOCIETY INC.
7 Washington Square North (21A), New York, NY 10003 6647
tel: (212) 254 4862 / fax: (212) 777 6754 / e-mail: irgeorgian@aol.com